THE HENRY A. WALLACE SERIES
ON AGRICULTURAL HISTORY AND RURAL STUDIES

IOWA STATE UNIVERSITY PRESS • AMES

THE HENRY A. WALLACE SERIES
ON AGRICULTURAL HISTORY AND RURAL STUDIES

Richard S. Kirkendall, SERIES EDITOR

Over-fulfilled Expectations

HAROLD F. BREIMYER

Over-fulfilled Expectations

A Life and an Era in Rural America

THE HENRY A. WALLACE SERIES
ON AGRICULTURAL HISTORY AND RURAL STUDIES

IOWA STATE UNIVERSITY PRESS • AMES

First edition, 1991

Library of Congress Cataloging-in-Publication Data

Breimyer, Harold F.
　Over-fulfilled expectations : a life and an era in rural America / Harold F. Breimyer. – 1st ed.
　　p.　　cm. – (The Henry A. Wallace series on agricultural history and rural studies)
　Includes bibliographical references and index.
　ISBN 0–8138–0856–1
　1. Breimyer, Harold F.　2. Agricultural economists – United States – biography.　3. Country life – Ohio – Fort Recovery.　I. Title.　II. Series.
HD1771.5.B74A3　　　1991
338.1′092 – dc20
[B]　　　　　　　　　　　　　　　　　　　　　　　　　　　　　　　　　　　　90–46633

FRONTISPIECE: *Harold F. Breimyer, 1989.*
© *Julie's Studio, Columbia, Mo. Reprinted with permission*

Dedicated gratefully to the memory
of four persons who influenced the
life and career of Harold F. Breimyer:

Christina Pauline Walter Breymaier
his stalwart grandmother

Lucile DeSelm Seedorf
his pert and inspiring high school English teacher

Oris V. Wells and Sylvester R. ("Si") Smith
his first and last mentors in government,
who taught without meaning to

CONTENTS

SERIES EDITOR'S INTRODUCTION

THE HENRY A. WALLACE SERIES on Agricultural History and Rural Studies is designed to enlarge publishing opportunities in agricultural history and thereby to expand public understanding of the development of agriculture and rural society. The Series will be composed of volumes that explore the many aspects of agriculture and rural life within historical perspectives. It will evolve as the field evolves. The press and editor will solicit and welcome the submission of manuscripts that illustrate, in good and fresh ways, that evolution. Our interests are broad. They do not stop with Iowa and U.S. agriculture but extend to all other parts of the world. They encompass the social, intellectual, scientific, and technological aspects of the subject as well as the economic and political. The emphasis of the Series is on the scholarly monograph, but historically significant memoirs of people involved in and with agriculture and rural life and major sources for research in the field will also be included.

Most appropriately, this Iowa-based Series is dedicated to a highly significant agriculturist who began in Iowa, developed a large, well-informed interest in its rural life, and expanded the scope of his interests beyond the state to the nation and the world. An Iowa native and son of an agricultural scientist, journalist, and secretary of agriculture, Henry A. Wallace was a 1910 graduate of Iowa State College, a frequent participant in its scientific activities, editor of *Wallaces' Farmer* from 1921 to 1933, founder in 1926 of the Hi-Bred Corn Company (now Pioneer Hi-Bred International, Inc.), secretary of agriculture from 1933 to 1940, and vice-president of the United States from 1941 to 1945. In the agricultural phases of his wide-ranging career, he was both a person of large importance in the development of America's agriculture and the leading policymaker during the most creative period in the history of American farm policy.

As farm editor, founder of a seed company and secretary of agriculture, Wallace participated in a revolution. In fact, he was one of its promoters. It changed farm operations, substituting machines and other technologies for human beings and animals, sharply reduced the number of people on farms, and increased farm productivity in equally dramatic fashion. It also restructured the agricultural system, substantially reducing the number and increasing the size of farms and making public agencies and private corporations more important in their relations to farmers and farming. In the new order, to cite one illustration, farmers, rather than raise their own seed corn as they had in the past, now bought it from firms such as Pioneer.

This new contribution to the Wallace Series, written by a person who began his career in Henry A.'s Department of Agriculture, offers an interpretation of the revolution. Harold Breimyer sees his life story as illustrative of "the saga of dramatic changes in the farming and rural life of the Midwest, and of major developments in the role of the United States government relative to agriculture." He has much of value to say about the public dimensions of the developing agriculture system, both the Department of Agriculture and the land-grant universities. Even more important, he shows what the revolution meant in the lives of individuals, especially those for whom it enlarged opportunities. In writing the memoir, he sees himself as "surrogate for a generation of farm youth whose lives were reshaped by a paroxysm of emancipation throughout the rural America of their time. He and his fellows saw and felt the rural community . . . emerge from circumscribed opportunity and outlook into vistas of worldwide dimension."

For some people of course, the revolution destroyed hopes of remaining farmers; for some, it meant migration to an urban slum, often from a rural one. Breimyer is not unaware of negative aspects. In fact, as an agricultural economist, he has been a critic of the structural features, especially the trend toward an industrial agriculture with farm operators controlled by outsiders.

Nevertheless, Breimyer is confident that "thousands of Americans of his day" had predominantly positive experiences similar to his own. For him and for them, the revolution elevated their status in life. As a participant in an era of rapid change, he attained more than he had thought possible. His story, as he sees it, is "the account of an entire generation of rural youth who found cultural emancipation during the years when it was a national purpose to help them do so."

This happy, fascinating, delightful, frank, and insightful memoir is a welcome addition to the series. Since the beginning nearly a decade ago, we have promised to publish memoirs, but this is the first to appear, at least the first full one. It seems certain to help scholars and general readers enlarge their understanding of the enormously significant revolution that swept across rural America during much of Breimyer's lifetime. Perhaps it will encourage others who experienced the phenomenon in different ways but share his talent as a writer to give us accounts of their lives.

RICHARD S. KIRKENDALL
The Bullitt Professor of American History
University of Washington

ACKNOWLEDGMENTS

AS I WROTE THIS MEMOIR of my life experiences, I was reminded, almost line by line, of the infinite ways other persons' lives have touched mine.

I am deeply grateful to the thousands of individuals who have made my life richer. Many were still present with me on our planet as I wrote the memoir; others had departed. They have been childhood playmates, schoolmates, members of my family, close and casual friends, fellow workers, professional colleagues, teachers, counselors, and ministers. They have provided companionship, empathy, instruction, counsel, and, occasionally, a bolstering of moral resolve.

A few are named in this memoir. Many more are worthy of mention. Some names are no longer remembered.

Each of them, in striving to fulfill his own expectations, has contributed to the over-fulfilling of mine.

In a different vein, I acknowledge my debt of gratitude to the individuals who helped in the production of this book. It is greatest to Jody Pestle, who converted every word of my cut-up, pasted, stapled, and interlined text to clean copy for the publisher. I thank Dr. Bruce Bullock, who as chairman of the department of agricultural economics of the University of Missouri—Columbia let me horse-trade my small services in exchange for that typography.

My wife, Rachel, pored over phrasing, punctuation, spelling. She sought out non-sequiturs, redundancies, and other flaws that creep into a manuscript. She is due, and has, my gratitude.

I will always stand in appreciation to Dr. Richard Kirkendall, editor of the Henry A. Wallace series published by the Iowa State University Press. He invited me to submit my memoir, contributed his suggestions for revision and his recommendation to the Press, and wrote an introduction to this volume. I am especially pleased for a new association with Dr. Kirkendall, once a colleague at the University of Missouri— Columbia, for whom I formed high respect as I read his splendid study of the New Deal era, *Social Scientists and Farm Politics in the Age of Roosevelt*. Having just completed thirty years experience in Roosevelt's Washington, I was strikingly impressed by how accurately he, a historian, had captured from secondary sources the atmosphere, the sense of mission, that I had felt as a participant. A considerable part of this memoir is devoted to the Age of Roosevelt. I would be pleased if I describe it with an insight matching Dr. Kirkendall's.

HAROLD F. BREIMYER

Columbia, Missouri
June 1989

Over-fulfilled Expectations

Prelude

A farm boy reared on Horatio Alger who later adopted Santayana (Last Puritan) and Henry Adams (Education) finds himself molded. Whether success as the world views it is thereby accounted for is moot; that outlook and character are influenced is beyond doubt. — biographical entry, *Who's Who in America, 1988–89*

To ask a reader to give undivided attention to the saga of a stranger is presumptuous. It is especially so when the narrator is no luminary of business or politics, as is Lee Iacocca of Ford and Chrysler fame or the string of legatees from the Reagan White House, writing their kiss-and-tell revelations; when the account is not of a rise from bleak obscurity to national prominence, as Booker T. Washington's; or when the story is not embellished with sidesplitting humor or racy revelation. None of those attractions will be found in this modest recounting of the life of an Ohio farm boy who lived in what surely was one of the most exciting periods in our nation's history, and who experienced handicaps, hopes, and eventual gratifications that parallel those of thousands of Americans of his day.

Everyone seeks satisfaction in what he does. The Greek philosopher Aristotle, in his *Nicomachean Ethics,* called happiness the universal goal of mankind. Happiness can be defined variously, but elevation of one's station in life surely is one of the most common ingredients. We can suppose that a person born to the top rung of the ladder strives only to avoid slipping lower. But to the majority who begin at a lower level, the urge is strong to climb higher.

The urge was strong indeed in the mind of the Ohio lad whose story this is. Recounted here will be the setting from which he began, his aspirations, successes, and disappointments. Successes there were; but they take on meaning not because they were grand or conspicuous but, rather, because they more than fulfilled what the boy had dared to dream of. What higher satisfaction can there be in anyone's life than to attain more than had been thought possible? To arrive at the denouement years with a sense of self-fulfillment is the richest reward in human existence.

The theme of an individual's rising out of nowhere to notable accomplishment occupies many biographical and autobiographical works. Very often, the hero or heroine was initially handicapped by being not only poor but a member of an ethnic minority as well. So it was that a century ago Booker T. Washington became a renowned educator after beginning as a slave. The late Theodore White, reporter of wartime China events and of presidential elections, told in his *In Search of History* how he, as a youth in the Jewish quarter of Boston, sold newspapers on a commuter train in order to buy food. In her appealing *I Know Why the Caged Bird Sings,* Maya Angelou describes the cage of being black in Arkansas.

Most of the success stories in current literature are urban. Usually the high achiever rose out of an urban slum. More rarely has a comparable rural story been told — or, in any case, not since the popularization a century ago of figures such as Abe Lincoln the rail splitter.

This is a rural story. In some respects it is a rural counterpart to the urban accounts in which second-generation Irish, Italian, Jewish, and black youth rose to fame.

But the differences are more than rural versus urban. Harold Breimyer was born white to parents of German lineage who were in the ethnic majority of their community. His family circumstances were modest but not mired in abject poverty of income or culture.

Moreover, this is the story of not just a person — or even primarily of a person — but of a community, of a time, and of a national ambience. No suggestion will be found in these pages that the author or any other human being can, as the bromide goes, pull himself up by his own bootstraps. The most ancient of enigmas is how to separate the autonomy of the human will from the environmental forces that either restrain or aid its expression. This story will focus mainly on the latter. It will be more sociological than psychological.

Harold Breimyer was born into a place and time that put a high premium on improving one's lot; his motivation reflected the mores of his native community. The community surrounded the sleepy village of Fort Recovery at the western edge of Ohio, so named because in the Indian wars following the American Revolution Anthony Wayne recovered a fort site that Arthur St. Clair had lost. By any test the community was unprepossessing. It had no place to go other than upward. Yet it was imbued with a confidence, as unsubstantiated as it was unsophisticated, that the future offered bright promise. Was not the United States the land of opportunity?

So it was that the community's farmers listened to the advice put out by George Henning, the first county agent of Mercer County in the new

Agricultural Extension service of the Ohio State University—and to Charles ("Nick") Nicholson, the first instructor in vocational agriculture at the Fort Recovery High School. Or if they did not hearken to those teachers directly, they watched the crops and cattle of neighbors who were more responsive.

Townsfolk pinned their faith in education. School teachers ranked with ministers of local churches as the recognized intelligentsia. Scholastic achievements of the brightest students were rejoiced in. A half-century before a Coleman report would tell everyone that formal education doesn't really escalate status, the burghers of Fort Recovery were certain that it does just that. And their faith made it do so.

During the 1920s, the decade of the farm boy's youth, the community was caught up in the effervescence of the time. The years were sometimes called "roaring," but Frederick Lewis Allen, their scribe, said they were "ballyhoo years." Victory in World War I had induced a national euphoria, a sudden new appreciation and confidence in what great things lay in store. Industrializing rapidly, the country saw ahead, in the words of favorite author Richard Halliburton, only Horizons Unlimited.

Ohioans of the community readily accepted as individual and collective destiny what Frederick Watkins, in *The Political Tradition of the West,* called the Judaic vision of a "future kingdom of heaven on earth" (p. 367).

These pages will chronicle the experience of Harold Breimyer as a product of that place and time. They will tell how he responded to the influences brought to bear on him as he moved first into scholastic achievement and then into positions of respect and esteem in public service and in university education.

And because his life experiences ran contemporaneously with major developments in U.S. agriculture and the public role relative to it, the personal record will be a vehicle for commentary on the farm scene and agricultural policy. After growing up during the heated but inconclusive political agitations in agriculture of the 1920s, Harold Breimyer, by good fortune, entered into the new and revolutionary New Deal farm programs as soon as they were set in motion in 1933. Thereafter he rarely was far removed from farm policy action. The story of his life is almost a story of the political milieu of U.S. agriculture from the 1920s to the 1980s.

CHAPTER 1

The Mettle of the Boy: A Vignette

SELF-CHARACTERIZATION IS NOTABLY UNRELIABLE. Centuries ago the Scottish poet Robert Burns wished "the giftie" had accorded mankind the power "to see oursels as others see us." The dispensation would from "mony a blunder free us, and foolish notion." The character of Harold Breimyer will be derivable from the experiences recounted in these pages. A brief confession, however flawed, may nevertheless provide an introductory focus to all that follows. It is confined to youthful years. Remembered behavioral patterns and emotional strains as lodged in a seventy-year memory will be described without pledge of exceptional insight.

Harold was the oldest child and only surviving son (a younger brother died in infancy) of a school teacher mother and a father who was a superb craftsman but an undistinguished farmer. The father had enticed the mother away from their comfortable home at 528 Grand Avenue in Springfield, Ohio, with promises of a better life, eventually, in the country. She found there only disappointment and near-privation. In the simplest emotional response pattern she sought compensation in the performance of her firstborn. The boy, as though to accommodate her psychic needs, showed an aptitude for learning. Coached by his mother, he was enrolled in the local one-room school already possessed of ability to read and to manipulate numbers. Thereupon he advanced fast.

During those years educational philosophy, as dependably cyclical as the locusts or farmland drought, had swung to the acceleration principle. Each pupil was to be pushed ahead as quickly as possible. Mothers, in sweepstakes conversations about their children's achievements, cited not scholastic grade scores but how many grade levels had been telescoped or skipped. Ella Breimyer could eventually say that her firstborn completed eight elementary grades in six years.

Through high school and college years the boy was to be two years younger than his classmates. He has never since been sure how severe an emotional penalty was paid.

If Ella Breimyer pushed her son to move ahead fast in school, her husband was no less aggressive with regard to farming skills. The father had even more community sanction for early training. Among farm families, children were rated by how early they learned to milk a cow or to drive a team of horses. Harold did not surpass neighboring farm youth as widely in farm chores as in book learning, but neither did he lag.

RESPECT FOR AUTHORITY

A moral trait showed up early that was to prove indelible. It was respect for authority and for social rules. When he was very young, the boy was coached into obeying not only the instructions of his elders but also the dicta of society. He was so sensitized that he lived in fear of being reprimanded. The paradigm is not rare. In his case, though, it metamorphosed early into attentiveness to rules as guides to his own conduct and into intellectual inquiry about their origin and composition. And it went beyond that, into believing that the most elevated human conduct not only conforms to society's mores but improves them.

Long before he enrolled in study of the interminable Great Books, he anticipated Immanuel Kant's one and only categorical imperative: to "act only on that maxim whereby thou canst at the same time will that it should become a universal law" (p. 421). Young Breimyer thought his pattern of conduct was merely what ought to be everyone's.

The trait has shown up in countless ways beginning from the boy's youth. When the custodian of Fort Recovery High School complained that some boys were pulling three or four paper towels from the dispenser to dry their hands even though, he said, "one will do," Harold found that indeed one towel sufficed. Sixty years later, at the University of Missouri–Columbia, he was still using only one. In his professorial years he also switched off the light when he left his university office, turned off other professors' air conditioning (Ph.D. professors seem to be capable of turning the air conditioning switch only to the ON position), never walked on the campus grass, and picked up stray newspapers and other trash on the front lawn of the university's Mumford Hall.

Anyone who respects society's rules must necessarily also respect the people and processes that set them. The young man, perhaps reflecting his Teutonic lineage, reserved his greatest homage to the highest authority—the United States government.

It was almost foreordained that a youth who was so concerned for social rules and behavior would find his employment in public service and his intellectual home in the social sciences. So it proved to be.

THE URGE TO WIN

Another characteristic that showed up in Harold Breimyer as a boy fit with the pressure brought on him to excel and to move ahead rapidly in all that he undertook. It was less consistent with his sensitivity to socially considerate behavior. It was an urge to win. He felt impelled to take first place in every contest in which he engaged and, moreover, believed he was able to do so.

As a ten-year-old he took part in a debate staged within the sixth grade. The school was the new Madison, Indiana, consolidated school, the most modern institution in the region. The class was big enough to have not only internal debates but three boys' basketball teams as well. The debate topic was, "Resolved, that life is better in the city than in the country." Memory does not reveal whether his team took the affirmative or the negative side, but it still records that when his side lost, the boy could not understand how such a dreadful outcome was possible.

Through the elementary and high school years he won most contests. During those years he trusted the encomiums that came from his parents and their close friends. Not until reaching adulthood did he comprehend that for every winner there are one or more losers, for whom defeat can be painful, especially when they experience it repeatedly. Nor did he know that his schoolmates wearied of his being at the top so often.

Once, following a 4-H Club event in which, as usual, he collected a blue or a red ribbon (first or second place), his father's cousin Albert suggested that instead of handing out two or three top prizes, the club leader should give a small reward to each boy or girl who successfully completed his or her club project. It could be only a pencil, Albert suggested.

The perennial winner was too polite to rebut the second-cousin, a formidable, handsome hulk of 76 inches height and 230 pounds. In later years, though, Albert's philosophy gradually sank in. The urge to win may have been the first of Harold Breimyer's boyhood traits to yield to perceptions learned as he matured. In college, as an editor of *The Agricultural Student* magazine, he editorialized on the theme, "Why glorify leaders so much? Why not applaud the followers?" He was ready to listen to cousin Albert.

In later years Harold Breimycr as philosopher-economist found similar reason to reject the Darwinian-survival thesis of the business world. The objective of a social system is not to enable a select few to win big at the expense of all others but instead to offer opportunity for all to employ their talents remuneratively. Such became the philosophy of his adult years. It took various forms including, in classroom teaching, his showing more interest in helping lagging students to upgrade themselves than in applauding already bright students who really did not need tutoring.

THE STRESS OF SHYNESS

Among all his self-perceptions, the one most difficult to account for is a shyness so intense as to be an affliction of Harold Breimyer's youthful years. It had follow-up consequences that persisted throughout his lifetime. As a boy he was sure he was lacking in attractive appearance, social graces, and capacity for small talk and repartee. His judgment was not entirely wrong. The puritanism of his parents that spurred his competencies gave little opportunity for cultivating the arts of conversational banter.

Classmates who lost in scholarly contests with the boy doubtless did not hesitate to get even by means of jibes or ridicule, thereby contributing to his social insecurity. The sensitivity of the boy is attested to by a recollection still vivid after sixty-five years. As a seven-year-old visiting his city cousin Paul Schulz, Harold heard a neighbor lady say, to his surprise, "Why, Harold is better looking than Paul." The boy had supposed he was not better looking than anyone.

The shyness retarded emotional development. His fear of girls delayed his dating until his senior year in college. Not until his early twenties, when he was professionally established in Washington, did he feel comfortable in the company of young ladies. The imbalance in which he was so successful in any structured situation and so ill at ease in amorphous social relationships stayed with him all his life. It doubtless contributed to his professional success. How much enjoyment it denied him he cannot know.

MATERIAL VERSUS SPIRITUAL VALUES

Yet another trait as perceived by Harold Breimyer himself is worth mention. Human beings can be identified by a large number of attributes, but surely one is the relative importance each individual attaches to material pleasures and indulgences relative to those of the mind and spirit. Indeed, the material-spiritual dichotomy can be drawn on to describe individuals, social groups and even whole nations. It likewise can be the nexus for delineating changes in the make-up of a society over time.

In Harold Breimyer's observation, the United States turned away during his lifetime from its professed asceticism of the 1920s that was epitomized in the Eighteenth Amendment to the Constitution (prohibiting manufacture of alcoholic beverages) and moved progressively to the sensual indulgences of the 1980s with their sexual libertinism, high consumption of alcoholic beverages, and drug culture. The drug experience of the 1980s is a logical extension of the trend that began in the 1920s when speakeasies took the lead in undermining the ban on alcohol ("prohibition") and billboard advertisements enticed young men and the most fashionable ladies alike into the pleasures of inhaled cigarette smoke.

Everything in Harold Breimyer's upbringing weighed in favor of spiritual rather than material values. Circumstances alone did so; few material comforts were available to him. Having lived satisfactorily without many material pleasures until he reached his majority, he found it easy in later years to discount their importance.

Yet the equation is not resolved that readily. Young Harold wanted a few things very badly. As a child he dreamed of getting in his Christmas stocking a wind-up toy train, on a track. He asked for it two or three years in succession. Always a note was found in the stocking: "Maybe next year." One time he was given a small pull-train instead. The pull-toy cost a dollar or less, a price his parents could afford. A wind-up version had a tag of two or three dollars, which was more than their means.

A little later he begged for a baseball and bat. He thought maybe the family's minister could somehow provide them. Although Harold Breimyer never did get his wind-up train, he fared better with baseball equipment. By chance his father's friend William Trautwein was coach at Wittenberg College in Springfield, Ohio. He sent the boy unclaimed equipment, including a couple of fielder's gloves and a catcher's mask. The father fashioned a bat from the roller of a grain binder. Thus the lad's emotional scars were partly erased and he gained an elevated social position in the neighborhood as custodian of the only baseball equipment available. When the bat had knocked the leather cover off the three baseballs, friction tape wound over the gummed cord kept the balls in use almost interminably.

Is there a moral? It could be trenchant. It's that no child born to American parents should be forced to accept too severe an austerity.

Every child should receive some wanted item in a Christmas stocking. A baseball and fielder's glove ought to be the legacy of every boy, and perhaps an optional choice for each girl. Most communities now have social agencies that guard against the worst deprivation of children. It ought to be possible to make sure that no child be over-victimized by the economic position of his or her family. The psychological damage is too severe, and in fact can be socially dangerous.

INQUISITIVENESS

Last, why do some people spend their lifetime inquiring into the working of any mechanism, be it a mechanical contrivance or a social institution? Why do they do that when the egocentrists ask only how well their personal wishes are met?

Individuals of the first category are of the scientific mind, the primary feature of which is its selflessness. The scientist is by definition forgetful of self. Contrariwise, anyone preoccupied with self cannot learn much about other persons, things, or the universe.

Many years later, on the downslope of his career, Harold Breimyer would describe to colleagues the personal qualities of the research scientist as "the sense of detachment, the curiosity and capacity to observe phenomena selflessly" (1971, p.2). He claimed no high research achievement for himself but thought he had something of the researcher's mindset and morality. The scientist's inquisitiveness is a mental posture that extends to physical and social phenomena equally. In this respect the physical and the social scientists are alike. There is little difference between the engineer who wonders about the intricacies of a computer and the economist who asks about the ultimate effects of a monetary policy as imposed by the Federal Reserve Board.

In an age of science, the scientific mind is properly venerated. It also is often self-proclaimed, sometimes falsely. Imposters are numerous.

Breimyer is convinced that the truly selfless scientist is a rare bird. Whether he himself qualifies is not for him to say, but he likes to credit himself with delving into how anything works, even the agricultural economy, just because he wants to know. He may have a second reason, consistent with a trait mentioned several pages back: the wish to make things better.

CHAPTER 2

Hometown in the 1920s

IN THE LORE OF THE AGES, cities are, at one and the same time, the center of commerce and culture and the breeding ground for turpitude. Social ills of all sorts — class distinction, lawlessness, and moral depravity — are said to originate or be exhibited there.

Rural villages, by contrast, are regarded as lacking in sophistication. But they are credited with being democratic, free of the city's vices, and supportive of their citizens.

Harold Breimyer was born into the environment of a village of 1,000 inhabitants, Fort Recovery, Ohio. His parents' farm was located three miles south of the town. His father had bought the farm the year before Harold's birth. Lacking enough money to buy a good farm, Fred Breimyer over-paid for a poor one. He thereby confirmed an adage in the economics of agriculture: When money is tight, good land is under-priced and poor land is over-sought and over-priced.

The farm's clay topsoil was only a thin layer; the black loam of neighboring Darke County was absent. Only when Fred's son Harold grew up and got book learning did the geological fact come to light — that the ridges south of Fort Recovery were a recessional moraine. There the glacier had hesitated a moment in stellar time to let its ice fringe melt and deposit junk of rocks and clay.

Like many of the world's less prepossessing places, Fort Recovery's main claim to a dim fame rested on its history. The name itself suggests the events. A military loss (actually a disaster) was gloriously reversed. Regaining what had been lost has invariably given cause for rejoicing, and Anthony Wayne's recovery of the area at the headwaters of the Wabash River that Arthur St. Clair had lost to the Indians put Fort Recovery on the map for all time. It also gave occasion to erect an obelisk of commemoration. Not many towns of 1,000 people can boast a spire reaching 100 feet into the sky.

Legend has it that George Washington, when he dispatched St. Clair to the Northwest Territory, warned him against an ambush. The warning was ineffective. Early in the morning of November 4, 1791, a cold day with snow on the ground, a force of 1,400 men together with, strangely, many women and children was quietly having a breakfast of short rations. Having just arrived, the troops had not yet thrown up barricades. Shouting war whoops, Indians from the Miami, Shawnee, Wyandot, and Delaware tribes attacked. They fired from behind trees and logs. St. Clair's troops fired in the open from the close order to which they had been trained. The result was carnage, a massacre.

More than two years later General Anthony Wayne, "the chief who never sleeps," retraced the route of St. Clair. When his troops reached the place of the earlier defeat, they buried the bones that littered the ground and erected a stockade. It was named Fort Recovery, commemorating recovery of ground that had been lost to the Indians.

Once again the Indians of the Miami and other tribes, urged on by British agents, sought to repulse the invading white men. On June 30, 1794, a force of 2,000 attacked the fort, whose defenders numbered 200. Fortunately, a pack train of supplies had arrived the previous day. The Indians suffered heavy losses as they were repulsed. The battle was decisive in stabilizing the Ohio-Indiana frontier, and the Treaty of Greeneville was signed the next year.

Except for the obelisk, the people of Fort Recovery remained indifferent to their history until the depression years of the 1930s. Building a replica of the original fort was in part a work project. Thereafter the townsfolk took more interest. The Ohio State Historical Society led in designating the place as a state park. When timbers of the depression-built fort rotted, a sturdier reconstruction of the original structure replaced it. A museum now tells local people and visitors about Fort Recovery's history (also recounted by Martha Rohr in her book, *Historical Sketch of Fort Recovery*).

The town has little other distinction to announce—except that since 1971 billboards have proclaimed to arriving travelers that in that year the boys' high school basketball team won the Ohio Class C championship. Thus, the town's only claims to fame are dated 1791 and 1971.

THE VILLAGE ECONOMY

Fort Recovery in the 1920s was a sleepy village that kept itself alive—barely—by servicing the surrounding farming community. Its retail businesses still enjoyed the protection of distance from larger competing trade centers such as Portland in Indiana and Celina in Ohio. The Model T Ford, ubiquitous emancipator of rural America, had by that time only closed the doors of country crossroads stores, such as the one at North Dayton to which Harold Breimyer was dispatched by bicycle to buy small grocery items and paper and pencils for his schoolwork. In the decade of the 1920s, villages remained virile, vital trading centers.

Not until 1928, when the Model A Ford replaced the Model T and a beautiful new Chevrolet came into showrooms, did county seat cities begin to displace villages such as Fort Recovery. A companion factor in the change was an orgy of projects to put a hard surface on gravel roads. Only persons old enough to have driven automobiles over country roads know how dramatic was the transformation. On the older roads the graveled surface was merely the width of a wagon or car, offering a pair of tracks marked by chuckholes that a careful driver steered dexterously to avoid.

The surface was so narrow because it was put in place by farmers who, between their planting and harvesting seasons, earned a few desperately needed dollars by hauling, in their farm wagons, gravel from local pits. The wagons were fitted with a special gravel bed. Their floor boards, six inches wide, could be removed singly, allowing the gravel to fall on the center of the road. A horse-drawn grader then smoothed the dropped ridge of gravel just enough to accommodate two tracks. When two vehicles, cars or wagons, met, the outer wheels were carefully edged onto the rough shoulder.

If the drivers were acquainted, the meeting could be a social event. The horses were reined in and the automobile motor stopped as the drivers exchanged the time of day. For the moment the road was blocked. If another vehicle appeared, the conversation ended.

Among county and state highway authorities a debate ensued as to whether the preferred paving material was concrete or blacktop—the latter often called, erroneously, macadam. (The original macadam road, named for a Scotch engineer of the nineteenth century, used broken gravel.) Within the limits of a town such as Fort Recovery, though, the streets often were of brick.

Until speedier cars and hard-surfaced roads doomed much of its retail business, Fort Recovery had three mom-and-pop grocery stores— Arnold's, Grevencamp's, and Zehringer's. Late in the 1920s a merchandising event excited everyone. Kroger brought in the first chain store, which offered discount prices but otherwise was indistinguishable from its competitors. Self-service was not even thought of. The grocer kept prices in his mind, a pencil behind his ear, an apron over his clothes, a sharp ear for the housewife-shopper's order, and a long wand with which to pull food packages off the top shelves.

Among other retailers were three clothiers—Sunderman's, Weiler and Long, and Reuter and Leonhard (pronounced Len'hart). Weiler and Long was modern: The customer's money was put in a cartridge and dispatched by overhead pneumatic conveyor to the office clerk. Change and a receipt came back.

John Adams had the older of two drugstores, or pharmacies, and over it was the Morvilius "opera house," the only village facility for a stage performance. The newer Zimmerman competitor had a soda fountain and an ice cream parlor. Dispensing sodas was the most prestigious after-school employment available to high-schoolers.

Frank Hoke sold jewelry. Adam Beach mended old shoes and sold new ones. Mike Velten had harness on display but by the 1920s sold little. He diversified into bicycle repairs. The first automobile sales and repair establishments were Leo Wagner for Ford and Lee Guggenbiller for Chevrolet.

A combination feed-mill and grain elevator, a cooperative, had only intermittent competition from the private St. Clair mill. The Hull brothers sold farm machinery, Emil Wangler hardware. And two lumber companies vied for the business of farmers who built new barns (often) and new homes (rarely). Two banks served the community's financial needs.

As long as purchases were standard items ranging from women's hat pins to farmers' binder twine, Fort Recovery businesses could supply them. Anything newfangled was unlikely to be on a tradesman's shelf.

Even as early as the 1920s, many villagers sensed that local retail trade provided a thin economic base. Long before rural development became a politician's chant but an intermittent national policy, Fort Recovery's more imaginative leaders sought to develop small local industry. The town's old guard was opposed. Ed Koch had made a tidy fortune with his small stirrup factory. When a company that called itself New Idea proposed to manufacture a new-style manure spreader in Fort Recovery, Koch and his henchmen kept it out. They feared it would increase hourly wage rates. New Idea went to Coldwater, fifteen miles distant, there to lift its community to a prosperity that to this day Fort Recovery has not enjoyed.

Division on the issue of a new factory reveals much about the sociology of a community such as Fort Recovery, and the separation of fact from carefully cultivated fiction. The grass-roots imagery, as noted, glorifies smaller habitations. There the air is said to be pure, the people egalitarian-democratic, and economic instincts nonexploitive. The reality is that in small towns social and economic stratification is endemic. Fort Recovery had its network of class distinctions, separating its lettered and unlettered, its gentility and plebeians, its rich and poor. And as to the folklore that in a small town "everyone knows everyone else," in Fort Recovery of the 1920s were pairings of individuals who in their lifetimes rarely met or conversed—perhaps, in a few cases, never.

The village's poor families were *very* poor and had few champions. Jane Addams and her counterparts were always big-city. Small towns had no equivalent. In Fort Recovery some families scrounged for the barest existence. To Harold Breimyer, already socially observant, the means of their survival were invisible. In a few cases they may have been illegal, and the Jean Valjean moral enigma of *Les Miserables* was sensed.

In his later years he understood, retrospectively, how intense was the poverty. A classmate was a girl named Joan Golden, whose father dealt in metal junk and rags and seemed to have no other livelihood. Rail thin, Joan came to class in the palest print dresses. Following graduation she entered nurses' training, only to die soon of "consumption," the term for tuberculosis of the lungs. The diagnosis was technically accurate, but she was really a victim of poverty and malnutrition.

RELIGION AND POLITICS

Fort Recovery abounded in churches. Many of the congregations were small and could barely give their minister even minimum support. The Lutheran church, to which the Breimyer family belonged, vied with the Roman Catholics for community recognition and height of the church steeple. Most of the town's upper-crust inhabitants were Lutherans, Catholics, Methodists, or Congregationalists. The town also gave sanctuary to noisier evangelicals, toward whom the Lutherans and other Protestants snubbed their noses. The Catholics simply disregarded them.

The rural community, for which the town of Fort Recovery was cultural and trading center, was half Roman Catholic, half Protestant. In the countryside a line of separation was as sharp as Rome's Rubicon or America's Mason-Dixon. In the early 1900s the Catholics had their own parochial elementary schools. They were intensely loyal to their priests and frequently stayed aloof from community-wide activities.

The Lutherans, remembering Martin Luther and his theses of opposition to the Pope, kept a mild anti-Catholicism alive. Harold's father, Fred, who had been reared at the community's Rubicon line and had good friends among Catholic neighbors, rejected all anti-Catholic sentiment. He refused to attend the service at his church on Reformation Sunday, when the minister delivered his annual denunciation of the Pope and his minions.

Religious friction was mostly confined to the outlying rural territory. Townsfolk were pretty much bored by it, and the more so as the town's Catholic priest, Father Greiwe, proved to be cooperative, even ecumenical.

Philosophical differences between Catholics and Protestants colored a growing interest in national policy for agriculture—an interest that had begun farther west in Iowa, Illinois, and the Plains states. Despite its near-poverty, the Fort Recovery community was politically traditional and voted Republican. At farm meetings and Farmers' Institutes of the 1920s, price parity and McNary-Haugenism eventually came under debate. Catholic farmers, schooled in a doctrine of mutual aid and less coldly capitalistic, were more favorable than their Protestant neighbors to proposals that, a decade later, culminated in New Deal farm programs. Now, more than a half century since that time, placards indicating membership in the aggressive National Farmers Organization are found on farms of Roman Catholics east of Fort Recovery. Few, if any, are seen on land of Protestant farmers.

Harold Breimyer as a schoolboy got his indoctrination as he attended the meetings and listened to the debates. And he did not fail to note that the farmer who called most loudly for government help to farmers was John Brockman, a Catholic.

THE COMMUNITY'S SCHOOLS

A temptation more insidious than any corporeal pleasure comes to anyone whose several ventures prove successful, whose bed is always of roses. Such a fortunate person is easy prey to doctrines crediting one's own valor, one's superior worth. It is the self-made-man arrogation, the poet's pretentious, defiant, "I am master of my fate."

The temptation must be resisted. It calls for a Faustian renunciation of the tempting devil. It is hereby renounced for purpose of this narrative. Nothing of the theme will be found herein.

On the contrary, this is an account of the good things that came to Harold Breimyer and were not of his doing. Credit is accorded his family, especially his heroic paternal grandmother. But crucial to his early development was a community dedication to education.

How could it be that a community so sparsely enriched materially should set such high store on acquisition of knowledge—book learning, and applied knowledge too? That enigma remains unsolved, although one hypothesis fits the theme of the mother of the Gracchi, whose statesmen sons were her jewels. Denied the financial means for material splendor, the community of Fort Recovery could hope only for costless cultural achievement. In Harold Breimyer's day not even athletic competition provided an opportunity to demonstrate prowess. The high school basketball championship dated forty-one years after Harold's graduation. In his time the old brick school building had no gymnasium. Nor was a football field or baseball diamond at hand. The only recognition available to Fort Recovery High School was scholastic.

For Harold, good fortune began at the elementary school. George Young was nearing the end of his lifetime career of teaching farmers' children the ABCs and numbers and a lot more besides. How many rural school teachers, then or now, would read to assembled pupils, once yearly, portions of the annual report of the President of the United States to the Congress? George Young did so.

College Hill School, located only a quarter-mile from the Breimyer farm, had a single room but was sturdily built and was the best equipped facility within a twenty-five-mile radius. The school was the cultural center of the immediately adjacent farming area. One evening event held periodically was a public ciphering contest. Pupils would go to the blackboard, write down numbers read to them, and perform at competitive speed the required calculation, usually addition. Then parents would join in the contest. By the time he reached the upper grades, Harold Breimyer could out-figure his classmates. By that time, too, he would win a community wide contest staged by the visiting Chautauqua. At College Hill School Ferry Benner, a farmer-parent, could out-cipher everyone.

In these days of the computer, when a newspaper cartoon shows a kindergartner punching 2 + 2 into a pocket computer, skills in mental manipulation of numbers are not appreciated. Nevertheless, Harold Breimyer as an old cipherer still gets smug satisfaction from his deftness with numbers. When a speaker announces that 7 1/2 percent of a Gross National Product of $4.2 trillion goes to national defense, then stumbles to convert the ratio to dollars, Harold Breimyer retorts instantly that of course he has $315 billion in mind. All he does is divide the GNP figure by 4, getting 1.05, multiply by 3, and point off appropriately. The process requires, maybe, two seconds.

During the fifth grade the young numbers-whiz had Bertha Stump as his teacher. She was truly excellent. Two years later, on returning from a year in Indiana, Alta Stump, Bertha's younger sister, taught him the seventh and eighth grade work in a single year. The Stump sisters were daughters of a local farmer who could barely keep body and soul together financially but made sure that his daughters attended "normal" school (teachers' college).

Dan Stump is remembered as the farmer who, when the Applebee knotter on his grain binder did not knot the twine, shrugged his shoulders and remarked, "It doesn't matter; the wife and girls will tie up the bundles." He did not acknowledge how arduous was the task.

College Hill was one of three one-room schools in Gibson Township. They were overseen by the Mercer County superintendent of schools, whose primary concern was for quality of instruction. A township school board of three members, invariably farmers, took their role as seriously as the Regents of any modern university. When Fred Breimyer was a member, his wife Ella, remembering her own standards, became convinced that Lela Alexander, a neighbor girl teaching at College Corner School, was ineffective. Harold and his sister Louise had attended her school briefly and reported that Miss Alexander spent much of the day reading *Black Beauty* aloud to the pupils and was casual about all else. When Fred initiated Lela's dismissal, he stirred a community resentment that quieted only when Lela departed for Dayton, the nearest large city. There she learned stenography, married, and presumably lived happily ever after.

What was taught in the country and small-town schools of Harold Breimyer's schooldays? Reading, writing, and arithmetic, of course, but values too — not as such, but implicitly. All College Hill families were of Christian faith and Protestant, and most were church-going. Even so, modern secularism was manifest in the absence of prayer or other religious activity within school walls. The moral code, together with patriotic symbolisms, was incorporated in the fabric of instruction. More specifically, the stories and poems in the texts for reading had moral content. A poem titled "Somebody's Mother" is still remembered. A boy volunteered assistance to an elderly lady whom he supposed to be the mother of another boy not at hand. The opening lines have escaped memory, but the last stanza read:

> And somebody's mother bowed low her head
> In her home that night; and the prayer she said
> Was, "God be kind to the noble boy
> Who is somebody's son, and pride, and joy."

Henry Wadsworth Longfellow, with his "Psalm of Life" and other poems, and John Greenleaf Whittier were mainstays not merely of assigned reading but of memorizing as well. In high school the plays of Shakespeare became the vehicle for moral instruction. Among passages mandated to be committed to memory was Portia's instruction to Shylock in *Merchant of Venice:*

> The quality of mercy is not strain'd,
> It droppeth as the gentle rain from heaven
> Upon the place beneath: it is twice bless'd;
> It blesseth him that gives and him that takes:
>
> And earthly power doth then show likest God's
> When mercy seasons justice. . . .

Throughout his lifetime Harold Breimyer never doubted that learning must have a moral quality. In the late 1950s, when he became a candidate for election to the Board of Education of Montgomery County, Maryland, he astonished the liberal establishment by defending nonsectarian prayer in schools. Professionally he took to the pages of journals to inquire into the principle of objectivity in economic research. He wondered how much of the research being done in agricultural economics would meet a stern test. In the 1980s religious fundamentalists, emboldened by what they took to be favorable signals from the Reagan White House, inveighed against something called "secular humanism." Harold Breimyer distrusted them, but he also read with approval the plea of University of North Carolina Professor Warren Nord: "Liberals should want religion taught in public schools."

A product of value-laden teaching, Harold Breimyer has stayed opposed to all talk about value-free instruction. Any society should be concerned for the moral culture that is nourished and communicated. Such has long been his conviction.

FARMING IN THE 1920S

Farms in the Fort Recovery area were typical of those of diversified agriculture. They ranged from 30 to 150 acres. The 1920s was a time of converting the power source from horse to tractor. The Fordson, exploiting the popularity of its cousin, the Model T automobile, gained a foothold first. McCormick-Deering's Farmall challenged quickly, but by the end of the decade, few farmers had converted fully. Most still had at least a team of two horses. The horses did the lighter work; the tractor was the power source for plowing and for harvesting grain.

Because grain yields on moraine soils were low, much of a farmer's income necessarily came from livestock and poultry. Wheat was produced for sale, but corn, oats, and hay became feed for livestock. Soybeans were being introduced only slowly, and at first were used mainly for forage, not as an oilseed.

Crops were rotated, for two separate reasons. As nitrogen fertilizers had not come into use, clovers were included in a rotation as a source of nitrogen. The best practice of all, according to speakers at Farmers' Institutes and the new county extension agent, was to plow-under a legume. Sweet clover provided the most "green manure" per acre.

The second reason for crop diversification and rotation was to lengthen the season of fieldwork. Horses were dependable, faithful animals, but they were slow-moving and could be worked only a limited number of hours a day. The Biblical injunction of one day of rest in seven was seen as necessary more for the horses than for the persons who drove them! Oats could be sowed following discing in March or early April, corn planted as late as early June, and wheat seeded as a fall crop. By spreading the fieldwork over so long a time, a farmer could farm 75 to 100 acres or more, especially if some acreage were left as pasture for dairy or beef cattle.

Nowadays, farmers boast about how many hundreds of acres they can seed and harvest with their giant tractors and matching equipment. If they were to return to diversification of crops, they could double the acreage. In the process they also would cut in half their machinery investment cost per acre.

Fred Breimyer's farm was about average in size and cropping pattern. On its 70 acres, which included 5 acres of woodland, were produced the usual mixture of field crops, plus truck crops (vegetables) for sale in the summer. An orchard provided fruit for home use, except in years of untimely frost. Four or five cows were milked, by hand, twice daily. Hogs, sheep, and laying hens, in addition to three or four horses, completed the farm animal inventory.

CLASS DIVISIONS AMONG FARMERS

A farming community is defined less by its tools and crops than by its tenure. Who owns the land, who farms it, and what are the terms of contractual relationships? Answers to these questions have defined the economics and sociology of rural communities from time immemorial.

The answers often are spun from imagery and folklore rather than derived from data. Farmers have variously been characterized as the dispirited dimwits of Markham's poem "Man with the Hoe," the impoverished transients of Steinbeck's *Grapes of Wrath,* ungrateful spongers off government programs as portrayed in much of the financial press of our day, or, as the exact opposite, as the only truly unspoiled exemplars of democracy, the Jeffersonian ideal.

Each characterization bears some validity. The outstanding feature of the rural community is its internal diversity. Perhaps the range of differences among farmers was even more striking in western Ohio in the 1920s than in farming communities of recent years.

In the Fort Recovery area were a few well-established farmers, who owned stock in one or both the local banks and whose primary business decisions were to decide when to buy more land. A handful of them took on the classic features of landed aristocracy, proud and disdainful. The vast majority of families who lived on the land were at the opposite end of the scale. Some owned their acreages and enjoyed the social status that goes with landownership, but they often lacked a matching financial security. A great many, though, were tenants; and among them were found examples of poverty so dire and distressing as to qualify for portrayal in the *Tobacco Road* genre of literature. The poorest tenants tended to be hidden. They attended no church, took part in no community social activities. Only the school system knew of their existence.

Although differences in tenure explained why some farm families were better off than others, a sequence of national events in the first three decades of the 1900s accounted for wide schisms even among farmers who held title to their land. The lessons learned in those decades were useful more than a half-century later, when U.S. agriculture repeated its pattern of the early 1900s. Harold Breimyer's experiences as a boy in the 1920s gave him a degree of authenticity when he, as a university professor, explained the debacle of agriculture in the 1980s.

After hard times in the 1890s, U.S. agriculture began to prosper in the first decade of the 1900s. Then the onset of World War I created a boom in values of farm products and farmland. The average U.S. farm price of winter wheat, which had been 80 cents a bushel in 1912, soared to $2.10 in 1919. Farmers who had got a good foothold before the war made it big. They were able, during wartime, to pay off their farm-purchase debts.

By sharp contrast, younger farmers who were not well-established and were less able to capitalize on the peak wartime prices entered the 1920s still owing a debt. They found themselves prostrate as commodity prices collapsed.

In 1921 winter wheat sold for 95 cents. Its price recovered only slowly over the next few years. The 1920s was a decade of rising industrial prosperity but doldrums on the farm.

Those farmers who in the 1920s had notes due at their banks tried all sorts of schemes to stay afloat. Fred Breimyer's neighbor, Roy Snyder, bought a Fordson and added more acreage to his farm. By the middle of the decade, he had given up and moved to a factory job in Middletown, Ohio. Fred Breimyer deplored his doing so; but, as will be said later, he himself took the same course in 1928.

Generally, farmers who began the decade in trouble ended it somewhere other than on a farm.

CHAPTER 3

Family History

IN AN EARLIER ERA when it was not so fashionable to attribute individual behavioral patterns and even career successes or failures to cultural environment, one's ancestors were put under scrutiny.

This account is oriented mainly to environmental influences. Nonetheless, Harold Breimyer's familial background is relevant. It is the more so because it is of a type. The German version of Protestant Puritanism as exhibited in the Breimyer family has colored many episodes in the history of the United States. It has done so particularly in the Midwest. An illustrative example, familiar to Missourians, is Carl Schurz's role in holding the state of Missouri loyal to the Union during the Civil War.

THE MATERNAL LINEAGE

Harold's maternal grandmother was Auguste Toussaint, daughter of a French family of Lyons, reportedly tanners, that migrated during one of the many German-French wars to Magdeburg-Neustadt in post-World War II East Germany. In 1865 she married Christian Friedrich Schulz. Seventeen years later the couple, with their five children, set sail for the fabled United States. According to family lore, their first motive was to spare their three sons from the Prussians' compulsory military service. They went directly to Springfield, Ohio, where Ella Anna Margaret was born in 1884. Ella was the only one of the six Schulz children born in the United States.

Ella Schulz's father Friedrich was a carpenter who had managed a lumberyard in Magdeburg. Only nine months after arriving in

Springfield, he fell while working on a building and was incapacitated the remaining thirteen years of his life. Springfield was an industrial city, and the Schulz boys became machinists, tool makers, and industrial craftsmen of the first order of skills. In the tradition of the close-knit German family, they entered "shop-work" at a young age and supported the family after their father's disablement.

Ella, favorite of her father and his companion during his terminal illness, was enabled to complete high school. Of a literary turn of mind, she qualified as a teacher in elementary schools and began teaching in 1902.

Active in St. John's Lutheran Church in Springfield, she met the handsome young Fred Breimyer, who had come to the city to learn a trade. Fred proved as adept as Ella's brothers at mastering the skills of industrial manufacture and quickly became an expert pattern maker. He shared Ella's religious affiliation but otherwise was of a different background. He had completed only five years of formal schooling, the first of which had been in the German language. He spoke the Schwäbisch dialect of German, learned from his parents. Even though Ella was born soon after her family arrived in the United States, the Schulz family had Americanized so fast that she learned no German in her home. Following many years of study in school, she gained proficiency in a Hoch-Deutsch — high German — that hardly accommodated conversation with Fred's Schwäbian patois.

Fred and Ella were married June 30, 1908. They built a modern home and remained in Springfield until Fred contracted so virulent a farm fever that they left their comfortable urban setting and moved, in 1913, to a shack on a Fort Recovery farm.

THE PATERNAL LINEAGE

The paternal root proved to have much more influence than the maternal on the personality of Harold Breimyer, principally because the boy grew up in the shadow of his father's family home and family members. Grandma's small farm was located only four miles distant from his father's, and the grandmother as well as aunts and uncles were a stable rock amid the turmoil of Harold's family.

John George Breymaier, Harold's grandfather, came to the United States in 1870 from Rotenacker in the state that is now Baden-Württemberg in the southwestern part of Germany. His family had crossed the Atlantic two years earlier, but George delayed to complete his apprenticeship in brickmaking. The family had left Germany for the same reason as the Schulzes—to avoid the sons' military service. The Breymaiers were prescient: The Franco-Prussian war broke out in 1870.

The Breymaier motive was especially noteworthy because the community they left had a long history of pacifism. That itself is a story worth the telling. First, though, a note on the spelling of the name. Exactness in spelling is a luxury of recent years. Until dictionaries came into wide use, most spelling was *ad hoc* phonetic. The German language allows for variety in spelling: the *ai, ei, ay,* and *ey* diphthongs are identical. The family crest carries the spelling Breimeier. The trunk in which the family's possessions were carted to the United States is lettered Breimaier. John George wrote his name Breymaier. Why did his son Fred spell the name Breimyer? No explanation was ever offered, but it is supposed that when Fred arrived in Springfield, he attempted to anglicize the name. The irony is that Harold, his wife Rachel, and their son and grandchildren have found themselves standing guard against yet another spelling that apparently has appeal—Breimeyer.

The orthographic issue might have been avoided had John George used the name of his natural father, Scherer. The story, handed down from generation to generation, is that in the 1840s Barbara Gerster was betrothed to a young man of that name and became pregnant by him. The pair would have married prior to the birth of John George had not her parents objected. The young man did not meet their criteria. Apparently the code of the day called for compliance with the parents' wishes. In any event, John George was born, and irrespective of the name given him as a baby, he eventually took the family name of Michael Breimeier, whom his mother married. Michael and Barbara and their four children eventually settled near Fort Recovery, Ohio.

The lineage of Harold Breimyer's paternal grandmother also goes back to the community of Rotenacker in southwest Germany. Her parents, Gottlieb and Susanna Walter, left Germany many years earlier than the Breimeiers. Gottlieb first settled at Bolivar, Ohio, near Canton, where Pauline was born. Later he moved to Huntington, Indiana. As Huntington is sixty miles distant from Fort Recovery, only through the intermediation of mutual friends did Pauline Walter and George Breymaier meet and, after a fairly brief courtship, marry.

THE SEPARATISTS OF ROTENACKER

As the Walter and the Breymaier, as well as the Scherer, lineages trace from Rotenacker, and for the further reason that the locality has a unique history, the Rotenacker story is told here. The village, located south of Stuttgart, sits atop bluffs that rise from the Donau (Danube) river at a point near its source, where it is narrow. In the eighteenth century the area was a refuge of Separatists, a religious colony in constant trouble with both political and clerical authorities. It was pacifist and disdained many of the rites of the church, such as baptism and Holy Communion.

One anecdote, presumably unembellished, is that a Johannes Breymaier was sentenced to Augsburg prison for his beliefs. One day Duke Frederick brought him before the Emperor Napoleon, who was paying a state visit. The Duke wanted to show Napoleon what sort of people the Separatists were. The Emperor asked Breymaier, "Who do you believe I am?" The Separatist replied, without observing the custom of bowing and removing his hat, "Ein Engel des Abgrunds"—meaning a devil. Napoleon told the Duke to punish the insolence. Later the Duke told Breymaier that because he treated Napoleon no better than he did the Duke himself (apparently the Separatists bowed to no earthling), he could go home.

The character of the Separatists of Württemberg is illustrated by the venture of a band of them who slipped away from their home by night to travel to the United States, there to found a colony in northeast Ohio. Aided by Pennsylvania Quakers, whom they resembled, the German group established at Zoar a farming and small-craft colony that remained cohesive and was sometimes prosperous from 1817 until it was dissolved in 1898. Although the group was headed, and virtually ruled over, by one Joseph Baumeler, Johannes Breymaier was a leading figure. Historical accounts do not make clear whether the man was the hero of the episode with Napoleon. At the time of the colony's dissolution in a public sale, another Breymaier, Joseph, was one of the trustees.[1] Zoar is now maintained as an Ohio State Park.

The Zoar Breymaiers were doubtless related to Michael Breimeier, who as John George's foster father established the Breymaier homestead in Fort Recovery. But there is no record of the connection.

By a fateful twist Harold Breimyer's Walter ancestors, rather than

---

[1]This account is found in *Zoar: An Ohio Experiment in Communalism* (Columbus: Ohio Historical Society, 1970), and in Hilda Dischinger Morhart, *The Zoar Story* (Strasburg, Ohio: Gordon Printing, 1981).

the Breymaiers (or the Scherers), had a clear tie to Zoar. Gottlieb Walter was a cabinet maker whose home in Bolivar was only a few miles distant from Zoar. He fashioned furniture for Zoar homes. There is no record that he was a member of the colony, but furniture now on display at Zoar is indisputable evidence of his contribution to the colony. It shows an unmistakable Walter style, and some pieces are identical to those Harold Breimyer and his sisters inherited from their grandmother, Pauline Walter.

LINES TO FRED AND ELLA

Does a cultural heritage linked so loosely to a distant community in southwest Germany and a communal experiment in northeast Ohio have a bearing on the life experiences of Harold Breimyer? The question is only asked here, not answered. Irrespective of what answer is correct, the culture of Rotenacker/Zoar helps to account for the contrast between the personalities and philosophies of Harold's father, Fred, and his mother, Ella. Southwest Germany has always been lowbrow, unsophisticated, economically stressed. Not far from Rotenacker begins the Black Forest, with its appealing mythology. Fred could have been a character in one of the Black Forest stories. Ella, despite a smattering of French blood, was typically Prussian. Straight-laced, stern, humorless, but bright and capable, she was of the aura of the Prussian Hohenzollerns.

RESOURCEFUL, TALENTED PAULINE

For many years the *Readers' Digest* magazine carried a monthly piece, "The Most Unforgettable Character I've Met." Grandma Breymaier was the most unforgettable character Harold Breimyer ever knew.

Growing up a city girl in Huntington, she was one of a family of five girls and two boys. She attended school and was fluently literate in both English and German. As teenagers she and her sisters "worked out" in homes of the more well-to-do families. On one occasion Pauline was a heroine in saving a baby under her care from being lost in a home fire. The girls were paid partly in kind. At least one of the homes in which Pauline worked was of a clockmaker, so the young girl accumulated a stock of pendulum clocks. Of the two such clocks Harold Breimyer has

had in his home, one or both originated with his grandmother's household employment in Huntington.

Human beings are said to resemble birds in that they don their
brightest plumage at mating time. George Breymaier put on his best
clothes and manners during his courtship with Pauline Walter. He was a
tall, well-groomed man, more handsome than his bride. Irrespective of
how fast a mated bird loses its colors, Pauline found George's to disappear almost instantly. He proved to be addicted to his pipe and chewing
tobacco, and even more to alcohol. Whether owing to his personal insta-
bility or to cycles in the construction business, his brickmaking was
marked by repeated ups and downs. So, too, it may be supposed, was
the marriage relationship.

In those days the kilns for firing brick were constructed on the spot.
When George Breymaier got a contract to make a lot of brick, as for a
new Catholic church, he found it easier to relocate his plant to the site of
the construction than to haul the heavy brick by slow-moving wagon. A
few years after their marriage, George and Pauline moved to St. Henry,
eight miles east of Fort Recovery, to make brick there. Later, George
built a brick home for his mother and foster father and his own family
on a 44-acre farm southeast of Fort Recovery, and he set up yet another
brick plant there. The two families lived together more or less amicably
until the parents died.

In his inaugural address President John Kennedy quoted a line from
Shakespeare's *Twelfth Night,* "Some men are born great, some achieve
greatness, and some have greatness thrust upon them." Pauline Walter
Breymaier certainly was not born to greatness, nor was greatness thrust
upon her. By the world's standards she did not achieve greatness. But, as
judged by her grandson Harold's standards, she achieved greatness of a
distinctive kind. She rose sturdily, even mightily, above trying circumstances.

Arriving at her new home and discovering to her dismay what she
had contracted for in the marriage vows, Pauline proved equal to the
demanding equation. She kept her errant husband on the job most of the
time. She bore six children, and made certain they attended school and
church. She became a matriarch, presiding over her unsteady husband
and his brick business, her children, and the 44-acre farm. And she gave
shelter to a succession of passers-through—a girl named Caroline, the
two daughters of her daughter Eda's fiance, Gard Yaney, occasional
hired hands in the brickyard, and her younger unmarried brother Da-
niel.

From some obscure source Grandma Breymaier acquired countless
skills of the country. Harold's mother Ella saved all discarded meat fat

and delivered it to Grandma, who made a soap from it strong enough to emulsify the dirt and grease of farmers' clothes. She dug roots with which to concoct the universal ointment, parsley root salve. When apples were to be cooked to butter in a huge iron kettle, Grandma explained the technique and presided over the cooking. She was an expert in butchering a hog or calf and preparing hams and bacon for smoking, stuffing sausage in the animal's own casings (actually, intestines), and, of course, rendering lard.

Where did the city girl who arrived naive and innocent learn all these skills? And where did she develop the fortitude that carried her through so much travail? Harold never learned, but he pondered the eternal question of where greatness comes from.

Pauline's husband was one of her heaviest burdens. One summer he had an especially good harvest of grapes, from which he fermented several barrels of wine. They were stored in the damp, cool cellar of the brick home. One day George had an unquenchable thirst for the wine, and when he tried to sate it, he became dead drunk. The tale, as since told in quiet family conversations, does not explain how Grandma got the drunk Grandpa out of the basement. Perhaps she left him there to sleep it off. If so, he slept in wine-soaked clothes, for Grandma went to the work shed, got an ax, and swung it into the wine casks. Grandpa drank no more wine that year.

Grandma's travails eased a bit as her husband lost his health in his late sixties. Harold has remembered him only as a gray-haired man with a long moustache, who, with the aid of a cane, shuffled about in carpet slippers. During the 1920s the Eighteenth Amendment, banning manufacture of alcoholic beverages for sale, reinforced Grandma's own prohibition on Grandpa. George begged his daughter Rena to buy him some beer, which doubtless was available from some illicit source. Rena came back from town with a beverage called "Neer-Beer." Her father complained that it was only a little better than water.

Grandma did not fail to expose her husband as a teaching lesson. Every one of her six children abstained from tobacco and from anything more than the most temperate drinking of alcohol. The instruction reached her grandson Harold, whose consumption of wine in a lifetime approximates the volume of one of the casks his grandmother sliced open with her ax.

Matriarch Grandma was stern, imposing strict behavioral rules on her children. Moreover, the Germanic tradition of family loyalty and mutual support was as strong in the Breymaiers of the southwest German culture as in the Prussian Schulzes.

George and Pauline thought education to be more appropriate for boys than for girls. Their three daughters, though literate, were un-trained for jobs other than those involving home skills, at which, like their mother, they were superbly proficient. One by one they migrated to Dayton, sixty miles distant, where they were welcomed as live-in maids in homes of higher-income families. Always, though, one of the three was required to remain at home, helping to manage the household there.

If the source of Pauline Walter Breymaier's home talents is obscure, that of her understanding of health rules and medications is even more so. She learned from some teacher or book. No germs escaped the boil-ing water that Grandma always kept in a tea kettle. Family members each had their own drinking cup, hanging on a nail over a pail of drink-ing water brought in from a drilled well, which was purer and safer than water from a dug well, as found on so many farms.

No farm home in the 1920s had a bathroom. Indeed, the idea of putting a toilet inside a home was repugnant. "Inside the house!" was the exclamation shouted by a farmer to whom the idea was broached.

Farm homes of the early twentieth century were classified by their toilet facilities, or lack of them.

The starkest tradition was that any structure was a luxury; people, even as animals, could use the barn. Gradually, small shacks were built, with one or two toilet seats carved out of wood planks. In mock humor they were called "Chic Sales." Toilet paper was the pages of Sears, Roebuck or Montgomery Ward catalogs—except that the slick pages were unusable.

Grandma Breymaier, by some divination, learned about toilet sani-tation. She had her sons construct a neat outhouse at the base of a slope that dropped sharply away from the house, so that all natural drainage would be toward the fields. When her daughters brought news from Dayton about toilet tissues, the catalogs were replaced. His grand-mother's home was the only rural one where Harold as a boy saw toilet paper.

But that was not all. A concrete walkway, itself exceptional, led from the outside toilet to the back porch. Grandma gave orders that a wash table be built where the walkway met the porch, and that a hand pump and pipe be connected to a cistern in which rain water was col-lected from the rooftop. Soap and towel were always present. Grandma admonished her sons and daughters—and grandchildren—to stop for hand-scrubbing on each return from the toilet.

To this day, when Harold Breimyer sees a student or, all too often, a professor complete his visit to a university men's room and walk out without washing, he reflects on how ignorantly gauche are those per-sons—and how inferior to his wise grandmother.

His grandmother, as might be surmised by now, was circumspectly safety-conscious. David Baker, extension farm safety specialist at the University of Missouri–Columbia, would have found her an enthusiastic cooperator. When a wooden structure was dismantled, all nails were removed at once lest a grandchild, or Grandma herself, step on one with bare feet. And Grandma made it a precept that a garden rake never be left on the ground with its teeth pointing upward.

In spite of her own heavy responsibilities, Grandma was always available when needed. When her daughter-in-law Ella, expecting a child, began labor, her husband Fred called the family's physician, their friend Charlie Watkins. Next Fred "went for" or called Grandma. If he only telephoned, Grandma would walk the four miles to her son's home. She would remain until things were in order again.

To Harold as a boy, Grandma's most appreciated contribution was the sympathetic ear she always had for him and, even more, the calmness and serenity that he found on any visit to her home. Everything was always serene there. Chores were done like clockwork. Voices were never raised. The boy sensed and appreciated Germanic rationality long before he learned the word and concept.

On any visit Harold was incorporated into the work force; his services were enlisted in whatever was going on. One remembered activity is picking blackberries. In the woodland area of the small farm were blackberry bushes. At midsummer Harold, his grandmother, and whoever among his aunts was at home would pick the berries into milk pails. A morning's picking would fill several pails. After a noontime meal Grandma would hitch old Jim (a lean driving horse) to the buggy to take the berries to town (Fort Recovery). There ensued the usual contest with the horse. The animal resisted running down the center of the gravel road, rough with stones. He preferred one of the tracks that wagon and automobile wheels had made smooth. But if he took to the track, the buggy wheels would lurch over the stones. As in almost all challenges, Grandma's will prevailed. Old Jim stumbled over stones, but the buggy rode smoothly.

In the village familiar and friendly buyers bought the berries. The few dollars received were a welcome addition to Grandma's meager income, which in her older years was almost confined to cream and egg money plus the few dollars her daughters sent her from Dayton.

Not least of Grandma's contributions to her oldest son's family was her hospitality on holidays. Thanksgiving and Christmas were notable occasions. A long dining table was loaded with food. Seeing it, Harold would remember lines learned in his *Beacon* reader:

> Pies of pumpkin, apple, mince,
> Jams and jellies, peaches, quince,
> Purple grapes and apples red,
> Cakes and nuts and gingerbread,
> That's Thanksgiving.
>
> Turkey, oh a great big fellow,
> Fruits all ripe and rich and mellow.
> Everything that's good to eat,
> More than I can now repeat.
> That's Thanksgiving.

Until the boy was seven years old, his father owned no automobile. On Christmas, when a horse-drawn carriage carried the family including the boy and his sister Louise to Grandma's, a still-familiar jingle applied:

> Over the river and through the wood
> To Grandmother's house we go.
> The horse knows the way to carry the sleigh
> Through the white and drifting snow.

The dinner was only part of the delightful day. Usually two or more of Harold's aunts and uncles joined in the holiday festivities. Among them, Dan, Otto, and Eda were gifted musically. Harold, who flubbed every attempt to master an instrument, marveled at his uncles' and aunt's skills with violin, guitar, mandolin, and piano. Furthermore, the aunts had brought from Dayton first a gramophone with a big horn, and then a neat victrola in mahogany. Later they added a player piano. Records and player rolls were marvelous media for pleasure in an era when radio was just being introduced and had not reached the rural countryside, and television was only someone's dream.

A proper question is what religious or moral philosophy Harold learned from his influential grandmother. Whatever it was, it was direct, simple, unsophisticated. To Pauline Walter Breymaier, life's code was clear-cut and free of philosophical calculation. A person, especially a Christian, did what was morally right because it was right. One was honest, sober, responsible; neither vanity nor self-indulgence was to be pursued. Harold's mother could equivocate, yet be awed by fear of eternal punishment. But in his grandmother's reckoning the devil complex and Hell's fire were absent. Perhaps the simplicity of her convictions made it easier for her to steer a stable boat through rough waters.

Grandma lived to be ninety-five. Cancer-wracked and blind, she once commented to her grandson, "I wish't I could die." (She tried to use in English the subjunctive by which Germans in their language avoid committing themselves.) To her grandson the sentiment was new and startling. Many years passed before he accepted the euthanasia theme. Birth and death ought to be sacraments; to accede to the wish of the aged and ill to be relieved of further sojourn would represent an elevated state of humanity. That advancement in civilized behavior lies somewhere in the future.

FRED, ELLA, AND THEIR EXODUS FROM SPRINGFIELD

Fred Breimyer was born at a decent interval of about a year after George and Pauline's marriage. His first schooling was in the German language, but he shifted soon to an English school. At his father's brickyard he did small chores and ran errands, among them carrying a tin pail to the local barkeeper to get a few cents' worth of beer for the father and his "hands"—the term for hired laborers.

By the time he became a teenager, the biennial arrival of a brother or sister crowded whatever house his parents were living in as they followed the brickyard caravan. He was dispatched to live with his father's half-brother Jacob, eight miles distant. Like George, Jacob was a strong, handsome specimen of manhood. In other respects he was George's opposite—abstinent, ambitious, resolute. He was also extremely capable. A farmer, he bought an acreage of Darke County's productive soils and set out on a course that has been memorialized in the chronicles of U.S. agriculture wherein industriousness—relentless hard work—was substituted for purchased farm resources.

Also, cash expenditures in living were minimized. In their first years together Jake and his wife Liz were so frugal that they made home-produced sorghum molasses to take the place of store-bought sugar. The farm's earnings were capitalized into the growing farm operation. Jake proved to have skills in operating farm machinery. He and his sons and nephew Fred became the threshermen for the neighborhood.

Jacob's efforts and practices paid off. A generation later the members of his family were the only Breymaiers having any financial means. By this time they could buy all the sugar they wanted and the best automobile in the neighborhood. Jacob, highly intelligent, may have sensed that he was aided by economic trends of the time. As prices and incomes in agriculture climbed higher in the 1890s and early 1900s, Jacob's net worth moved upward with them.

If Jacob Breymier (his spelling) were that perceptive, he was far ahead of most savants of agriculture, of his day or this. It is still hard to convince farmers, or anyone else, that farmers' fortunes are made during inflation and lost during deflation; and the latter can thwart a farmer's management skills.

When Fred arrived at the home of his uncle and aunt and younger cousins, he was charmed by the atmosphere he found there. It was as warmly cordial as his own had been austere. From his uncle he learned the practices of farming, but even more the mechanics of farm machines including, especially, steam engines and grain separators. The knowledge was to serve him well later.

Fred did not cut all ties to his own family. He felt close to his mother and returned to his home for an occasional Sunday visit. He got there by walking the eight miles.

The experience that shaped Fred's life most, and indirectly his son Harold's, was a twelve-year residence in Springfield, Ohio. How he chanced to drift first to Lima and then to Springfield, both industrial cities, is not known. It was probably in his twentieth year, 1901, that he arrived in Springfield with a small bag of belongings. There he found a job, a hospitable home that provided room and board, and before long a church affiliation with St. John's Lutheran. He quickly took advantage of the instructional and recreational facilities of the YMCA (Young Men's Christian Association). He also made a good friend in his co-worker Fred Kramer, who taught him the skills of making patterns for sand-lined molds in which iron was cast. Fred Breimyer (the newly chosen spelling) developed mechanical and craftsman skills rapidly, studied mathematics at night classes, and within a few years was working for the International Harvester company at an attractive wage.

Fred learned with alacrity the sophisticated manners of Springfield. At the YMCA he discovered that he had athletic ability, notably in gymnastics. Many years later his son Harold put on display six blue, red, and yellow ribbons and a bronze medal his father had won in the Y's Athletic and Gymnastic Meet of 1906. The blue ribbon came from the half-mile run. Two reds signified second place in parallel bars and horizontal bars.

Extremely strong, Fred was the center man in human pyramids. Perched atop the pyramid was the small Bobby Clark, who soon left Springfield for New York, where he gained fame as a song-and-dance man in musical comedy and revues. Years later, when Harold and his wife Rachel saw Clark in a production of *Damn Yankees* at Washington's National Theatre, Harold wrote Clark a note extending his and his father's compliments. Clark's acknowledgment was cordial.

The strikingly handsome Fred must have wowed the girls at St. John's church. One of those impressed was Ella Schulz, newly an elementary school teacher. In 1906 she had the exceptional experience of taking her mother to Germany for a visit with relatives there. Ella was tall, with a high forehead, stern carriage, and a cranium packed full of knowledge. The two were married June 30, 1908. They built a home. After a baby girl was stillborn, Ella, literary and sedentary in her habits, did not readily conceive again.

It's only a guess that some marital discord may have been involved, but for whatever reason, Fred developed a nervous tic and hurried to the shelter of his revered Uncle Jake, staying there part of a summer and glorying in the restorative quality of work in the open air. He also noted that his uncle, after his Spartan and unstaked start, had achieved financial stability and was enjoying comforts of living. The farm fever set in.

It's an exercise in surmise to suggest how Fred convinced his city-bred wife that their future was on a piece of land near Fort Recovery. He doubtless stressed the healthful aspects of country living. He almost certainly promised that even though their first home would be modest he, even as had his uncle Jake, would be able to replicate on their farm the modern home they were enjoying on Grand Avenue.

Ella doubtless had some misgivings but she acquiesced, and to her eternal credit she "gave it a good try." Fred bought the 70 acres that Harold would eventually know so well, disregarding his Uncle Jake's warning that the tract was unproductive. We cannot know whether Uncle Jake also pointed out that farming is cyclical and the good times then experienced would not last indefinitely. He probably did not; most wisdom in agriculture is retrospective, not prospective. The good times lasted seven more years. They were followed by the lean years of declining asset values, beginning in 1921, that were so instructive to Fred's son, Harold.

As Fred held his uncle in high regard, it is surprising that he was not dissuaded from buying the farm for which he was negotiating. But his farm fever was at high heat. In 1913 he and Ella moved into a three-room house on 70 scrabble acres.

Whatever else was negative about the farm experience, the physical activity improved Ella's ability to conceive. She did so regularly, for ten years. In 1914 Harold was born.

CHAPTER 4

Boyhood on the Farm

ALL WRITTEN THUS FAR, like the opening pages of Chaucer's *Canterbury Tales,* is prologue. Now begins the saga of the life and times of Harold Breimyer, which is also the saga of dramatic changes in the farming and rural life of the Midwest, and of major developments in the role of the United States government relative to agriculture.

The confidence that led Harold's father Fred to seek his future, if not his fortune, in farming is explained in part by his progressiveness. Fred was sure that most farmers stayed with outmoded practices too long. He would update, modernize. He sought to learn the latest practices, including those that agricultural colleges declared to be scientifically sound. He was a natural target for the Extension counseling that was beginning to arrive. This personality trait was later transmitted faithfully to his son. In the 1920s the Breimyers, father and son, were quick to adopt whatever farming practice the county agent and vocational agriculture instructor were advocating.

Although his intentions were admirable, Fred fell prey to two mistakes. He sometimes adopted a new practice before it had been tested thoroughly. And he overcapitalized his operation.

In the annals of U.S. agriculture, early adopters—the first farmers to try out a new practice—are properly lauded. They are also said to be the only contingent that makes any money from the practice. By the time everyone adopts it, an increase in national production has shrunk the marginal value of the practice to the farmer. Thereafter, only society benefits. Therein lies a rationale for public funding of agricultural research.

Less often advertised, notably by the research community, is how often a new practice proves to have bugs. Early adopters find the bugs, and without intending to be eleemosynary, they perform, at personal cost, the public service of disclosing them.

As an example, sweet clover as a high-yielding legume enjoyed a brief fling of advocacy. Fred Breimyer, always receptive, seeded the crop and indeed found the hay yield to be high. But he soon learned also that the heavy stems slowed curing. The practice of the time was to cure hay in the field, often in small, rounded cocks. Fred's experience was that the heavy stems of sweet clover delayed curing so long that a summer rain was likely to damage the hay before it was hauled to the hayloft.

After two successive summers of using his sweet clover "hay" to fill gullies and arrest erosion in them, he went back to the lower yielding but readily cured red clover.

His more egregious error, though, was to overcapitalize. Although Fred bought secondhand machinery, his total investment in machines and small tools was excessive for a low-yielding, 70-acre operation. His even more flagrant error came about as he built a barn to replace his original one, destroyed by fire. Most farmers of the community who needed a new barn would tie some heavy timbers into place on level ground, get help in "raising" the skeleton into vertical position, then attach siding and a roof. Finally they would splash on the cheapest red paint. The more prominent farmers would engage a professional painter to add, in white paint, the farmer's name and the year. A decade or two later, when hard times came to farming, the faded white letters on its barn would reveal the last year of the farm's prosperity.

Fred Breimyer was not satisfied with an inexpensive barn held together by heavy beams. He built a splendid hip-roofed barn, and he painted it white. Had it housed pure-bred livestock on a productive 200 acres the barn would have been economic. But Fred had neither fine livestock nor high-yielding land. Years later his son, observing and teaching about the economics of agriculture, declared that overcapitalization is the most nearly universal mistake that U.S. farmers are prone to make.

THE FIRE

Building a new barn became necessary because, in the summer of 1917, the night after threshing the farm's grain crops, the old barn burned.

The event was the most traumatic single one in the life of Fred and Ella. And it had indelible effects on their son because it converted the hopeful outlook of his parents' first years to a desperate struggle to stay alive financially. Moreover, the event was the first in Harold's memory. He has remembered being rocked by his mother on the front lawn of their home as flames consumed not only the barn and its grain but also an old church building that housed the family's fine Springfield furniture. The furniture had been stored there in anticipation of building the comfortable home, similar to Uncle Jake's, that had been the young couple's dream.

It never was known whether the fire was arson, set by a neighbor with whom Fred had feuded, or was ignited by a lingering spark from the steam engine that powered the threshing separator. In any event, the fire was devastating because Fred's biggest harvest to that time was lost and because money had to be borrowed to pay high wartime prices for livestock feed and for materials to build the new barn. No benefits from fire insurance helped defray costs, because Fred had none. He had not taken out one of the mutual fire and windstorm policies that were coming into adoption. It's surprising that he failed to do so inasmuch as he was progressive in other respects. But farmers have long been quicker to plant a new variety of seed than to change a practice in financial management.

Up to that time, disaster was regarded as a signal for mutual aid given informally. The night of the Breimyer fire, flames in the sky communicated to farmers for miles around that a building was burning. Their height suggested that it was a barn. Even as the flames continued, farmers came to the Breimyer home, some by buggy and others in newly purchased automobiles. Checks were written and promissory notes handed over. Albert Meuthert set the standard by writing a check for one hundred dollars, an enormous amount as viewed at the time.

Voluntary contributions nevertheless paid only a small fraction of the cost of rebuilding. Owing to the debt he incurred, when prices of farm products collapsed following war's end, Fred Breimyer found himself trapped. He tried valiantly but vainly to recover stability.

The fire and its financial aftermath took a heavier emotional toll from Ella than Fred. She could no longer dream of the new home, and the fine furniture saved for it had only been fuel for lighting the sky.

The fire compounded the problems with which Ella was struggling. She had tried hard to fit into country living. She learned to milk a cow. Neighbor wives explained that care of chickens is reserved for the female sex, as is the egg income coming from it. So Ella looked after chickens. Previously, farm wives had churned butter and sold it pound by pound, and that income was theirs, too—hence the phrase "butter and egg money." But in western Ohio by the early 1920s, sale of farm-churned butter had moved into the history books.

One country-wife skill that Ella learned to perfection was canning foods from the summer garden and from winter butchering. In the annals of farm life before electric power put refrigeration in farm homes, canning foods for the family's winter needs was a ceaseless test of ingenuity. As grains were non-perishable, bread and cereal foods were a staple of wintertime diet. A reliable source of meat was the ham that was smoked following butchering of a hog. If stored carefully, potatoes would last until spring and cabbages could be kept well into the winter. But most other vegetables were denied the family during the winter — until home canning became practicable.

The mason jar with its glass-lined zinc lid was the magic device that allowed farmers to include vegetables in their winter diets. Ella Breimyer remembered the instruction of her high school teachers that vitamins were essential to good health, and that many came from vegetables. She made sure that her husband and children were not deprived. Neighbor ladies were amused by her insistence that stewed tomatoes be a part of so many winter meals. As her family grew, Ella had a second reason for lining cellar shelves with hundreds of quart jars of vegetables. Except for replacing the rubbers for the cans, the process was costless, and the Breimyers had almost no money.

The canning process was laborious. Ella had only a wood-burning range and no pressure cooker. Canning tomatoes in a hot kitchen on a summer day was enough to test the mettle of even a native of the country. A city-bred transplant found the task onerous.

Ella could milk a cow, feed chickens, and can tomatoes, but she found it hard to adapt to the rural culture. She never ceased being an alien. Some of the neighboring farm wives, such as the angelic Alice Heis, were understanding and sympathetic. Others were not.

Her son Harold remembers an incident at the rural school that illustrates the assimilation dilemma. One of the annual social events at the school called for each schoolgirl to bring an iced cake, which would be auctioned to the fathers present. Ella learned about having to bring a cake but did not understand that only girl pupils did so. She dutifully baked a cake, which her young son put up for the auction. Only on arriving at the school did Ella learn the details of the fund-raising event. She was embarrassed, for perhaps the twentieth time since her arrival at the farm in 1913. Sensing her distress, Ed Heis responded sympathetically, bid for Harold's cake, and generated tension-relieving humor in the situation. Some people deserve Heaven's blessings. Ed and Alice Heis were two who did so.

THE FAMILY'S FARM AND FARMING

Even at the date of writing this saga, Harold Breimyer remains astonished by the revolution in farming practices and country life that has taken place during his lifetime. He knows, though, that many authors have introduced nostalgic reflections in almost identical language. The story of the transformation of agriculture during the 1920s has been told often. The account here will be cursory.

Until Harold was seven years old, his father depended on horses for farm work and transportation. He usually had a team of two draft animals, of mixed Belgian and Percheron breed, and one driving (or "buggy") horse. He bred the mare, Daisy, that he used to pull a buggy or a light spring wagon, to a stallion of a draft breed. She was able to give birth to a filly that proved as fleet of foot as her mother, yet strong enough to join the draft animals to make a three-horse team. Occasionally even Daisy would be added as a fourth horse. But a skittish buggy horse does not work well alongside a Belgian.

Draft power was needed most to pull a moldboard plow, and a grain binder. The binder mechanism cut the standing oats or wheat and elevated it on canvas for packing and tying in bundles. It was driven by a heavy, cleated center wheel and required lots of draft power. The binder was the implement that Dan Stump could not get to work. Fred Breimyer, having helped manufacture the tool in Springfield, had no trouble.

Daisy took the family to Fort Recovery for shopping and to attend church, and to Grandma's. Most farm families had a one-seat open buggy. The ornately fringed surrey of the musical *Oklahoma!* was rarely found in Fort Recovery. Fred had bought an enclosed cab, plain but protective of riders' comfort during rain and snow. Although Daisy was fast afoot, Fort Recovery and Grandma's were about the limit of her range.

Chronicles of farm life tell the horse-and-carriage story repeatedly but typically omit mention of the bigger limitation of the horsepower era, namely, means of transport of freight—grain, feed, hay, or animals—for market. During Harold's earliest youth the horse and wagon provided the only drayage. The draft animals bred for pulling plows and binders were painfully slow on the road. A trip by farm wagon just to Fort Recovery consumed most of a day. Historians wax panegyrical in relating what the advent of the automobile and tractor meant to farmers and their families. They should save some of their eulogy for the farm truck.

When Harold and his father made their occasional horse-and-wagon trip to town they would usually finish their business and be ready to start homeward at about the noon hour. The village had a restaurant, Meinerding's, but the father and son never ate there. Fred thought it might be a vendor of the illegal beer. Irrespective of that hunch, it was less expensive just to buy some bologna at Vonderhaar's meat market, and rolls from the bakery. They cost very little and could be nibbled during the drive home.

Horses traveled gravel roads often enough that they had to be shod with iron shoes. Frequently the drive back from town included a stop at Thurman Graf's blacksmith shop. Using his hammer and forge, Thurman could do just about anything with metal. Henry Wadsworth Longfellow described the New England smithy in terms that fit Thurman Graf's shop. If memory is accurate, though, the tree over Thurman's shop was a catalpa, not Longfellow's chestnut.

Longfellow omitted one feature of the blacksmith shop. When Harold was old enough to drive a team, he drew the assignment of getting the horses shod. He usually was about fourth in line for service, and he learned that farmers ahead of him converted the shop into a neighborhood news and gossip forum. Not only was Graf's arm the most skilled in the area, but his head held the most information about the community goings-on.

In the technology of farming, field operations were modernized earlier and faster than the care of livestock. Fred Breimyer's white, hip-roofed barn accommodated four horses, six cows, at times a veal calf or two, brood sows, and even sheep. Although Fred tried to be up to date, he had not learned about stanchions for milk cows or concrete floors and gutters. His cows were bedded down on straw. More straw had to be added frequently to cover the animals' bowel droppings, which, mixed with the straw, constituted manure to be hauled to fields as fertilizer. Hand milking the cow was a constant game to avoid getting droppings on the shoes, and the cow's swishing tail in the milker's face and eyes. If the animal had eaten laxative feeds, the tail could even swish some droppings into the milker's face. During summer months, spraying a cow with an insecticide to discourage flies momentarily reduced the incidence of tail swishings.

Manifestly, all considerations of sanitation in handling the milk were either not in the farmer's mind or were disregarded. The significance of the neglect was confined to the farmer's family and any guests at his meals. Milk was produced only for its cream content. Except for that put aside for the family meal, the milk was separated into cream and skim by hand-cranking a centrifugal separator. The cream was delivered to a creamery. The skim milk was poured into troughs, where its valuable protein made young pigs grow fast. The whole milk set aside was drunk, raw, at the dinner table. A high incidence of tuberculosis caused by drinking raw milk brought pressure, during the 1920s, to test dairy cows for tuberculosis. Later, milk-drinkers contracted undulant fever often enough to force the initiation of programs to test cows for brucellosis.

THE TRAUMA OF BEING MONEYLESS BUT NOT IMPOVERISHED

The story of Harold Breimyer as a boy growing up in the 1920s combines the account of his parents' attempt to accelerate his development and the account of the family's financial stresses into which they drew their son.

Although this is a personal account, a great many farm youth were caught in a similar situation, a trap. During the 1920s the cash incomes of most farmers were meager. And although the new technologies that were being introduced promised higher productivity and incomes, they invariably required new capital investment. The cash-flow payoff was delayed. For many farmers, the benefits came into prospect about the time the Great Depression of the 1930s dispelled all hopes. The timing contributed to the receptiveness that even politically conservative farmers gave the farm programs of the New Deal. But that takes us ahead of the story.

The irony in Harold Breimyer's experiences is that his family's critical shortage of money was not linked with cultural poverty. Partly because of his mother's literary interests, in some years enough dollars were scraped together to pay for a subscription to the daily newspaper of the city they had left, Springfield. Ella became a one-person agency for the Curtis Publishing Company. She sold enough subscriptions to the *Saturday Evening Post* and other journals to keep a few magazines coming to the farm home. Harold read them avidly. He remembers the stories of Irvin S. Cobb, and of Octavus Roy Cohen, who told about a club of black members (called Negroes in those days), "Sons and Daughters of I Will Arise."

On farms of western Ohio in the 1920s, boys were an asset. Few fathers were so bold as to declare girls a liability. But when Fred Breimyer, public-spirited and cooperatively minded, tried to sell stock in a new cooperative creamery, he received a conditional response from a Catholic farmer, Charles Keller. In the 1980s Charlie's stance would be called sexist. His wife was expecting a child, Charlie explained. If the baby proved to be a boy, he would buy a $100 share. If the baby were a girl, he would not see his way clear to do that.

Boys were valuable because they provided labor. They did so beginning at an early age. Often their tasks on the farm took priority over attending school. The school calendar itself was drawn up to fit farming practices. The year was of only eight months. School ended in late April so schoolboys could be released in time to plant corn. School reopened in September, but attendance often was poor until the corn that had been planted with schoolboys' help was also harvested ("cut") with their assistance.

Farm parents who boasted of their sons' accomplishments in helping on the farm were silent about the risks of injury to which they exposed the youth. At a family dinner Fronie Green declared proudly that her Edward could hitch a team of horses. That meant the stripling of about nine years would step behind the mammoth horses and hook the chain trace into the singletree. One move of the horse's leg would have sent the boy to the hospital with crushed bones, or to eternity.

At eight or nine years of age, Harold Breimyer was given, one fall day, the task of cultivating a neighbor's rented field. The implement was a "roller," which consisted only of four cylindrical drums mounted on an axle. Supposedly it would crush clods of dirt and smooth the seedbed. It was an ineffective tool and soon dropped out of the farmer's equipment inventory. But it was pulled easily, and Fred Breimyer's second team of horses, including the driving mare Daisy, could pull it.

With Topsy and Daisy responding to tugs on the line, Harold rolled the field with dispatch. But when he guided the frisky team toward home, it asserted its own preference and broke into a gallop. It cut the corners at a gateway, whereupon the end of the roller climbed the fence and corner post. The boy was thrown off the seat. As he fell, his head hit the corner of the implement. His memory to this day is of his mother's picking him up; of the ether with which Charles Watkins anesthetized him preparatory to stitching the wound; and finally of the intense pain he suffered later when the good doctor, having failed to remove the stitches cleanly, had to fish in the unhealed wound to find and remove the remnants.

That incident slowed Fred and Ella's use of their boy as a field hand.

Harold was luckier than some farm youth. Then and now, farming operations classify as hazardous. A schoolmate, Don Painter, lost part of a finger in a mower accident. One boy, enlisted to help dynamite tree roots, was crippled for life and lost the sight of an eye. A generation later, when social consciences was stirred by the observed exploitation of farm youth, farm leaders shouted protests on two false grounds. They denied that their children were exposed to significant danger. And, reflecting a relationship akin to that of property, they objected to social concern for what they did to *their* sons and daughters.

Slowly, though, rules concerning youth employment in farming came into being. They were overdue, and in the early 1990s were still too lax.

THE FORD AND FORDSON

Harold was pressed hardest to learn how to drive not a team of horses but an automobile—specifically, a Model T Ford. His father, always short of money, could not buy his first Ford until 1921. Until then he borrowed his brother's Model T on occasion, and Harold's first instruction was with it. In an emergency experience, he was told to press first the clutch pedal and then the brake as his father used a rail borrowed from a fence to pry a front wheel out of a ditch.

The first Breimyer car had had two previous owners. It was a touring car, with a fabric top that could be folded back in pleasant weather. In unpleasant weather, when rain pelted or snow fell, side curtains were snapped into place to moderate the inclemency. The car was a pre-storage-battery model and the motor was started by hand-cranking. A Breimyer neighbor, Perry Lotz, suffered a broken arm when the motor backfired. A magneto generated the only electric current. Headlights showed bright or dim in conformity with the speed of the car, and therefore of the rotating magneto.

Henry Ford's Model T was a phenomenon of its age. Its planetary transmission was a marvel, but of more engineering significance was the casting of all four cylinders in a single block, with a separate bolt-down cylinder head on top. Henry Ford used vanadium steel newly produced in Canton, Ohio, for the engine. He claimed credit as the first automobile manufacturer to use vanadium.

At the age of eight, Harold was driving the Model T. For the first year or two his mother always accompanied him, more as a gesture to the neighborhood than for practical purpose. She had no knowledge of the car's engineering or locomotion.

Harold learned how to change a tire, which could be done only on the wheel. Henry Ford's first automobiles had no detachable rims or wheels. He also gained the knowledge that if the motor failed to respond to his cranking, lifting a rear wheel with a jack, blocking the opposite wheel with a piece of wood, and putting the hand brake lever into high gear allowed him to start even a balky Ford motor. A crucial part of getting the spark plugs of a Model T to fire was to choke the carburetor just the correct amount, enriching the gas-air mixture. A bent wire was pulled as the crank was turned. Too much choking would flood the motor. All that could be done then was to wait until some of the volatile gasoline had evaporated.

Although Harold's mother was innocent of mechanical knowledge, her demands for transportation — and her husband's impatience in providing it — explain why her son was tutored so fast in a chauffeur role. For six or more years Harold drove his mother in accord with her instructions. Eventually his sisters, Louise, Ruth, and Mildred, progressively, relieved him of the duty.

Harold spent even more time driving the Model T's cousin, a Fordson tractor. It, too, had only a magneto and was started by hand-cranking. A small tank of gasoline was drawn on to aid in starting. Once the motor was running, the fuel line was switched to kerosene. In cold weather, starting a Fordson was a major challenge. A combination of four dry-cell batteries, called a hot-shot, wired into the ignition could be crucial in supplementing the magneto. On coldest days a fire under the crankcase heated the oil enough to allow the crank to be spun faster, thus improving the odds that the motor would start.

The Fordson of those days had no power take-off. The mechanism of the grain binder, for example, was still set in motion by the binder's own big driving wheel.

The Fordson's near monopoly was eroded gradually as McCormick-Deering, along with Case, Massey-Harris, and other manufacturers, introduced more versatile tractors. A neighbor, Carl Denney, bought a Moline that combined a power plant mounted on only two wheels with plow, disc, and other implements. The driver sat atop whatever implement was attached, manipulating a steering wheel and other controls attached to the motor by a long neck that resembled a giraffe's stretched horizontally.

On a 70-acre farm in the 1920s, much of the fieldwork was still done by hand. Hay was lifted onto a wagon by pitchfork. It was unloaded and lifted into the hayloft by a rope-and-fork mechanism utilizing pulleys and a track suspended from a timber at the peak of the barn roof.

In all farm operations Harold Breimyer worked as a field hand. He also hauled manure from stables, cleaned the chicken house, and, if the truth be told, was assigned many of the mean little jobs his father did not like to do. In the farming of the 1920s, the farmer performed the more basic and visibly respectable tasks. His wife and children were bade to do the unpleasant, unrewarding odd jobs.

The regime was similar for all the farm boys of his neighborhood. If anything, Harold's was less dreary than theirs, as his parents allowed interludes for attending the summer Chauauqua and participating in 4-H Club activities.

ALLEGED MERITS OF FARM UPBRINGING

For more than fifty years — ever since 1933 — the federal government has taken an active hand in determining prices of farm products and incomes of farmers. Running as a thread through all the arguments waged during those years has been the policy question of what kind of agricultural system, organizationally, is to be defended. The Congress has routinely declared that the objective is to preserve a system of family farming. Critics accuse drafters of farm laws with hypocrisy. The laws have not preserved family farming, they say, but have undercut it.

A majority of farmers, and an equal plurality of city people, genuinely want to keep farmland in the hands of family farmers. A number of people who call themselves sophisticated, including professional agricultural economists, take an opposite stand. They contemptuously deride all pro-family-farm philosophizing.

Throughout his professional career Harold Breimyer has taken an interest in the topic called the "organizational structure of agriculture." He has written about it more often, perhaps, than any other agricultural economist. He has defended the traditional structure and so has differed with many agricultural economists.

Many of the popular debates about country life and family farming have turned on the idea — a claim made so often — that farm experiences cultivate personal morality and, particularly, a sense of responsibility. Harold Breimyer has not pitched his defensive argument in those terms. Yet there is irony in that he and his fellows were ingrained, deeply, ineradicably, with the notion of responsibility. A cow had to be milked twice on each of the 365 days in a year; in a leap year, two more times. Likewise, all farm animals were necessarily fed and watered on schedule. Grain was harvested when ripe. And so on.

His defense of proprietary farming may appear strange for the further reason that he did not enjoy his own farming days. He found gratification in successful ventures, to be sure, and even as a boy, reflected cosmically on the miracle of producing life-sustaining foodstuffs by implanting germplasm in soil or in the uterus of female animals. But the farm duties into which his parents forced him were uninteresting, devoid of any artistic or spiritual uplift. They did not exceed his physical capacity, but they were boring. He remembers to this day how tiresome it was to walk behind a spike-tooth harrow that his team dragged over a 20-acre field. The operation seemed interminable. He sought to relieve the tedium by changing the geometric pattern of the laps as the implement was pulled up and down the field, or across it. He found it helpful to estimate a countdown of how many circuits were left, although he invariably underestimated the number and was too optimistic as to the time it would take to finish.

But the most unattractive feature of farm life was its social isolation. Herein, too, lies a contradiction. Harold Breimyer has never been gregarious; he is capable of working on his own, even as a loner. Nevertheless, to be mired in farm chores day after day, seeing no human being other than parents and sisters, was for him an austerity, a penance paid without a prior transgression. On a rare occasion when he spotted his vocational agriculture teacher or county agent walking across the field toward him, usually to enlist him in a 4-H Club activity, his heart leaped up. The monotony was broken.

Sociologically, isolation of the farm family has taken its heaviest toll on farm wives. Surprisingly, that feature of farm life has not been exposed widely. It's as though a blanket of silence has been dropped on it. Some years ago, however, Carl Kraenzel, a rural sociologist at Montana State University, won acclaim for his studies on the psychological damage incurred by wives of farmers and ranchers in the Plains states. A few other scholars addressed the social costs of space. It was high time, thought Harold Breimyer, that the subject be illuminated.

Most historical accounts of U.S. agriculture are male-chauvinistic. Much has been written about how new tools and technology have relieved the farmer, a male, from drudgery. That story is correct, to be sure. It's easier and more pleasant to milk cows by a machine than by hand, and to bale hay in the field instead of pitching it onto a wagon. But surely it's equally significant that life has been made a lot better for the farm wife. It's not just that she no longer has chickens to feed and water, or that garden produce can be dropped in a freezer instead of cooking and sealing it in glass jars. It's also that the automobile, paved roads, and the telephone have given her a release that previous generations did not know. Perhaps the radio and television should be added as farm-wife emancipators. For farm as well as city wives, though, they have an ersatz quality: The voices heard are surrogate for persons in the flesh. They do not keep farm living from being marked by more than a taint of isolation.

THE BURDEN OF SHARED RESPONSIBILITY UNDER STRESS

It's easy to observe that clockwork farm duties such as twice-daily milking of cows breed dependable behavior by farm youth. That manifest feature of farm life falls far short of characterizing the personality-molding experiences of Harold Breimyer as a farm boy. The gripping phenomenon of his youthful years was that his parents and he, too, saw his contribution to the farm as critically essential. He knew that his father was struggling to avoid foreclosure. He was aware that no money was available for buying anything other than what was absolutely necessary. He never wheedled his father out of a dime. He knew his father did not have an unallocated dime in his pocket.

Furthermore, Harold was sensitively aware that the friction between his parents was caused almost entirely by the constant financial exigency. He also learned early that his mother had a better head for financial management than his father did. Her heroics may have saved the farm, though at a high emotional cost to everyone.

Every veteran of past generations has a private stock of examples of self-denial and abstemious living. Purchases for daily living in the Breimyer home were nearly confined to flour, sugar, baking powder and soda, and supplies for kerosene lamps. As his mother had scholarly inclinations, Harold Breimyer remembers as better examples of self-deprivation the absence of stationery items other than paper, pen, and ink. Flour and water substituted for library paste. Neither paper clips nor a stapler was available; they could not be afforded. If papers had to be hooked together, folding a corner tab might work, or, if not that, a straight pin would serve. Sometimes gummed labels were needed, as for identifying glasses of jelly. Harold's mother carefully inspected all incoming mail for envelopes that were not tightly sealed. Flaps with unmoistened mucilage were scissored into strips that could serve as labels. Such are the laborious practices resorted to in a household that is not culturally impoverished but has no spending money.

Black-letter days in the household were those when notes at the bank were due. In the early years the notes became due frequently, as Fred Breimyer relied on individual short-term obligations. About midway in the 1920s he applied for a loan from the Federal Land Bank. That cooperative credit institution had been in existence for a decade but had not yet won wide acceptance. Fred and Ella rejoiced when his application was approved and a loan was advanced. Thereafter, loan payments would come due only twice a year. A further attraction was amortization of the loan. Part of each payment was allocated to reduction of principal. Thereby the family farmer was aided in becoming a debt-free owner of his farm.

The scheme was beautiful. For the Breimyers it had only one drawback. The semi-annual payment was more than Fred Breimyer could readily assemble. He was not disciplined enough to build up a reserve in his checking account in anticipation of the payment obligation. Twice each year a script was repeated that son Harold will remember forever. When the payment date arrived, Fred would instruct Ella to write and mail a check. "There's not even close to enough money in your account," she would protest. "Send it anyway; we'll get more in it before the check clears," was her husband's instruction. On the first go-round Ella did not explode in vituperation. Always, the check would reach the bank and be returned because of insufficient funds. The Land Bank would send it through again. Harold Anthony of the Fort Recovery Banking Company would send a sharp warning, usually via Harold, whom he accosted as the boy deposited a dribble of money to his father's account: "Tell your father he can't do that. It's illegal, and it will get us into trouble," instructed Anthony. On and on, this litany was repeated twice yearly until Harold escaped to Ohio State University as a freshman student.

After two rejections of the check, Fred, and especially Ella, went into their emergency tactics. They began with Ella's almost hysterical complaint about having to struggle with their "God-forsaken farm." Her phrasing was stereotyped. Naturally, during the crisis period nothing was bought. All cream and egg income went into the checking account. Anything salable was sold. Rags and old iron were delivered to the junkyard for a few paltry coins. Any calibrated medicine bottles went to the local veterinarian; under protest he usually paid fifty cents for the lot.

Another measure taken is less defensible. If Harold and his three sisters had any money for their savings account on hand, it was borrowed. Always their mother promised to repay as soon as solvency was reestablished. Harold estimates that his mother defaulted, over time, on about fifty dollars of repayment due him.

The scenario repeated so often left Ella distraught. The climax was an incident when she left Sunday church to walk the country roads. Brought back to her home, she recovered her poise. Once again Grandma Pauline was the heroine. Knowing that the extra travail was traceable to menopause, Grandma recounted how she, too, had found the change of life to be distressing. Strong, imperturbable Grandma could establish a bond stemming from a time when even she was scarcely equal to the stresses on her.

All these memories resurfaced in Harold Breimyer's mind during the 1980s as thousands of farmers in Missouri struggled with financial pressures similar to those in the Breimyer family of the 1920s. The external origin was similar—a nationwide devaluation of farm assets. The internal consequence also differed little. Rural sociologists such as the Heffernans at the University of Missouri–Columbia reported the trauma, the emotional distress, experienced in countless families. Not only were parents' lives torn asunder, said the Heffernans, but children's too.

After sixty years Harold Breimyer could still empathize. He found himself supportive of public measures to relieve some of the distress, and aligned against other economists who dismissed the whole debt crisis as just a quirk of the wonderful capitalistic system. But most of his professional adversaries had never experienced financial stress of an intensity equal to that of his own family in the 1920s.

FINANCIAL RELIEF

The culmination of the Breimyers' financial problems, their easing, was Fred's decision in 1928 to go back to industrial employment. The industrial prosperity of the 1920s was still in full swing, and he was welcomed by the Portland Forge and Foundry. At the drop-forge plant in Portland, Indiana, fourteen miles distant, Fred began work on the night shift as a die sinker. In the years following Fred's leaving Springfield, much metal work had changed from casting to forging. Fred quickly proved adept at guiding the cutting edge of a huge lathe across the surface of a block of steel. He demonstrated also his various mechanical skills. Gradually his financial problems were relieved.

"Get a city job!" was in the 1980s the monotonous mandate to insolvent farmers. It was advanced by university professors who were themselves shielded by tenure, or by business people with a lockbox full of securities. Fred Breimyer was able to get a city job, a good one. He was only in his forties and possessed of superb craftsman skills. Had he been ten years older and without experience or training other than planting corn and milking cows, he likely would have retreated into impecunious obscurity. His wife would have departed to some destination, possibly Springfield, to resume teaching. His children would have scattered, probably without attending college. Missouri farmers of the 1980s who were of the second category retreated into their private hideouts.

Fred's decision to go back into the shop had a double meaning for his son. On the one hand, as financial problems faded, so did the emotional tension in the family. A few family activities became affordable, including travel for a holiday. One episode fits with a theme, or social question, of how severe a limit to children's experiences is socially tolerable. Fred took his family to Dayton, where he had reason to visit what was known as the "soldiers' home." It probably was a Veterans' Administration facility. Alongside the hospital and rest home was an amusement park. Harold and his sisters were familiar with the merry-go-round and whip at county fairs. But the interesting rides and other attractions of an amusement park were fairyland given materiality. The intense delight in indulging in all the rides and treasures the family budget would allow was for them a once-in-a-childhood experience, never forgotten.

The second meaning for Harold of his father's taking off-farm work was that Harold graduated from a part-time hand to a full-time farmer. His father was able to devote a couple of hours a day to helping with farm work, but the continuing responsibility was the boy's. Was the load put on the fourteen-year-old a step that furthered the maturing process, or did it run a risk of overload and of unbalanced emotional and psychological development?

The question will not be answered here — at least not conclusively. But the risk was high. His parents were fortunate that the consequences were not more than some arresting of their son's progress in acquiring social amenities.

A further hypothesis is that the issue so posed can be applied universally. As the children of a family move through their teenage years, how can the proper balance be established between imposing duties, responsibilities, and challenges that further their development, without inviting disappointments and defeats that can impede that development?

Harold Breimyer suspects that countless farm youth of his generation — those who were forced to cut corn instead of attending classes during fall months — were in fact repressed. In the agriculture of the 1980s and early 1990s, young people reared on farms appear to be relatively free of the cultural inhibitions that were so common in an earlier day. It's possible that the analogy with the farming community of the 1920s fits better the youth of cities, especially black youth of the ghetto. They may now be the repressed ones.

Be that as it may, this recounting of stresses and strains that Harold Breimyer somehow survived introduces the last and most positive part of his boyhood history. It is the role played by institutions of social intercourse.

SOCIALIZATION AND A TOUCH OF CULTURE

Rural America has always devised ways to interrupt monotony and relieve isolation. Mutual aid activities such as barn-raisings were one type. Farm wives had their quilting bees. The rural church, including *ad hoc* tent meetings, was a fulcrum of social release. The rural school also has served as the center for a wide variety of community get-togethers, including the cake social and ciphering contest at College Hill School.

Threshing. During the 1920s in western Ohio, an activity that was as
social as it was technical was the threshing of grain. Fred Breimyer was a member of a threshing ring. A ponderous coal-burning steam engine, a separator, and a water wagon were stored over winter in a shed on Jack Brock's farm. All were put into use at midsummer to make one circuit among members to thresh the earlier-maturing wheat, and then another to thresh oats. Floyd Brock was the permanent fireman/engineer. One or two of the farmer-members were routinely assigned separator duty, or to the water wagon. Horses pulled the wagon to a source of water nearest the farm where threshing was being done. Water was laboriously lifted by hand pump into the tank, then taken to the steam engine for refilling its boiler.

The rest of the members of the ring either provided horse and wagon for hauling bundles of grain from the field or were pitchers. One farmer who had lost a hand in a farm accident was always assigned to pitch the sheaves of grain onto a wagon.

Harold Breimyer began his threshing duties when his father took the drop-forge job. The tasks proved within his capacity. The experience was memorable. He learned about men. He heard lots of profanity, absent in his own home and prohibited in his grandmother's. He learned about the human male's preoccupation with sex — at least conversationally. Sexual stories and the banter of accusations about the various farmers' proclivities were stock conversational items. That, too, was new, as his father and mother rarely mentioned the topic. And as to the boy himself, he had been immersed in the natural process of reproduction in farm animals. At age nine he had begun midwiving ewes, which have more trouble giving birth than do cows or sows. Sixty years later he found himself nonplussed by a prevailing preoccupation with the salacious aspects of human sexuality and a national hand-wringing over the penalties for promiscuity. He was sure the origins were all urban; farm folk, as the threshermen of his youth, are too earthy for that.

Alien as he was to much of the threshing crew's daily subject matter,

Harold was intrigued by it, and entertained by the joke-making and the practical jokes played. He relished the subtle boasting by which farmers sought to hide their problems and distresses. Every farmer was preparing to buy some fine new piece of machinery, or a draft horse of unparalleled strength—every farmer, that is, except one. Russell Potter, fat, slow-moving, tobacco-chewing, and probably the most inept farmer in the ring, admitted in appreciated candor, "I owe everybody." He did, of course—including Harold Breimyer, from whom he had bought a couple of used Model T Ford tires (for one dollar each, never paid). Most of the other farmers also had sizable debts. Unlike Russell, though, they kept silent about them.

Though himself innocent and even naive, Harold had a subtle sense that most of what he heard was game-playing. He was virtually certain that the men who talked most boisterously, or roisterously, about their sexual exploits were the most faithful to their wives and considerate of them. He was less trusting of the silent types. The cautionary pose has never left him.

The threshing ring taught Harold a lesson about human behavior and about political staging that proved lifetime-indelible. Tradition has it that preparing dinner for threshing crews was the occasion for competitive display of farm wives' culinary talent. Threshers' dinners had long been over-sized, over-rich, over-caloried. But not those in Fred Breimyer's ring. Fred pushed through a rule calling for the farmers to carry their lunches. His rationale, accepted by a narrow majority, was that a morning dew could delay threshing so that the farmers would be at one farm while the dinner was cooked at another, and that overeating on a hot day was just not a good idea.

A few of the threshermen never stopped voicing their disagreement. Harold noted that the few who stayed rancorous had no visible problem with the lunch-carrying arrangement. They would be first to grab their lunch pails when the sun hit its vertex. Quite possibly, in a new vote they would stay with the lunch pail. In their protest they were indulging in a relished pastime of costless advocacy. They were secure in the knowledge that the stand they enjoyed voicing would never be put to test.

In sixty years of witnessing stance-taking in the politics of farm policy, Harold Breimyer has found the paradigm demonstrated countless times. The American Farm Bureau Federation, for example, loads its policy resolutions with a variety of pronouncements, each of which caters to some constituency but none of which will ever be a part of the Bureau's political agenda. Political declarations are cheap.

He saw, in 1961, a flagrant failure to distinguish between political puffery and serious advocacy. As newly elected President, John Kennedy named the neophyte Orville Freeman as his Secretary of Agriculture. Freeman hastened to grant all concessions within his power to farm groups that had supported Kennedy in the narrow election. A wise old political hand observed, "That's a mistake. Political groups should be granted only enough to keep them begging." The groups' professional spokesmen were crestfallen. They thought they had been safe in making their puffed-up pitches. When Freeman gave them more than they really wanted, they themselves became supernumeraries. They had nothing left to advocate, to justify their role or salary. More than one lobbyist likely was dismissed as no longer needed.

Not least of the social aspects of a mutual threshing organization was the ice cream festival held at season's end. Big blocks of ice were brought from the town icehouse, and freezers were hand-cranked to churn the egg-and-milk-rich confection. Wives contributed their home-baked cakes. All appetites, even teenagers', were sated that evening. The occasion, by rural standards, was gala.

In the summer of 1933, Harold Breimyer, by then a nineteen-year-old veteran thresherman, was offered a summer job in Columbus, Ohio. His threshing career ended. So did, a year or two later, the threshing ring itself. It gave way to the modern technology of the grain combine. The combine may be a marvelous advance in engineering, but its introduction was a social catastrophe.

Chautauqua. In the annals of rural America, chautauqua deserves a strong, positive note. Harold Breimyer was fortunate that his life-time overlapped chautauqua's, though not by much. At midsummer in years of the early and mid-1920s, the imminent arrival of the big tent with its cultural performances would be announced with all possible salesmanship. Harold rode his bicycle to the homes of prospective ticket buyers, hoping to sell enough to pay for his own ticket. During mornings of chautauqua days, organized recreation was offered to children of the community. Afternoons and evenings brought the more appreciative among town and country folk into the big tent, there to sit on slatted wood folding chairs borrowed from church basements to listen to a musical performance, a lecture on public affairs, or a stage drama.

Most persistent in memory is a performance of Channing Pollock's *The Enemy.* The work had a moral message, but one incident in it stuck in the mind of a future agricultural economist. Not long after World War I a German farm wife called on her banker, telling him she was prepared to pay the principal of the farm mortgage. She would do it in kind, she said. She handed over three eggs.

At the height of the German inflation after the first war, a few eggs would indeed lift a farm mortgage. From the play Harold Breimyer learned about the German experience with runaway inflation. He did not yet comprehend that the U.S. farm distress of the early 1920s was largely traceable to deflation.

Also remembered is an evening of songs from opera and musical comedy, sung by a quartet. The honcho of the group was an aging bass named, appropriately, Alexis Bass. He displayed his veteran talents that, unfortunately, were marred by an occasional breaking of the voice. The other three vocalists were attractive college students, for whom the chautauqua circuit was valued concert training. The most colorful rendition that evening was an aria from Victor Herbert's *Blossom Time,* always a showpiece for quartet harmony.

Fort Recovery was not a profitable chautauqua stop. Year by year the attendance dwindled, and the summer of 1927 went by without an announcement that chautauqua was due in town. Nationally, the institution was about to complete its record of providing a major cultural uplift to rural environs.

The Victrola. The wind-up victrola was a gadget, not an institution, but
its production and the outflow of records was an institutionalized contribution to relief of tedium in rural parts. Harold Breimyer's first acquaintance was not with a victrola but with his grandmother's gramophone. From a huge horn atop a small box came a scratchy reproduction of recorded music. A bit of marvelously good fortune is dated about 1925 or 1926. Harold's Aunt Rena told his father that a victrola was available to him at the Wuichet home in Dayton, where she was a maid. Mr. Wuichet had died. He had been a lover of classical music, but his widow had no interest in music or in her late husband's victrola. The instrument and a collection of records came into the possession of Harold's family.

Wuichet did indeed have an ear for the best classical talent. Harold Breimyer as a boy listened for hours to the acoustically recorded renditions of Ernestine Schumann-Heinck, Fritz Kreisler, John McCormack, and various bands and orchestras, not to mention the Scotch singer-comedian Harry Lauder. Most treasured of all, though, was a record, still possessed, of a duet by Caruso and Scotti singing an aria from *La Forza del Destino.*

What a cultural addition was that victrola, with its records, to an isolated country home!

Treasured Interludes: Visits to City Cousins. Harold Breimyer as a boy
had one advantage over other farm boys of his neighborhood. He had city cousins, whom he visited once a year. They lived in his mother's

home city, Springfield. Even the trip to the city was an event. Suitcases
were lashed to the running board of the Ford, and early in the morning
the seventy-mile journey was under way. Roads were gravel until the
travelers reached U.S. highway 40. Harold's anticipation waxed when he
saw the count of telephone lines increase, indicating that the city of
60,000, huge to him, was becoming close.

His city cousins were the epitome of urban enlightenment. They
lived in a home with electric lights, running water, and a bathroom. Aunt
Rosa was a favorite aunt. Although both were available to her, Rosa had
neither an electric washing machine nor a refrigerator. She did the washing in an appliance driven by the pressure of tap water—invariably, early
Monday morning. As countless other Springfield wives were equally
chained to that day of the week, the water pressure was so low the
agitator would scarcely turn. "Aunt Rosa, why don't you wait until
Tuesday to wash, when the pressure will be better?" asked her sensible
nephew. "Oh no," she replied, "Monday is the day for washing." She was
German, of course, a Mayer.

Harold's aunt did not see why she needed an electric refrigerator
when she had an icebox. On hot summer days the vendor of blocks of ice
would announce, as noisily as possible, his presence on the street. Wives
would watch carefully as he weighed the vended ice. All the kids, including Harold and his cousin Paul Schulz, would beg for a splintered chip
of ice, good for fifteen minutes of cool sucking. Some vendors were
generous, others not. It was an interesting daily game.

To this day, Harold Breimyer regards the absence of refrigeration as
one of the worst hardships of country life in the years before electric
power. Unlike his Aunt Rosa, farm wives did not have ice as an alternative. Only a damp cellar floor slowed the souring of foods—but not for
very long.

By chance, several of the Breimyer family visits to the city spanned
the Fourth of July holiday. Harold helped his cousin Paul pick the ripe
cherries on a neighbor's tree to earn enough money to buy firecrackers.
Farm youth scarcely knew that the nation's natal day could be celebrated
in so exciting a fashion. The farm boy was enraptured.

FORT RECOVERY HIGH SCHOOL

The people of Fort Recovery recognized only two pedestals. On the
lower were their ministers. The higher was reserved for school teachers.
Education was the magic formula for achieving success and enjoy-

ing a good life. A good life was defined not just in material success or social status but also in appreciation of "higher values" in living. The theologian Paul Tillich has said that education is the language that liberates from situational bondage. The main thought-leaders and opinion-makers of Fort Recovery saw it that way.

Thought-leaders there were. The town may have had two pedestals, but below or alongside them was a tier of platforms. The community was highly stratified. In the highest stratum were a few dozen individuals, not knit in any formal way, who collectively gave leadership to community-wide activities and especially those of uplifting nature: John Premer, who sold cemetery monuments; Guy Reuter, who wanted to build a community arts center and who went broke in a haberdashery but caught on as postmaster; the wife of Dennis Honn, the Lutheran minister; Martha Rohr of the Fort Recovery Bank. These and a few others bestowed leadership that prevented the town from drifting into an abyss into which its economic failings would otherwise consign it.

Therein lay a moral conflict, a contradiction, that bothered Harold Breimyer even as a high school student and has burdened his political thinking ever since. It may be the nub of all social-political philosophizing. It's the contest or distinction between egalitarian democratic values and their opposite, meritocracy or elitism. Harold Breimyer is a lifetime subscriber to the democratic postulates of Thomas Jefferson. But he knows that in his native Fort Recovery, and in every more prestigious community in which he has since made his home, a congeries of imaginative, progressive, and even courageous individuals have worked to make their own tiny patch of planet Earth a better place in which people can live. What motivates them? Where do they find psychic rewards?

Public-spirited elitism may be essential to civilization itself. From whence does it arise? What prevents its being quenched?

Harold Breimyer thinks he may himself have caught some of the spirit. And his philosophical misgivings were assuaged when he learned that his model, Jefferson, with whom he shares April 13 as birthday, was able to reconcile elitist performance with democratic values. Jefferson, sensitive to his own quandary, regarded democracy as requiring an aristocracy of virtue and talent. His objection was to an elite "*born* booted and spurred," that is, to a hereditary aristocratic class.[1]

Thomas Jefferson and John Adams, erstwhile antagonists, found it possible late in their long lives, both of which ended on the anniversary

---

[1]Max Lerner, "Our Constitutional Government: Of, By, and For the People," mimeographed notes from Gerald Engelman, taken in Graduate school, U.S. Department of Agriculture, April 23, 1965.

day of July 4, 1826, to agree on the role of a meritocracy in a democratic nation. The theme embellished the correspondence of their final years.

The quality of Fort Recovery's leadership contributed mightily to the good education that was made available to the youth of the town. The principal limitation to schooling of the youth in those days was physical—transportation. The percentage of boys and girls of high school age who completed the four years was correlated not with IQ but, rather, with miles to be traveled. No public transport was provided. Among the thirty members of Harold Breimyer's graduating class, none came from a home more distant than five miles. A majority lived in the town or close by.

Harold himself traveled three and a half miles. The first year or two he rode his bicycle, in company with a neighbor, John Patton. On winter days of bitter cold, John's or Harold's father would take compassion and drive the two boys to school. Later, two older boys, Ronald Heis and Edward Frommel, took turns driving to the school and provided Harold the luxury of a ride, for which the payment probably was five cents. In his fourth year his sister Louise was a freshman. By that time his father, relieved from poverty by Drop Forge income, paid $35 for the nearly exhausted Model T Ford of L. N. Geiger, successor to Charles Nicholson as vocational agriculture teacher. Harold drove his sister to school.

In some respects Fort Recovery's faith in education was self-fulfilling, as the esteem in which it was held contributed to high morale in the school and modest but adequate financial support—and to that intangible quality, companion to high-pedestal respect for teachers, of pride in students' scholarly achievements. And how did it happen that outstanding high school teachers such as Pearl Wagner, Ethel Johnson, Lucile DeSelm, the two Darsts, and a dozen others would not only come to drab Fort Recovery but would remain there at least a few years?

The sardonic suggestion can always be offered that because the hamlet had no basketball gymnasium or other athletic facility, its only alternative course was to pursue academic achievement. The notion is not frivolous.

But that flip note distracts from the community self-assessment that led to putting so much emphasis on education. Citizens knew that their local resources were few. Their own horizons rested on common uplift more than individual heroics. In such a setting, only when the common weal improves can individuals soar.

Famous persons often are asked to name who contributed most to their success. The non-famous Harold Breimyer can readily pinpoint much of the credit for the modest acclaim that has come his way. It goes to a pretty, pert, bright teacher of English, Lucile DeSelm, who arrived at the Fort Recovery school directly from DePauw University in Indiana. She quickly became the darling of Harold's class, if not the entire school. She found Harold to be a quick learner and gave him every encouragement. When the boy later enrolled as a freshman at Ohio State University and sat through the mandatory freshman English course, he learned nothing new. From Lucile DeSelm he had learned previously the rules about grammar and parsing a sentence.

In the 1970s Harold Breimyer reestablished a relationship with his beloved teacher. In May of 1980, he visited her at a retirement home in South Bend, Indiana, cutting a tape to convey her greeting to members of the Fort Recovery graduating class of 1930, which would soon hold its fiftieth reunion. Much of the visit was given to reciting to each other remembered lines of poetry — Thanatopsis, Hamlet's soliloquy, Portia's discourse on the quality of mercy. When his teacher faltered, Harold corrected, and heard the response that follows all successful teaching: "And now the pupil corrects the teacher." They were the last words of Lucile DeSelm Seedorf to her onetime pupil.

In those years the Ohio school system held a scholarship contest. Each high school would select its brightest pupils in each of several subjects, who would take a competitive examination at a district center. Harold and his sister Louise were among the Fort Recovery High School students nominated in the spring of 1930 to do their best by their school's colors in examinations held at Bowling Green State College, seventy-five miles distant. The school's representatives won awards out of proportion to the school's size. Their tally is given in a newspaper clipping, yet retained.

Harold Breimyer's score in American History was high enough to win for him the top grade statewide. He has proudly displayed in his home a certificate certifying, "First Place in American History in the State of Ohio." Harold believed at the time that he outdistanced other contestants by denying, in a multiple-choice question, that the Civil War came into being over slavery. He targeted the issue of the constitutional right of secession.

Except for the puzzle of why a town with resources as limited as Fort Recovery's could offer its youth such good education, the experience of Harold Breimyer in high school was not exceptional. But he later found himself well-prepared for college, and eventually for a professional career.

4-H CLUBS

Harold Breimyer believes that 4-H Clubs were his salvation. They opened for him a world that lay beyond his everyday confinement to milking cows, plowing fields, and doing the homework for school assignments by the flickering light of a kerosene lamp or, when it would work, a gasoline lamp.[2]

The 4-H Clubs were a route to escape from cultural confinement for literally millions of rural youth. Credit for initiating the 4-H movement is given to A. B. Graham, a sometime teacher and superintendent of schools in Clark County, Ohio. Springfield, the home town of Ella Breimyer, is in this county.

In a broader sense 4-H Clubs captured and reflected the drive in opening decades of the twentieth century for cultural emancipation of rural America. It was expressed in the American Country Life movement, epitomized in the American Country Life Commission appointed by President Theodore Roosevelt and headed by Liberty Hyde Bailey.

In the spring of 1923, Mercer County Extension Agent George Henning induced Fred Breimyer to form and lead a pig club. Fred did so. Always progressive and cooperative, he wanted his son to have the experience. The prescribed minimum age was ten and Harold was nine, but the boy knew how to take care of a pig and could keep records.

Fred Breimyer was surprised by the number of farm boys who leaped at the opportunity. Boys joined from families located in the community's sticks, many of whom Fred had never known. Del and Emma Schlamb, good farmers but childless, invited the club to meet at their home, and they showered the kids with confections that some had never tasted.

At summer's end the pigs were shown at the county fair. Fred borrowed a Model T Ford truck from Fred Ulmer, a local grocer, and loaded the bed with the boys' animals. The Model T motor was not designed for heavy freight. Memory is still clear that the travel distance of ten miles to assemble the pigs and of twenty miles to Celina, the county seat, required much of a day.

Not etched in memory but a valid speculation is that most of the boys managed somehow to travel to the fairgrounds, each to see his pig snug in a pen and competing for a blue or red ribbon. It's probable, too,

---

[2]The Coleman gasoline lamp. That lamp was a technological boon before electric power came to farm homes. Air pumped into the gasoline-filled base would generate fuel for fabric mantles. Their bright white light was immensely more satisfactory than yellow kerosene light. Trouble was, the gasoline lamp could not be kept functioning. Its internal tubes clogged repeatedly.

that some had never before traveled as far as Celina.

Fred Breimyer found 4-H leadership to be too demanding of his time and did not continue as leader. But in 1926 his son joined a dairy calf club. By that time Harold was twelve. Also, by that time Fort Recovery High School had introduced new vocational education programs in both home economics and agriculture. Jessie Nichols had come from Ohio State University as the home economics teacher. She married Arden Beach, the shoe man, and remained in the village the rest of her life. Charles "Nick" Nicholson taught vocational agriculture.

Even though the community was progressive, it would be historically inaccurate to report that the two new programs were endorsed enthusiastically, or that the new teachers were embraced warmly. Some members of the community were sure that mothers could teach their daughters all they needed to know about cooking. Ignorant of nutrition themselves, they could not comprehend what nutrition education meant. There was less skepticism about teaching agriculture. Even so, partly because Nicholson was of Roman Catholic faith, a cross was burned on his lawn. Education about a scientific agriculture has since become so ingrained that it is easy to forget early discord when its sponsors had to fight traditionalists.

Undaunted, Charles Nicholson ingratiated himself in the community almost at once. He made 4-H Clubs one of his responsibilities. When he formed the dairy calf club that Harold joined, the response was enthusiastic. Even some girls enrolled. Nicholson insisted that purebred Guernsey heifers be bought. A truckload came from dairy farms in northeastern Ohio. When the calves were unloaded, the 4-H members hurried to make their choices. The girls opted for animals with bright splashes of white in their coat. Harold, coached by his father, who had read Ohio State University bulletins, looked for depth of chest and other traits that the dairy husbandrymen called "good conformation." He did not mind that the calf of his choice had a coat of plain fawn color.

Judges at the year's Mercer County Fair were concerned for conformation, not color, and Harold's heifer placed second in the judging ring. Because his record book graded high, the combined score earned a blue ribbon.

The week at the county fair was memorable. The boy bunked in an empty calf pen, making a bed on the straw. Food service tents hawked hamburgers and chili. All sorts of candies, ice creams, and soft drinks were dispensed for nickels and dimes. But Harold's fare was the sandwiches, hard-boiled eggs, and garden tomatoes brought from home. Inured to the financial discipline of his family, he allocated one dollar of spending money for the five fair days. Cold root beer sold in mugs at five cents was his favorite indulgence. An occasional frankfurter, at ten cents, was a luxury.

Charles Nicholson included Harold and his calf in an expedition to the state fair in Columbus. At midnight one night Nicholson set out with a carload of 4-H boys. A bundle of energy, he had played cards with friends until the hour of departure. But sleepiness caught up with him. When he nodded, Charles Wertz grabbed the steering wheel and prevented a potential tragedy.

The Ohio State Fair was a county fair magnified manifold. Harold was most impressed by a display of the dairy science department of Ohio State University. In a glass-enclosed refrigerated space students sculpted a cow of butter. The dairy display was attractive for yet another reason: It sold milk ice cold, probably the boy's first exposure to refrigerated milk—which proved even more refreshing than the county fair's root beer.

The Mercer County calves won a few ribbons. Among them was Harold's pink fourth-place one.

When the Guernsey heifer became a cow, she again was shown at the county fair. Judges gave her no prize because her udder was unbalanced. The impressive milk production record her owner put on a display card was disregarded.

A wish without fulfillment is that the dairy calf project initiated by Charles Nicholson would prove to be a community-development miracle. It did not, because Nicholson, in his ebullience, failed to ask for a Bang's disease test from the source herds for the beautiful Guernsey calves. The 4-H project introduced brucellosis into the low-producing but brucellosis-free dairy cows of the Fort Recovery community. As the disease swept all of Ohio, it would have reached the area in any case, but the happenstance that it entered via a 4-H project was regrettable.

Our era has worshipped at the shrine of technology, and the 4-H movement is often viewed, favorably of course, as a means of introducing farm boys and girls to the wonders of modern technology in farming. It did that. But let it be said again: For millions of 4-H members, the clubs were first of all a route to cultural emancipation.

For Harold Breimyer even the local meetings and especially the occasional picnics were exciting experiences. In his elementary school he had played group games, such as scatter base, but 4-H offered a repertory of games and activities unheard of in staid German-Lutheran families.

And the first state convention Harold attended! In the fall of 1926, he was named a Mercer County delegate to the 4-H convention in Columbus. His father drove him to Wapakoneta, where a dozen or more

4-H members from surrounding counties boarded a train destined for Ohio's capital city. At Columbus the boy was lodged not in a tent as at the state fair, or even in a crowded college dormitory, but in a single room at the Neil House, a first-class hotel on High Street opposite the State Capitol. He had his first experience with a shower equipped with a single handle that blended hot and cold water. But what he remembered most were the many notices telling that Charles Dickens had once lodged at the Neil House.

The Ohio Farm Bureau hosted a banquet, held in a hall of unimaginable size. The printed program carried data on the tonnage of foodstuffs required to serve all the 4-H appetites. The youth were impressed!

One evening Harold was accosted in a cafeteria line and asked to report to the desk the next morning. After a sleepless night, when he wondered what his infraction had been, he was asked to take part in a tableau. In it he posed as Whittier's barefoot boy with cheeks of tan. He must have displayed a complexion of suitable hue. But his alarm illustrates his sensitivity to any rebuke or, in this case, hint of one.

The episode, however, did not detract from his evangelistic excitement of the conference. Included in the program of several days was inculcation of a 4-H theme song:

> A waking day and a breaking field
> And a furrow straight and long.
> A summer sun and a lifting breeze
> And we'll follow with a song.
>
> Sons of the soil are we,
> Men of the coming years.
> Turning our sod, asking no odds,
> Lords of our land we'll be.

The Mercer County delegate joined with enthusiasm, doubtless off-key. He could not have guessed that the song would disappear later from 4-H lore, as clubs invaded the cities and as the masculine focus ("sons," "men") was found objectionable.

The next year proved even more memorable. Harold teamed with Ernest Heiby in a 4-H demonstration contest. They chose to demonstrate how to produce clean milk. In 1990 the instructions would appear antique, but in 1927 it was novel to tell farmers to wash the cow's udder, to use a pail with a partial cover (requiring a little more accuracy in squirting the milk from the teat), and of course to sterilize all milk-handling utensils. The boys must have told the story well, as they were judged the best demonstrators at the Mercer County fair and then at the

Ohio State Fair, which they attended for the second successive year. The reward for the latter achievement was a trip to the National Dairy Show in Memphis, Tennessee. For the first time the boys, accompanied by their county agent, O. H. Anderson, and vocational agriculture teacher, L. N. Geiger, traveled beyond the bounds of the states of Ohio and Indiana.

In Memphis Harold enjoyed once again the comforts of a downtown hotel. He heard fire sirens and watched fire engines in the middle of the night—a first. He and Ernest attended one of the earliest talking-picture movies, *The Trial of Mary Dugan*. In it the villain was identified when he caught with his left hand a knife thrown at him. It had been shown that the victim was killed by a left-handed knife wielder. More cultural emancipation.

The two demonstrators from Ohio won no laurels at the National Dairy Show. Unwisely, they decided to go modern, borrowing from display booths of DeLaval and other distributors the latest equipment in milk handling. Unfamiliar with the newfangled gadgetry, their previously smooth demonstration with a half-covered bucket and simple strainers turned into an awkward bungle.

The return trip revealed something about the state of highways in the South in 1927. Choosing to return via Chattanooga, Anderson and Geiger set out on a highway leading due eastward from Memphis. After sixty miles they encountered a roadblock and had to return to Memphis. They then took a road that would conduct them eastward through northern Mississippi and Alabama. They got only as far as Tupelo, Mississippi, the first night.

Highlights of the return trip were a stop at Muscle Shoals in Florence, Alabama, and a ride on the inclined railway at Chattanooga. The hydroelectric dam at Florence was an exceptional engineering achievement. Harold, already a social scientist at heart, or perhaps just humanitarian, still remembers the statistic that fifty-six men died in its construction. Almost sixty years later he saw the movie describing construction of the St. Louis arch and was impressed to learn that the arch was built without a single fatality.

Later Harold was leader for clubs in the Fort Recovery community. Those experiences were not exceptional. But 4-H was yet to hold further meaning to him—a story that awaits an account of his college days.

VOCATIONAL AGRICULTURE

For rural youth in the 1920s, vocational agriculture was companion to 4-H in Operation Uplift. It was a school-year undertaking, complementing the summertime 4-H. A high school pupil enrolling in a class in vocational animal husbandry, for example, was required to undertake a livestock production project; in crops, he was to plant a specified acreage of an agreed-on crop. Records had to be kept. The vocational agriculture instructor was not just the preceptor of the classroom; he was also counselor, business advisor, and confidant. Charles Nicholson, Harold Breimyer's first vocational agriculture instructor, was followed by Harold Hersch, Wilbur Bruner, L. N. Geiger, and, in his senior year, C. E. Pope.

Harold first chose a hog project. He bought two purebred Duroc gilts. The animals were productive enough, but Nick Nicholson's training was entirely in farm production. He knew nothing about price cycles. Worse, the high prices of the time led him to see a hog project as attractive. By the time the gilts' progeny were of market weight, the price cycle had corrected itself. Thus, the young student learned that the best production techniques in the world are unavailing when the price cycle swings unfavorably. He could not have guessed at the time that twenty years later he would be the country's best known authority on price cycles in livestock.

And Harold's later potato project was no more successful, even though his father made available the best acre of soil on his farm. It was the best because it was at the bottom of a slope, alongside a stream. But, by virtue of its topography, it was also subject to flooding. The principal lesson learned from the project was that the sprouts of Russet potatoes imported from Michigan will not survive flood water.

The boy's only profitable undertaking in vocational agriculture proved to be the raising of broiler chickens. The technology of producing chickens for commercial sale already had undergone dramatic changes since filo coops were advocated early in the 1900s. In 1930 the recommended technique was to put 500 baby chicks in a brooder house. Fred Breimyer constructed a splendid octagonal house, following, as always, the instructions and architectural plans obtained from the Ohio Agricultural Extension Service. A small stove burned hard coal, at a height of flame controlled by a wafer thermostat. As long as it worked properly, it kept the chicks comfortably warm, but the mechanism was delicate and required lots of attention. When cold, chicks crowd against each other and smother.

Early in 1930, 525 baby chicks (a bakers' dozen count) were lifted carefully out of cardboard boxes that had been punctured with air holes. Soon the cheeping of the chicks filled the air of the brooder house. Harold fired the stove, then began his vigil. Each night just before going to bed, he looked into the brooder house. He set his alarm clock for two o'clock in the morning. At that hour, shielded from chill winds by an overcoat and "arctic" boots, he made his way, often through snow, to the house holding the chicks that were to stake him to the first year of college.

If farm life in the 1920s trained farm boys for responsibility or, conversely, revealed their lack of mettle, the ultimate test was caring for baby chicks in winter. Harold Breimyer, at age fifteen, met the test. From the 525 biddies he raised almost 500 birds to market weight. Unlike the hog and potato enterprises, the broilers made money for him. They also capped his first venture into borrowing money. Although he had dollars enough in savings to pay for the chicks, he was not able to finance the cost of feed. So he asked the manager of the local equity cooperative elevator, Floyd Freemyer, if he could get feed on credit. The man let the young entrepreneur borrow on his own signature up to a maximum of $100. Chances are he would not have done the same for Harold's father, as Fred Breimyer's credit rating had not yet improved much. Not long before the broilers were ready for market, the manager called Harold to his office and told him he was over the $100 figure. Harold assured the manager that he was solvent, and two weeks later the high school senior had a song in his heart when, following his good luck in hitting a high price market for broilers, he could pay the Equity and put another $100 or more into his savings account. He then refilled the brooder house with White Leghorn chicks, to be raised as replacement stock for the farm's egg enterprise.

The boy was luckier than he could have known at the time. The Depression was only getting under way. In a later year the bottom would have dropped out of the broiler market and the young poultryman would have found himself bereft of college funds.

FUTURE FARMERS OF AMERICA

If de Tocqueville, the French visitor to the United States, was impressed in 1839 by the propensity of the provincials to congregate in clubs, he would have been astonished by the proliferation of organizations in the 1920s. Ladies who were otherwise unemployed were even more aggressive than the men. A veteran of those years, Helen Hooven Santmyer, gained fame in the 1980s, a few years before her death, by writing an account of ladies' clubs.

Rural America was not far behind. These pages have already dwelt at length on 4-H Clubs. During Harold Breimyer's senior year the impetus of the FFA—Future Farmers of America—carried as far as remote Fort Recovery. Harold joined instantly. The big FFA event of the year for him was a public-speaking contest. The pattern continued of his being named the Fort Recovery candidate and winning at the regional level. Thereupon he took part in the statewide contest. By that time a trip to Columbus was no longer a novelty, but the public-speaking experience proved to be that. He had chosen for his topic the losses of farm products attributable to insect damage. He dug up data on crop values and found it easy, aided by charts, to reveal the enormous dollar worth of grain and other products ingested by the insect world. Unbeknownst to him, he chanced upon price statistics of an earlier and happier day for farmers, so his data had an implicit upward bias.

But flaws in data were not his Waterloo. The judges were Leo Rummel, field reporter for the *Ohio Farmer* magazine, who was later to be named dean of agriculture at Ohio State University; Guy W. Miller, Extension farm management specialist; and a third person whose identity eludes memory. During the question period Guy Miller shot this one: "But if crops were saved from insect loss, would not their price be lower, so that crop values to farmers might not be affected much?" The high school senior was nonplussed. He had studied no economics and stumbled with a non-answer.

He did not forget. Almost exactly a year later, when the high school senior had moved to the exalted status of a university freshman, he was employed in the farm accounts office presided over by Guy Miller and three associates. He came to revere the lanky, cigar-chewing, superb extension man and remained his friend until his death in 1985. Not fewer than a dozen times he reminded the man of the upsetting question asked in the FFA contest. Guy's invariable response was an admission, with a chuckle, that the question was too difficult for a high-school student.

FURTHER MUSINGS ABOUT THE 1920s

The year 1930 was a turning point in the life and career of Harold Breimyer, as he left high school and matriculated at Ohio State University. It was also a momentous year in the nation's history, as the emerging

Great Depression became more visible. It was manifest first, in the young university student's eyes, by haggard men selling apples, for five cents with hope of overpayment, on sidewalks in Columbus.

Nonetheless, the exceptional years of the 1920s merit a little more mention. Anyone born late enough to have grown up in that decade, rather than earlier, was fortunate indeed. The account just completed emphasizes the meaning to farm youth of new institutions such as 4-H clubs and vocational agriculture. Boys born a decade earlier would have been denied those felicitous aids to personal growth and social release.

In many respects the 1920s were a pivotal decade in the history of our country. World War I woke up the drowsy nation, which got a glimpse of its destiny. The decade has often been reported, and even rhapsodized. Frederick Lewis Allen's *Only Yesterday,* written soon after the decade's end, remains the sublime testament. Recent efforts to reassess the decade, such as Geoffrey Perrett's, are comparative flops.

Around rustic Fort Recovery, changes taking place in styles of living, in the economy's infrastructure, and in political thinking were perceived only dimly and, often, whimsically. Only the automobile and paved roads permeated the place and were received appreciatively. But even those hallmarks of the 1920s did not mean a great deal until 1928, when the Model A Ford and a new Chevrolet became available.

In Fort Recovery the Eighteenth amendment (prohibition) was endorsed matter-of-factly, though more affirmatively by the local WCTU (Women's Christian Temperance Union). The WCTU was given several inches of lineage in the *Journal,* the local newspaper. The law was observed reasonably well in the Protestant half of the community, and less faithfully by the Catholics.

SCHOOLDAYS' READING

Newspapers carried the column of Arthur Brisbane, who purred the conventional conservative wisdom of the time. Even though Fort Recovery qualified, in the lexicon of a later day, as underdeveloped, it was a politically conservative town. It supported Ohio's Senator Simeon Fess, even concurring that the man of unexceptional talent and unimaginative mien might qualify for the presidency. It voted for Harding and then for Coolidge. In 1928 its Protestant contingent could not even consider seriously the candidacy of Al Smith, who was a Catholic and, worse, a "wet."

The gentle, and almost prostrate, people of the town were fatalistically reconciled to the doctrine of an inactive government. They accepted the dogma that any action of government to improve economic conditions would be as ineffectual as it would be inappropriate. Few of the town's citizens likely were familiar with Andrew Mellon's dictum, doctrinal emblem of the decade: "The prosperity of the middle classes depends on the good fortune and light taxes of the rich." Were they to have heard it, they would not have demurred. Fort Recovery was not sure many of its citizens qualified as middle class.

The town's intelligentsia nevertheless kept up to date on the flow of literature. Ella Breimyer stayed in fairly close touch but had to depend on books borrowed from a library. She and her husband were financially unable to buy newly published books of high literary quality. Each Christmas they gave their children the latest of the Bobbsey Twins books. For Harold they bought Horatio Alger books, which allegedly had a moral message—but also were inexpensive. Harold all but rebelled. For reasons he cannot explain to this day, he did not like the Alger books. Perhaps he did not believe that simple virtue always brought handsome financial rewards.

One incident fictionalized by Alger stays in his mind. One of the author's simple-minded honest types was a country boy who, having sought his fortune in the place fortunes were to be found—a city—was hired temporarily to fill in as conductor on a streetcar. A lady passenger lost a dime, which the youth found and faithfully returned to her. Fortuitously, a company official observed his conduct. The reward was an offer of permanent employment as conductor. By Alger standards that was high reward for a bumpkin fresh out of the country. Implicitly the author was demeaning the rural culture. Harold Breimyer's indignation at the put-down, felt as sharply then as later, probably accounts for its staying in his memory.

Lucile DeSelm prescribed the conventional English-class readings: *Last of the Mohicans, Ivanhoe, Silas Marner,* and lots of Shakespeare. Gene Stratton-Porter was popular; she wrote of the Limberlost swamps, located only forty miles northwest of Fort Recovery. She died in an automobile accident at about the time.

In English classes it was prerequisite to a good grade to recognize the existence of Theodore Dreiser, Sherwood Anderson, John Dos Passos, and other protest writers, but their writings were never assigned. A physician friend of the family gave Harold a copy of Bruce Barton's *The Man Nobody Knows,* which made clear that Jesus was really the first capitalist. The high-school student lacked the critical capacity for misgivings. He was in the intellectual grip of a Fort Recovery too insecure for nonconformity.

Later, during his college years, Harold Breimyer read *Main Street,* *Babbit,* and other books authored by Sinclair Lewis. He did so with sharp appreciation of Lewis's satire.

Literary reading matter in different form—and price—came to Harold Breimyer and other impecunious young people from an exceptional source. The Haldeman-Julius Company of Girard, Kansas, merchandised Little Blue Books through nationwide mailings. The price of the small, thin paperbacks is not recalled, but it may have been ten cents. Among the titles were a number on astrology and the publishers' religious philosophy, but also the Shakespeare plays and hundreds of the shorter classics that teachers of English love to assign. The *Literary Digest* met the competition by putting out its miniatures of literature bound in red leather-like covers. Between the Blue Books and the *Literary Digest's* red ones, Harold Breimyer acquired reading matter of literary merit at a pittance in cost.

Of contrasting content and singular emotional effect was a small volume, *The Little Minister,* written by Sir James Barrie. The book came as a gift. In the culture of Fort Recovery, it was surprising to read of a love story surrounding a labor union's activities and strike. In its insularity the town scarcely recognized the existence of organized industrial labor, and surely granted it no charity of acquiescence, not to mention approval. *The Little Minister* opened a new avenue of social philosophy.

CHAPTER 5

College and Depression Years

THERE NEVER WAS QUESTION in anyone's mind that Harold Breimyer would go to college. And there was little question about the identity of the college—Ohio State University—or of the curriculum—agriculture. If the boy had any doubts, they were resolved by another success in scholarship. The Ohio State University asked of its students only an "incidental fee" of $20 per quarter, and occasional laboratory fees. The institution offered scholarships that remitted even the modest incidental fee. When a test was given at Fort Recovery High School, Harold received a score high enough to qualify him for remission of the incidental fee for the full twelve quarters normally required to obtain a bachelor's degree. To the boy, whose financial resources were confined to a couple of hundred dollars earned in his broiler and dairy enterprises, the $240 scholarship was a godsend, manna from heaven.

The only curricular decision was choice of a major. It need not have been made at once, but when the college catalog described in six lines of fine print the offerings of the Department of Rural Economics (renamed Agricultural Economics several years later), the prospective freshman made up his mind instantly. He remembered that his good productive effort in hogs had been annulled by a downward swing in price of hogs. The Depression was already undercutting farmers' incomes from grain and livestock. He also recalled hearing debates about farm policy at Farmers' Institutes held in the Morvilius Opera House. It's exceptional when a 15-year-old high school student chooses a field of specialization that he will hold to unswervingly throughout his lifetime career. But Harold Breimyer did so.

In September 1930, college life began. It began with Freshman Week, marked by getting lodging, a job, and the Ohio State fever. In those years universities acknowledgcd a sheltering responsibility toward their female students but denied any concern for the males. The girls' dormitories, modern and attractive, were located at the edge of the campus, and presided over with the best matronly protection. Male students found lodging where they could. Harold Breimyer's former vocational agriculture instructor, L.N. Geiger, guided the new freshman to the home of his friend Wallace Binegar. There Harold shared a room and bed with Virgil Bumgarner, also a freshman in agriculture. Harold's monthly rent was $9.00.

The room had closet space for six or eight garments (for both boys), two small tables, each with a reading light, and a shelf for books. Most of the clothing was kept in a suitcase that was slid under the bed. Harold and Virgil were two of five students living in the home, the Binegar family numbered seven, and the house of average size had a single bathroom. Yet the conditions were not regarded as exceptionally crowded, as judged by standards of the time — or by Harold's home on the farm, which was even more cramped and had *no* bathroom. He did not feel himself underprivileged.

EMPLOYMENT

The young freshman's concerns lay in another direction, that of employment. Scarcely more than sixteen years old, he set out to make his way. The university YMCA had an employment service. One afternoon he helped a lady dig dandelions out of her yard. The blisters from the paring knife earned him thirty cents an hour. Another day he helped a returning professor of sociology, Herman Adolphus Miller, put his home back in order. The good professor had just come back from a globe-circling trip, during which he learned that colored races had a basic intelligence equivalent to that of whites. He told his classes of that observation. For that insolence the trustees of the great Ohio State University, seat of scholarship, bounced him within the year.

Sigma Phi Epsilon Fraternity needed kitchen help during Freshman Week. So the new freshman got a job with a seven-day security. He left with the plaudits of Miss Woodruff, "You are a good worker." Harold had no idea what he had done to win the praise.

The YMCA came through. A restaurant in the lower level of an apartment house at Neil and Woodruff avenues lacked a dishwasher. Harold must have looked honest to Mrs. Dutt, who promised him meals in exchange for four hours of kitchen duty daily. The meals were good, and Mrs. Dutt a kind employer. Harold Breimyer had accepted enough of the Horatio Alger philosophy to know he was morally obliged to feel grateful for the largess that came his way. Social concerns did not yet lie heavily on his consciousness or conscience. He gave no thought to how low his compensation was. At the price of Mrs. Dutt's meals, he earned about twenty cents an hour.

His first budding sensitivity attached to the fortunes of the cook, Fannie Shields. A widow, she worked six long days a week, doing all the cooking for the miserly wage of $17.50 a week.

At the end of the school year, Mrs. Dutt lost her lease. So Fannie lost her job. As the Great Depression worsened, Harold Breimyer wondered what fortunes lay ahead for her. He wondered, too, about Mrs. Dutt, also a widow, who was responsible for rearing her thirteen-year-old daughter. The next year Mrs. Dutt opened a small eatery in residential housing, with prospects that could not have been better than minimum survival. What becomes of a proud but resourceless middle-aged woman when economic recession envelops?

Harold Breimyer, himself scarred by the long financial struggles of his family, gradually came to understand that not only farm families can be beleaguered. Industrial recession claims urban victims numbering many thousands.

Recession also invites inhumane, uncivilized business conduct. Harold learned this the next year. In the fall of 1931, finding Mrs. Dutt's Neil Avenue restaurant closed, he first petitioned Mrs. Anderson, who operated a small, clean place on High Street. As one of his credentials, he cited his good student record. Thereupon he got a response that shocked him. Mrs. Anderson did not hire good students; they were too likely to fail to show up when preparing for an examination.

Wiley O'Hara had no such concerns. Sure, Harold could work for him. The emolument would be seventeen-and a-half cents an hour, taken in meals. The O'Hara establishment was, in the vernacular of the time, a greasy spoon, a joint. His employees were unskilled, low-paid, and callous to O'Hara's abuse. One of Harold Breimyer's duties was to close up the restaurant each evening, ending with mopping the entire floor space—all for seventeen-and-a-half cents an hour paid in the plainest food.

The social conscience began to activate, particularly as Harold learned something about life in the stratum of low-paid menials. One kitchen worker was a lady of about twenty-five years who resembled in appearance the comic strip character Olive Oyl (as thin and straight as a board). She was a fairly dutiful worker, except that she had to be reminded to comb her hair in the bathroom rather than over the food table. She was married to a burly man who delivered ice, packing it with a pick on his shoulders. The two shared a single room in a rooming house. The Olive Oyl lady probably was not paid more than twelve dollars a week. Her husband was lucky if he earned twice that. What kind of life did they lead? There was no sign of debauchery. A waitress was a redhead named Verna, a grandmother at forty-five, whose husband had disappeared. Life must have been circumscribed for her.

The O'Hara instruction in the busiest private business practices took place in the dreadful economic winter of 1932. It was his standard practice to fire his employees periodically and take on a new gang. One day he summarily did so. The Depression was deepening. In what manner did those individuals survive until economic conditions improved? Wiley O'Hara did not care.

By that time Harold Breimyer had gleefully escaped the O'Hara guiles and returned to farm account mill employment (see below). He lost touch with Olive Oyl, Verna, and the others. But the sequence came painfully to mind a year later, when he met Mary, the former head cook, on the sidewalk. Correction: he almost met her. The lady crossed the street to avoid being seen and greeted. She was emaciated and dressed in rags. The brief episode exemplified the intense human cost of the Depression before relief measures were put into operation.

THE OHIO STATE SPIRIT

Freshman Week was intended to acclimatize incoming freshmen students to the huge Ohio State campus and its institutional workings. It also served as a screening device. Harold Breimyer learned, to his astonishment, that a few of his fellow greenhorns who came in on Monday morning had departed by Friday evening, permanently. They could not accept the institutional clime.

A second purpose of Freshman Week was to inculcate the Ohio State spirit. It's hard to explain why Ohio State, a large state university, should have made such a point of developing—nay, inspiring—so close an allegiance between student and school, a loyalty that was intended to be lifelong and often became that. Conceivably, the origin lay in the university's earlier fight for public recognition. In the later 1800s the fledgling public institution had to contest with older private Ohio colleges of high fame, such as Oberlin and Ohio Wesleyan. It did so, vigorously.

Whatever its history, the indoctrination during the seven days of

Freshman Week was intense and effective. By the time they entered classes, the novice scholars knew they were allying with a great seat of learning. It had good football teams, too!

At a huge rally Olive Jones played the piano accompaniment for singing "Fight That Team Across the Field" and other songs, ending, of course, with "Carmen Ohio." The secular tabernacle won its converts.

Fifty-four years later Harold Breimyer, as a graduate of the class of 1934, returned to his alma mater to join in a fiftieth anniversary celebration. He found, not to any surprise, that the school spirit had not languished. Ohio State was still conveying to one and all that it is one of the best institutions of higher learning, or maybe even the best. The experience was to Harold almost as electrifying as the Freshman Week rallies of September 1930 had been.

THE FARM ACCOUNT MILL

Harold Breimyer discovered early that he encountered no problems in the classroom. His tribulations centered on income, and on social maturity. The former was resolved by employment in the so-called farm account mill of the university's Extension Service. For the latter, campus organizations were to play a major role.

Is life a lottery? Does the turning of the wheel of fortune have more to do with individuals' life destiny than any preparation and planning they may do, and any resolute exercise of will power?

It was a lottery datum that his vocational agriculture instructor L.N. Geiger was a classmate of Carl R. "Cap" Arnold, professor of rural economics and chief of Extension Farm Management at Ohio State University. It also was fortuitous that a few years before, the farm management office had initiated a record-keeping service for farmers that included an annual summarizing of each farmer's account book. The first objective was to help the account keepers manage their business. The secondary purpose was to obtain data as raw material for Extension education.

The approximately 1,000 farm account books that came into Arnold's office were audited and summarized with the help of students employed for the purpose. The new freshman, with his facility for numbers, was a natural. So declared Geiger to his friend Arnold. Arnold gambled on the recruit, who in March 1931 notified Mrs. Dutt that he would leave her employ. The new job carried the handsome wage of forty cents an hour.

On arriving at the desk of Margaret Judd, who presided over the auditing, Harold and Ralph Crooks (a redhead also newly employed) were given instructions and a sample record book. Harold's competitive instincts came into play. With intense concentration he followed instructions in recording the numbers, hoping he could finish the assignment before Ralph did. He won the contest. Actually, for Ralph it was no contest. The amiable young man sought only to do competent work, not to be acclaimed champion. Some years after graduation Crooks served creditably as head of an egg marketing cooperative.

The farm account mill provided employment from January to June during each undergraduate year. The hours worked varied from twenty to twenty-four, or even, during rush periods, twenty-eight. A twenty-hour week brought a check for $8, or a little more than $32 monthly. Of this, $9 was paid for room rent, first to the Binegars; to Tom Swan when the Binegars moved to a farm north of Worthington; to Harold's cousins Bob and Otelia Trump; and finally to the Stouts, who lived next door to the Binegar home.

The biggest expense was, naturally, food. Harold Breimyer did not short-ration himself as severely as some students did during those Depression years, but his diet was barely adequate. Breakfast was hot chocolate and a doughnut, or, alternately, hotcakes at the White Castle. His lunch consisted of cookies bought at a grocery, combined with a slice of cheddar cheese from the dairy counter in the basement of Townshend Hall. Frequently the evening meal was canned foods, obtained from A.R. Cook's family grocery. Sunday noon, though, called for splurging. A restaurant on High Street offered a tasty Virginia baked ham dinner for forty cents.

A careful nutritional analysis probably would have shown only the breakfasts to have been unacceptable. But the experience was Spartan, and at best borderline in nutritional adequacy.

Other living expenses were minimal. They included postage for mailing dirty clothes to Harold's mother, who dutifully washed and ironed them and, in the manner of the majority of mothers of college students, often sent back with the clean clothes some confection. On one occasion, though, her kindness outran her probity. She put fresh strawberries in a Rumford baking powder can. The juice escaped and colored the clothes, and her son spent much of an afternoon borrowing his landlady's washing machine and, probably a few spoonfuls of bleach.

He bought clothing at a so-called workingmen's store, and cleaned the pants and suits only when they took on odor. In that regard, the economizing tactics of Ella Breimyer showed up in her son: He saved the hangers on which cleaning was returned, and when he had accumulated twenty or so, he took them to the cleaner and asked to be credited at the price the shop paid. The proprietor was astonished, but he complied.

Any student must buy books, and laboratory fees were attached to enrollment in several courses. Harold Breimyer paid those costs from the savings with which he began his college career. Moreover, although his father made no direct contribution to his son's education, he implicitly helped a little. For two or three years he continued to milk the cow that Harold had raised from a 4-H calf, and to remit the income received from the cream—or, later, the milk (for manufacturing)—that was delivered to the local creamery. As the father did not deduct the cost of feed, his financial aid was the equivalent of the cost of feeding a Guernsey cow.

The sharpest limitation was in money for any kind of diversionary pleasure. The deprivation began with near-denial of sweetstuffs. Harold Breimyer was born with a craving for sweets. In high school he would walk to the town's variety store and ask kindly Mary Brock to sell him two cents' worth of candy. She did so, probably not watching the scale as she weighed the precious caramels. In college years he drooled for an ice cream cone or candy bar, and drooled over it when he could afford to purchase it. He suppressed the craving for a candy bar a thousand times, as the nickel would have exceeded the carefully calculated food budget.

Soul satisfaction, a variety of pleasure, sometimes can be found without cost. Or it may just extend the good luck that began with Aunt Rena's making available the wind-up victrola with its classical records. One day during the depth of the Depression, placards on campus announced that the famed Polish pianist Ignace Jan Paderewski would give a concert in downtown Columbus. The local producers were listed as Messrs. Hast and Amend. Harold wrote to the gentlemen. Could he do any chores in order to hear the concert? Yes, indeed, he could. He helped the pianist's manager place the piano and bench so they would not rock on the rickety floor, begged neighboring shops to break big bills into smaller ones, and stood ready for any menial tasks.

In the next several years he heard Rachmaninoff, Jeritza (so far past her prime that her voice broke on high notes), a striking young pianist named Poldi Mildner (never again heard from on the concert circuit), Fritz Kreisler, and a dozen other concert artists. How lucky can an eighteen-year-old college student be?

Harold Breimyer budgeted every dollar, but he was not flat broke. He was not impoverished as severely as some students were. Pages could be written about students who at times had no money, even for food. One youth, Martin, also had worked in Mrs. Dutt's restaurant but had to discontinue, presumably because work hours conflicted with his class times. Months later he dropped in on Mrs. Dutt with a polite request for some task with which he could earn a meal. He had not eaten for three days. Mrs. Dutt gave him the meal. How the young man scrounged to stay in school is hard to imagine. It was gratifying, fifty years later, to note that the list of 1934 graduates included Martin's name. Somehow he had continued and graduated, on schedule.

THE FORD AND OTHER AUTOMOBILES

It may seem incongruous with this account of Harold Breimyer's money struggles to reveal that in 1932 he bought what every young man wants above all other material goods — an automobile. To get it, he rode the streetcar to an automobile junkyard in southwest Columbus. The least costly Model T Fords on the lot, both touring models, were priced at $10 and $20. The $20 one appeared to be the better, but either was a gamble, so why not gamble with the cheaper one?

The newly purchased ten-dollar jalopy could not be driven from the lot because the fuel tank was empty. When asked for a quart of gasoline, the proprietor replied, with impeccable logic, that at the sales price he could not afford to provide gasoline. A can of fuel from a nearby gasoline service station powered the bargain-basement car to its new parking spot, the curb of West Lane Avenue.

His Uncle Otto had taught Harold Breimyer how to service and overhaul a Model T Ford motor. The following Saturday, having bought piston rings, brake bands, and two new tires (paying $5 for the two) at a cut-rate automobile supplies store, he enlisted the aid of friends in performing an instant overhaul at the Binegars' farm home.

Finishing the task about midnight, the boys got a little sleep and then early Sunday morning set out on a holiday trip through southern Ohio and West Virginia. Harlan Binegar and George Patterson were travel companions. They painted appropriate slogans on the side of the vehicle, such as "Nowheres or Bust." At Waverly, on their southern route, they picked up Harold's former roommate, Virgil Bumgarner. The four made it to West Virginia by nightfall. They slept on the ground at a schoolyard — on the soft side of a rock, Patterson reported.

The return was uneventful, or almost so. Near Athens, Ohio, the newly overhauled engine suddenly stopped running. Harold had an idea as to the cause. He had once ridden with the driver of a Model T truck when a similar casualty proved to be caused by a break in the wire spring of the timer. When the spring broke, the rotor no longer made contact, in rotation, with the points that established electrical connection with the spark plugs.

The timer spring had indeed severed. The *ad hoc* mechanic carefully hooked the broken ends together as the truck driver had done. When he pressed his shoe heel on the floorboard starter button, the motor responded. He and his passengers continued their return to Columbus. A self-debate was whether he should stop enroute and try to find a garage that could replace the broken spring. The reasoning, like that of automobile drivers ever since Duryea put the first internal combustion passenger car on the road, was that disaster (that is, engine casualty) would never strike twice in the same place. It did not strike the Ford's timer spring. The travelers reached Columbus.

The Ford touring car, never garaged, provided acceptable transportation until a cat jumped on the fabric top and tumbled through it. By that time the pit of the Depression, with its early-1933 bank holiday, had passed. (The holiday had come at a time when Harold Breimyer, fortunately, had more dollar bills than usual in his pocket—maybe five or six.) By the summer of 1933, the Ford's owner had put together enough dollars to warrant another visit to the junkyard. He was able to buy, for a few greenbacks, the body and running gear of a Ford sedan. Walter Stout helped him transfer the often-overhauled motor. Thereafter, Harold and any passengers were shielded from the elements.

After another year or so, when a period of full-time employment provided still more spendable dollars, the Ford and $50 were exchanged for a 1927 model Davis. The Davis, an assembled automobile with a Continental motor, was almost an elegant car. It served Harold until he drove it to Washington upon his employment there in 1936. The only epilogue is to confess the regrets of later years, that the Davis was consigned to a Washington junkyard instead of being retained to become a classic. In 1990 the rare and beautiful Davis would have value equivalent to a new Mercedes-Benz.

SHYNESS, LONELINESS, AND STUDENT ORGANIZATIONS

In Harold Breimyer's undergraduate experience he mastered class work easily. And personal finances were manageable thanks to the farm account mill. But social insecurity persisted.

Being young and socially immature, the student benefited initially from his familial living arrangements. But midway in his undergraduate years he admitted to himself that he was not developing confidence in social relationships. An occasional Friday evening found him despondent. He was still too frightened to ask a girl for a date. Although it's an old saw that intellectuality hinders emotional development, in his case the opposite rule proved applicable. He reasoned that organized activities were his best hope. He tried young people's groups at the campus Lutheran church. Although Paul Bierstadt was an attractive minister, Harold did not warm to social activities there.

His father's grand experience in the YMCA of Springfield lent that organization some appeal, so he joined it. One evening the Y had a picnic that began with a hike. Uncomfortable with the repartee, Harold lagged behind. Thereupon occurred an incident that was trivial at the time, but almost pivotal. The Y secretary was an understanding man, Finky Willet (his actual first name, seldom used, has been forgotten). Noting that a tall, lean member was not joining in, the secretary drifted back, engaged Harold in intimate conversation and, probably without knowing what he was accomplishing, initiated the beginning of Harold's social involvement and restoration of confidence.

One wonders how often pivotal experiences redirect the lives of individuals. Advocates of born-again Christianity assert the validity of the thesis, and they self-appoint as executors. It's likely that in reality those experiences are more adventitious and subtle than the born-againers proclaim. They may resemble the Finky Willet instance.

Harold Breimyer treasures the plaque he eventually received for his YMCA activities. Nonetheless, neither the Y nor any church was most instrumental in bringing him partway out of his cocoon. The university's 4-H Club and, most notably, university Grange were the more effective. No account of his growing leadership roles is needed here. What is significant is that the troubled student decided, by cold logic, that he must lift himself out of his enervated state by forcing himself to attend those organizations' meetings. After he got into the swing, and was appointed to committees, the upward path became easy.

Yet one more extracurricular activity merits note. It, however, only took advantage of a scholarly aptitude. The *Agricultural Student* was (and, slightly renamed, remains) the student-produced magazine of Ohio State's College of Agriculture. Writing news stories, articles, and editorials was a natural for Harold Breimyer, who became an assistant editor. Eldon Groves wanted to groom him to be editor, but fear — once again — of personal relationships, together with his respect for the aspiring Bill Zipf, led him to deny an interest.

ECONOMICS AS TAUGHT DURING DEPRESSION YEARS

In October of 1929, the stock market plunged. Collapse of stock values brought to an end the rollicking 1920s, when ecstatic middle-class investors who previously had held no paper other than a bank's passbook found they could get rich by buying common stock on margin. During a few days of that fateful October, their gilded dream world vanished. They were wiped out. Some of them then wiped themselves out. At Fort Recovery High School, Maurice Warnock, a classmate, guffawed at news stories that some frustrated investors who faced margin calls chose to jump from the top floor of a tall building. The high school seniors could not conceive of turning to suicide just because stock values depreciated. To them it was all make-believe, akin to the Edgar Allen Poe and Guy de Maupassant stories that Lucile DeSelm required everyone to read. It is likely that families of the high school seniors owned not a share of stock other than that in a local farmers' cooperative.

Fort Recovery's seniors could not know what a frightening episode in the life of their nation lay ahead. They could not have guessed that a fourth of the working population would be unemployed, or that political movements of a hundred ideological colorations, each with its cell, would come into being. Advocacies were to range from communism to fascism. Nor could the students even surmise that a New Deal would revolutionize attitudes toward the economic role of central government.

At first, Harold Breimyer, too, was innocent of direful forebodings. He had got his first inkling of what was happening when, upon arriving in Columbus for Freshman Week, he applied for employment at the university's YMCA desk only to learn that wage jobs formerly available to students were being reserved for men with families (hence his accepting the only job he could get — washing dishes in Mrs. Dutt's restaurant).

How did a seat of higher learning, the proud Ohio State University, react to the strains and alarms that were enveloping the nation? The answer: about the same as similar institutions elsewhere — which is to say, variably.

Someday a social historian will investigate and report the record of institutions of higher education during the cataclysmic days of the early 1930s. An intrepid sleuth will find, doubtless, a highly mixed pattern but no overwhelming perceptiveness. After all, most professors have tenure and are shielded well from economic vicissitudes.

ECONOMICS OF THE FIRM AND OF THE ECONOMY

One explanation for such an erratic performance by university scholars lies in the schizophrenic make-up of economics as a discipline. From the time of ancient Greece until the day these words were written, or the day they are read, the field of inquiry now known as economics has been torn by disputes as to whether it is directed primarily to the management and functioning of economic units, or to the performance of an economy.

What, really, is the meaning of *Oekonomicus?* The Greeks saw it as the principles for management of an estate. As the city-state emerged, becoming the unit for collective survival, it was natural to recast the teachings of estate management into those of policy for the city-state economy.

In early decades of the 1900s, the ancient debate was phrased, drawing on the eminent Alfred Marshall, in terms of partial versus general equilibrium. The language was changed later to microeconomics versus macroeconomics.

The flaw in the intellectual controversy is that an economy is not a firm magnified a thousand, or a thousand-thousand, times. In a brief 1981 note, "The Fallacy of Macroeconomics," Harold Breimyer deplored the use of the term macroeconomics. The economy, he wrote, is not an entity that can be reduced to a few Greek letters. All the talk about macroeconomics, he added, is gamesmanship, "an attempt to dignify our unsureness about economy-wide behavior by coining impressive terms." An economy does not perform as though it were a single economic unit.

Ohio State professors of the early 1930s responded so variably to the emerging economic crisis for a reason that has been a career-long obsession for Harold Breimyer. It's that their ideological preferences obscured their observations and tainted their analyses and prescriptions.

For the more timid souls, the easiest response was to confine attention to narrow spheres — the economics of the firm, or of a sector such as livestock production or all agriculture. Then, as now, it was the safer haven. It was sought and occupied by most professors of rural (agricultural) economics at Ohio State University in 1930–1935, the years Harold Breimyer was a student.

Cap Arnold, for example, had taken his master's degree under the tutelage of old-school professors at Cornell University. He was well-instructed in the virtues of untrammeled open markets and saw the Depression as only an episode in progressive deflation. In a paper written in early 1932, Arnold rejected the popular idea that agriculture's price troubles were traceable to overproduction. He did admit that the three-year drop in prices was the worst ever. The January 15, 1932, price of corn in Ohio, he reported, was 64 percent lower than three years before. The wheat price was down 61½ percent. But Arnold called it incorrect to say that farmers were overproducing. Average U.S. production of wheat in 1928–31, Arnold wrote, was 20 million bushels less than in 1926–28 and population had grown. Corn production had decreased 90 million bushels.

After defending against charges that overproduction caused agriculture's woes, Arnold used less than a page to give his two diagnoses: "two rather significant factors [in] our drastic decline in agricultural prices . . . are the drop in the general price level of all commodities and the loss of export trade." Arnold could not have guessed that the weak-export argument would resurface during every low-price episode the rest of the century. He was not entirely mistaken; farm product exports in 1931 were a third smaller than five years previously. But relative to export volumes of the time, the fall-off in trade was a minor element in the severe price break.

Arnold and his fellows put out an advice sheet for troubled farmers. Its admonitions were the conventional ones, to keep records and raise more cash crops — advice to be repeated a half-century later during the distress of the 1980s. They included, though, an injunction of another genre: "If your wife can't can so things will keep, learn to do it yourself." We can wonder how many Ohio farmers (males, that is) rushed to the cookbook to find out how to cold-compress tomatoes. The number doing so probably was fewer than those who rebelled at the brazenness of crazy Extension guys in their swivel chairs at Ohio State. Livestock sent to market sometimes did not bring a price equal to the cost of transportation. So Extension advised learning how to can!

Harold Breimyer accompanied Cap Arnold one evening when, in the best Extension tradition, Arnold spoke to a meeting of farmers held in Licking County, east of Columbus. There, Arnold gave his deflation thesis. He implied, if he did not say outright, that nothing could be done about it. Harold wondered if those farmers too were turned cold.

Best remembered from the Extension meeting was a pitch made by an older man for identifying farm homes by a geometrically designed system of numbers. He buttonholed the Ohio State student as a convenient quarry. The student thought the idea to be far-out. He could not guess that years later such a system would be adopted, so that persons looking for Farmer Brown's home need not be directed in terms of an oak tree and a narrow bridge. Probably every innovation requires such a gestation — advancing of an idea by individuals who do not live long enough to receive credit upon eventual adoption.

Teaching of Principles. Courses in general economic theory were taught in the College of Commerce. Professors there did not insulate themselves as carefully as those in rural economics. A few stayed with the dogmas of Frank Taussig of Harvard, which were the centerpiece of the pre-Depression economic theory. But others did not.

Ohio State was more alert to ongoing events than was the University of Chicago, about which the eminent economist Paul Samuelson has written. Samuelson reports that during his student years there, which were contemporary with Harold Breimyer's at Ohio State, he half-listened as professors droned on about how free was market capitalism of widespread unemployment — it couldn't happen. The instruction was of a kind with an alleged scientific report, popularly ridiculed, that anatomically a bumblebee is unable to fly. Samuelson and his iconoclastic fellow students needed only to look out the window to see bread lines. They rejected the Chicago-school teaching, which in fact invited derision. Samuelson himself, drawing on the writings of John Meynard Keynes, developed his own set of principles by which an economy functions. Wide adoption of his textbook made him wealthy.

At Ohio State the daily class in principles of economics was taught by a lean, fast-talking instructor named John D. Blanchard. He asked not to be confused with "the other John D." — by whom he meant Rockefeller. The time was the fall of 1932, the pit of the Depression and presidential election season. Blanchard vainly tried to disguise his preference for Franklin D. Roosevelt as presidential candidate. Harold Breimyer, who had been reared in a Republican environment, had ambiguous reactions. He thought it inappropriate that Blanchard expose his political leanings, yet he found himself concurring.

Showpiece, and show-person, in economics at Ohio State was Professor H. Gordon Hayes. His two-volume *Our Economic System* was the assigned text. The eloquent Hayes was a once-a-week lecturer. His text, published in the pre-Depression year 1928, ranks as a vintage piece, for it contains nary an economic formula and only a few charts. It is highly empirical. It describes the economic system of the 1920s.

Hayes was obsessed with the monetary system, explaining that "no one economic institution has such commanding importance in our economic life as has the system of money." Moreover, "the industrial life of a modern nation is so delicately adjusted to its money system that merely the fear that a change may be made may disarrange the economic life of a nation" (p. 415). The system in use was, of course, the gold standard. Gold was particularly appreciated for settling international accounts.

Hayes wrote respectfully of the role of the Federal Reserve System and its "considerable power over the supply of our money through the control of the rediscount rate, and through open market transactions" (p. 518). Was the Federal Reserve able to keep the price level stable? Hayes gave much attention to this issue, which was to be a topic of debate from his day through the rest of the century. Hayes was skeptical: Federal Reserve banks "may not be able to control [the price situation] sufficiently to maintain a stable price level over a long period of time" (pp. 535–36).

H. Gordon Hayes was more prescient than many economists. Even though he wrote before the Depression broke, he noted "another proposal for price control," namely, "that gold should be abolished as money and that irredeemable paper money should be substituted for it." He credits the plan to "a brilliant English economist, J. M. Keynes." Not many economists yet knew of Keynes. Hayes saw problems in management of money, yet suggested that "major fluctuations in the level of prices might be prevented" (p. 538).

Monetary policy thus got a good going-over in Harold Breimyer's undergraduate instruction. Fiscal policy was scarcely recognized. Yet the imaginative Hayes, after reviewing the tendency of the economy to go through business cycles, concluded a chapter on public finance with the note that "during periods of unemployment . . . the issue may be . . . whether men shall work at government account or be unemployed" (pp. 309–10). Anticipating by a half-dozen years the New Deal's Public Works Administration that put people to work, the liberal H. Gordon Hayes was well ahead of most of his contemporary economists.

Even though the 1920s were marked by prolix glorification of U.S.-style capitalism, not everyone was convinced or silenced. H. Gordon Hayes devoted 150 of his 1,116 pages to the (mal-)distribution of wealth and income. The concluding section was titled, "A Critique of the Present Economic Order." He expressed that critique in terms of comparative economic systems and described three alternative systems: socialism, syndicalism, and communism.

Therein may lie the sharpest contrast between how economics was taught in the 1930s and the typical instruction of the 1980s and 1990s. It is no longer appropriate, or in some places even safe, to raise questions as to how our U.S. system compares with alternative ones. The most publicized agnostic about the blessings of modern capitalism, John Kenneth Galbraith, has had to cloak his critiques in ingenious phrasing, clever riposte, and subtle innuendo. In the 1930s, study of comparative economic systems was a part of the bill of fare in economics.

After more than sixty years, Harold Breimyer believes that the starting point for studying our economic system, or anyone else's, is to view and conceptualize it broadly. The particulars can be delved into once the system as a whole is comprehended.

GOING TO WORK FOR THE TRIPLE-A

A chance development that could not have been imagined did much to fashion Harold Breimyer's career. In late July 1933 he was asked if he would like to come into the office of Dillon S. Myer, newly appointed chief of the Ohio wheat program of the new Agricultural Adjustment Administration.

The letter of invitation arrived on a hot day when the farm boy was guiding a two-horse, two-row corn "plow" (cultivator) down the rows of pale-green corn that offered little promise of high yield. During the Depression years the Fred Breimyer farm, like virtually all neighboring farms, was over-cropped and under-fertilized. Also, in those years the summers were hot and dry. And the price of corn was low.

The letter promised a salary of $100 a month, less the Hoover deduction of 10 percent. Under the stringencies of the time, President Hoover had reduced all government salaries by that amount. Inasmuch as deflation was under way and the cost of living was declining, government servants were not hurt.

A response required no deliberation. The refugee from cornfields would pack his clothes and drive the beat-up Model T to Columbus. In keeping with the German tradition, because he had implicitly contracted to do his father's farming during the summer, the boy arranged for his third-cousin Paul Smith to take his place. He paid Paul's wages out of the $90 monthly check. Obviously, he paid Paul a low per-hour wage. It was the end of Harold's farming; he never again harnessed a horse or tried to start a balky tractor motor. He did milk a cow occasionally when visiting his grandmother.

Times were hard. They were so hard in agriculture that when the new President Franklin Roosevelt asked Congress to enact the domestic allotment plan as devised by Mordecai Ezekiel, John D. Black, and Milburn L. Wilson, that legislative body hastened to do so. The Agricultural Adjustment Act was signed into law May 12, 1933.

Times were so hard in agriculture that militant movements and protest demonstrations were popping up in farming country. Farmers armed with shotguns would stop the auction sale of a foreclosed farm, bidding it in at a couple of dollars, threatening violence to any competitive bidder, and giving the farm back to the farmer.

Milo Reno was converting *ad hoc* protests into a National Farm Holiday movement. In a radio address of July 20, 1932, Reno declared that the "Farmers' Holiday association proposes to fix a fair valuation on farm products, based on production costs, and to refuse to deliver until those prices are conceded." "Some may call this a strike," he acknowledged. But it's no more a strike for a farmer to refuse "to deliver his products for less than production costs," he argued, than for a merchant to decline to sell goods for less than their cost to him.[1]

Conventional wisdom has it that President Roosevelt advocated and Congress enacted the Agricultural Adjustment Act because of the persuasiveness of Black, Wilson, the new U.S. Department of Agriculture Secretary Henry Wallace, and several farm leaders. It's more accurate to say that Congress passed the new law because it was scared.

Harold Breimyer was acquainted with the despondence some of his father's neighbors felt, but he had not witnessed a penny auction with its guns and violence. The closest he came to such an exposure was his attending an organizational meeting of the Ohio Farmers' Union.

In the early 1930s the National Farmers' Union (NFU) was more aggressive than the two other major farm organizations, the American Farm Bureau Federation and the National Grange. Its secretary was a near-militant, Edward Kennedy. The years of the statesman-quality leadership given by James Patton as NFU president had not yet begun. Harold Breimyer made Patton's acquaintance many years later and respected him.

The Farmers' Union met at Urbana, Ohio, for the two purposes of giving a rostrum to William Lemke and his debt moratorium, and of according official status to the fledgling Ohio unit of the organization. The firebrand Lemke, a congressman from North Dakota, was co-author of the Frazier-Lemke Act, which was invalidated by the U.S. Supreme Court only a few months after its enactment. At Urbana, Lemke heaped scorn on the Agricultural Adjustment Act and its production control. His later efforts to win support for a new, Court-proof bankruptcy bill proved unavailing, as the Triple-A programs successfully boosted the prices farmers received for their products.

Harold Breimyer was puzzled by Lemke's opposition to the Triple-

---

[1]Contained in Wayne D. Rasmussen, editor, *Agriculture in the United States: A Documentary History,* volume 3 (New York: Random House, 1975), p.218.

A. He had not yet learned that a true apostle brooks no competitive dogma.

Memories of the radically oriented Farmers' Union meeting center not on the political arguments heard but instead on the abject despair witnessed in the faces and mien of the farmers who attended. Five years of the declining prices that Carl Arnold reported had taken an emotional as well as a financial toll. The farmers were dressed almost in rags and drove automobiles that appeared to have been bought at the junkyards where Breimyer's Model T Fords were bought. The farmers were desperate to hear any promise of political activity that would give them hope.

On only one other occasion during the Depression years did Harold Breimyer see so much defeat in visages. It was a meeting of the Socialist Labor Party, held in Columbus. The industrial workers present, probably unemployed, were scarcely distinguishable from the farmers at Urbana.

Times were hard. If they had not been so hard in agriculture, a program so untraditional, even revolutionary, as that of Agricultural Adjustment would not have been possible. The idea that farmers should leave land idle and fail to produce all the life-sustaining food of which they were capable was unattractive and even objectionable. Only under stress would it be accepted.

And the magnitude of such a program! A boy of nineteen just released from servitude on a 70-acre farm could not conceive of enlisting several million farmers in a program that was strange and new not only to them but to the entire agricultural establishment. Administratively the AAA was heroic derring-do.

M.L. Wilson, John D. Black, Howard Tolley, Chester Davis, and George Peek were not repelled. Incredulously, by early August, when Harold Breimyer arrived in Columbus to do his small bit in the wheat program of Ohio, the Agricultural Adjustment program was well under way.

The Ohio wheat program was small stuff relative to the grand design nationally. Harold Breimyer reported to the office of Myer, a highly personable man who had been County Agent supervisor for northwest Ohio Extension. Harold's first task was to help give sign-up instructions to county agents. The agents were involved because the Agricultural Extension Service had been drawn on to help administer the acreage-reduction program. County extension agents became the program's field agents.

Utilizing Extension to administer the AAA was as radical as the Act itself. But times were hard even for Extension. In county after county, funding of the county agent's office was being discontinued. AAA money put into counties to service the agency's programs was critical to getting a quick sign-up by farmers in the acreage programs, as well as salvaging county agents' jobs.

In Washington the choice had been whether to draw on state departments of agriculture for field-level administration of the new programs or to turn to Extension. According to the historian Theodore Saloutos, when M.L. Wilson and Chester Davis heard about proposals to put the program in the hands of commissioners of agriculture, they hit the ceiling. Only the Extension Service had a field force on location, they pointed out. Saloutos reports, however, that although the Extension offices of most states cooperated, "there were states in which the cooperation was lukewarm or indifferent, and one or two states in which there was outright hostility" (p.49).

County agents were well-suited to carry out a notable feature of the new AAA, which was to enlist farmer-elected community and county committees in the administrative process. Those committees were voted into office and put to work immediately. Cooperative Extension bowed out of the picture very soon, but the committee system has remained in place until this day.

The instant success of local AAA committees was followed a little later by a similar experience in conservation and electrification. From the farming community came forth a corps of leaders that organized soil and water conservation districts and rural electric cooperative associations. It may be easy, in drawing rooms of the supercilious, to scoff at the alleged virtues of agrarian democracy. No doubt, monolithic corporate capital could take over the countryside and feed citizens well. But the resource for responsible rural leadership demonstrated by the AAA, Soil Conservation Service, and Rural Electrification validates much of the Jeffersonian philosophy and gives cause to regret the transformation of rural America that is surreptitiously under way in the last years of the twentieth century.

Administering the new AAA acreage-control programs by means of farmers' committees brings to mind a philosophical conundrum that has sparked debate over commodity programs ever since the days of the Federal Farm Board of 1929. Are those programs "government" programs, in which the benevolent or heavy hand of government "manages" the nation's agriculture? Or are they instruments of farmer cooperation? The Farm Board of the late 1920s and early 1930s was viewed as an extension of farmers' cooperative movements. The Agricultural Adjustment Act made special provision for farmers' cooperatives in several commodity programs, notably those for cotton and tobacco. That law and its successors also authorized marketing orders, which were most applicable to specialty crops that often had strong marketing cooperatives. In his classroom teaching of later years, Harold Breimyer called the orders "government enforced cooperation."

The mandatory acreage-reduction programs that were authorized until the early 1960s always required a favorable farmers' vote, usually two-thirds of votes cast. Government programs for agriculture have had a considerable grass-roots character.

Farmers' Philosophy versus Practice. Ohio's wheat farmers signed up for the 1933 wheat program in droves. Many of them likely had ideological reservations. But few let those leanings keep them from trekking to the courthouse to sign to reduce wheat acreage—and qualify for a badly needed check.

Harold Breimyer's reflections on the connection between farmers' professed value system and their behavior were to continue throughout his lifetime. He believed then, and still accepts as valid, that farmers are sincere and not hypocritical in the values they profess. But seldom are their convictions strong enough to control behavior in the face of strong counter attractions.

A note published in *The Atlantic* more than a century ago (September 1886), and reproduced in the same magazine in 1986, is of interest partly as whimsy but also as a suggestion that human nature is unchanging. George Frederic Parsons wrote:

> In settled times men come to hold their political opinions far more as a matter of custom than of conviction. That they should do this in politics is not remarkable, seeing that the same practice is often followed in regard to religion. The tendency to take the line of least resistance is very strong in the average man . . . . (p.12)

To Ohio wheat farmers in the summer of 1933, the line of least resistance was clearly visible. It was to sign up for the program. Economic incentive proved powerful.

A few farmers nevertheless stayed out. Not infrequently they announced that they "didn't believe in it." Thereupon a salty skepticism arose in the mind of Harold Breimyer. Some non participators who said the program violated their faith chose to stay out because their wheat acreage base was small and they had planned an expansion. Even more often, they calculated that if enough farmers signed, production would be reduced and the prices would rise. They could then profit without participating. The free-rider syndrome appeared almost instantly.

Forty years later Breimyer generalized more broadly about the cold calculations that enter into farmers' behavior. Not only do farmers often act in violation of the values they profess but they also can use the latter as a smoke screen. In writing *Farm Policies: 13 Essays,* published in 1977, he borrowed a phrase from the political scientist Don Hadwiger, who had written of "the paradox of denied dependence." As Breimyer put it, as long as the government shells out money to them, farmers "can safely proclaim their ideological conservatism. They can announce their conservative purity even as they take their government check to the bank — or even their private check that is larger because of some government program" (p.39).

Secretary Wallace Comes to Ohio. To stretch his $90 monthly check, Harold Breimyer stayed with the Binegar family on their farm north of Worthington, sleeping as third person in a bed. The Binegars were as hard-pressed as Harold and welcomed the few dollars he paid them. In the fall quarter, when he remained in the AAA office instead of returning to his classes, Harold moved once more to Columbus, living in the hospitable home of the John Stouts, on West Lane.

Some time later Secretary of Agriculture Henry A. Wallace breezed through Ohio on his return from a circuit through the Midwest. Everyone in Columbus who was associated with the farm program motored to Camp Ohio. Wallace appeared as a tousle-haired man driven by evangelistic fervor. He explained the purpose of the acreage-reduction programs and the attempt to restore farmers' incomes. Most remembered is the frequency of his Biblical references. Wallace drew on the Old Testament for parallels, anticipating, perhaps, his later anointing of grain storage as an updated Joseph Plan. In the later 1930s, when Wallace made the Ever Normal Granary his signature piece, he struck a parallel with the Genesis account of seven fat and seven lean kine. He apparently anticipated seven — or at least a few — years of lean crop harvests. As events turned out, his strategy was sounder than his forebodings were accurate. Grain stocks were boon for the nation a few years later as there came into view not new droughts, but World War II.

A SECOND AAA EMPLOYMENT

In 1934 Harold Breimyer discontinued his work in the office of Dillon Myer and resumed his classes. As he had a twelve-quarter scholarship, he accumulated graduate credits while remaining in undergraduate status. In December 1934 he received his B.S. degree, then continued graduate work at Ohio State. For a graduate research assistantship he updated previous studies on the expenditures of the Ohio agricultural industry. The work was done under the tutelage of J. I. Falconer, chairman of the Department of Rural Economics. J.I. was an aloof, self-contained New Englander who always pronounced the word creek as though it rhymed with trick, and whose affections were as warm as his manners were chill. He had the distinction of having received the first Ph.D. degree ever awarded in agricultural economics, following graduate study at the University of Wisconsin.

In the summer of 1935, as he was completing his master's degree work, Breimyer once more became an employee of the Agricultural Adjustment Administration. The role was a new one; he took part, along with several classmates, in the Ohio portion of a national Regional Adjustment Project. The Project was initiated by the Program Planning Division of the AAA, an office that would, a year later, offer the beginning of career employment. Kenneth Nicholson, the field man on the project, would become, in 1936, Harold Breimyer's co-worker.

The Project was hardly one of deep meaning, and to some extent was intended as an instrument by which the AAA, with its well-filled pockets of federal funds, sought to establish cordial relations with land-grant universities—relations that, it was hoped, would also be supportive.

Yet, in another sense, the project addressed an important principle that has been alternately invoked and rejected ever since the first Agricultural Adjustment Act was enacted: the principle of incorporating soil conservation in acreage reduction. Reducing the acreage of row crops, such as corn and cotton, to strengthen their price will contribute to conservation of soil, as they are among the most erosive of all crops.

But crafting a soil conservation effort also involves retiring the most erosive soil first. The Regional Planning Project was intended to provide estimates of how much erodible land ought to be retired from cropping, or at least from row-cropping, for each type-of-farming region of the United States. What would be a desirable pattern of land use in each farming region of Ohio, and of other states? Estimates were made in matching research projects carried out in the various states.

Harold Breimyer was happy to get the salary dollars, which were always in short supply. Otherwise the value to him of the brief research experience lay in orientation. Thinking about how the agriculture of a region, or of the nation, might be reorganized to fulfill a meritorious public purpose was a new, engaging, and instructive mental exercise.

A master's degree was forthcoming in August, but otherwise

Breimyer was footloose. When he received flyers from the University of California, telling of the availability of graduate assistantships, without much premeditation he sent an application to the faraway school. The applicant was first approved for alternate status; a little later, he was accepted.

A YEAR AT BERKELEY

At three-thirty one morning in August of 1935, Breimyer boarded a Greyhound bus destined for fabled Berkeley and its university. After continuous night and day travel, the student traveler arrived at the beautiful Berkeley campus. He slept a long night, then reported to the Giannini Foundation.

The contrast with the Department of Rural Economics at Ohio State was striking. The Foundation was housed in a gleaming white marble edifice. It was an another-world contrast with Ohio State's dull, gray Townshend hall, with its oiled but squeaky floors and crowded plywood-paneled offices.

The intellectual atmosphere proved to be equally contrasting. Professors at Ohio State had won few scholarly distinctions and were reconciled to their run-of-the-mill-ness. Harold Breimyer is not sure to this day whether the faculty at Berkeley was truly eminent, but its members carried on as though theirs was the seat of knowledge. Their pretensions were not modest.

The new environment was well-suited to the incoming student's needs. Although the faculty had an oversupply of pedants and prima donnas, his own closest association was with four competent, well- balanced individuals. His research adviser was Henry Erdman. He studied with Murray Benedict, a distinguished scholar, and with Harry Wellman, who was later to become university vice president. The department chairman was Howard Tolley, a short, pot-bellied Irishman whose grin reached from ear to ear. He had come to California from Washington, where he had been one of the leading minds in the Bureau of Agricultural Economics. During periodic absences from the university, he helped set up the new Agricultural Adjustment Administration. He may have found Berkeley even more turbulent than Washington, as he sought to impose administrative discipline on Giannini anarchists such as Professor George Peterson.

The year 1935–36 at the Giannini Foundation was post-Galbraith (as a Ph.D. candidate) and pre-Mehren. John Kenneth Galbraith had left a reputation as an indefagitable graduate student. George Mehren, equally brilliant, came along a couple of years later to add to the Giannini reputation for intellectual licentiousness.

The year at California was all a plus for Harold Breimyer. His most developmental experience was not professional, but social. He took a room in a large boardinghouse on College Avenue. Its proprietor was the comely Mrs. Elliott, who had two children and a mother to support. Residents were undergraduate and graduate students, and also a few secretaries and young professionals. A man named Tweedle daily took the Key system trolley and ferry to the Federal Reserve Bank of San Francisco. A social worker whose name is remembered only as Ferd drowned in alcohol his despair about the hopelessness of his clients.

Among the graduate students were three of outstanding caliber who were majoring in physics: Dorr Etzler, Leon Jaehle, and Glenn Seaborg. Seaborg would later become distinguished as an atomic physicist, and he would win a Nobel Prize. His success was not surprising to those who knew him at Mrs. Elliott's. He was truly brilliant.

One of the undergraduates was a stunning red-headed senior, Florence Frederickson. Another was blond Eleanor Oechsley, daughter of a minister, who did wonders in drawing Harold Breimyer out of his reticence. An additional value of Berkeley and Mrs. Elliott's was his learning to play bridge. As still another, enough money remained from his $55 monthly assistantship stipend, after paying for board and room, that he could join Dorr Etzler and Frances, a secretary, in an occasional game of bowling.

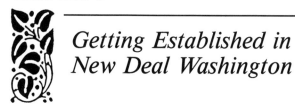

CHAPTER 6

Getting Established in New Deal Washington

DEAN ACHESON, President Truman's secretary of state, titled his autobiography *Present at the Creation*. Acheson was not only present at the creation of the Truman doctrine of Soviet containment but also was a participant in the process.

It can almost be said that Harold Breimyer was present at the creation of a national policy for U.S. agriculture. He arrived a little late, and his participation, unlike Secretary Acheson's, was obscure. But for fifty or more years following his arrival in Washington in the spring of 1936, he has been close to the center of the making of a public policy for agriculture and rural America.

Even though the New Deal was three years old in 1936, it was still at a formative stage—politically insecure and tentative in economic policy-making. All was in flux. Creativity ranked higher than conformity.

Moreover, it was Breimyer's good fortune that the office in the Department of Agriculture to which he reported one sunny morning in late May proved to be the nerve center not only of the Agricultural Adjustment Administration but of the entire USDA. It was there that dreaming and calculating and forecasting for farm programs were going on—internally, and in collaboration with Secretary Wallace's chief economist, Mordecai Ezekiel.

THE ODYSSEY–BERKELEY TO WASHINGTON

Even though life at Berkeley was easier and more rewarding than that at Ohio State, by the spring of 1936 monastic self-denial was beginning to pale. One day Elmer Braun of the AAA in Washington appeared at the Giannini Foundation, recruiting for the General Crops Section. He wanted economists who could help administer marketing order programs in fruits and vegetables. He was commissioned also to look over promising young graduate students who might be suited to other parts of the agency. He spoke with Harold Breimyer, youngest of the grad student clan.

On his return to Washington, Braun offered employment not to Breimyer but to Henry Stippler, an older, more experienced student who had received his first economics instruction in his native Germany. Meanwhile, Harold Breimyer reflected on Henry Erdman's suggestion that Harold could probably qualify for a Swift and Company job that would pay a hundred dollars a month. That was almost twice the amount his assistantship paid but scarcely more than the monthly salary in the Ohio wheat program three years earlier.

The stage was set for jubilation when, about May 1, Harold Breimyer received a telegram from F. F. Elliott, director of the Program Planning Division of the Agricultural Adjustment Administration in Washington. Would the addressee accept a position as assistant agricultural economist at the salary of $2,600 a year? Silly question; of course, he would! Arrival on May 18 was hoped for, but May 25 would be acceptable, read the telegram.

With money borrowed from his sister Louise, the ex-student bought a train ticket for the luxury of travel by Pullman. An incident in Chicago was instructive as to the depth of the lingering Depression. A ten-block transfer between stations was necessary. As his luggage was not excessively heavy, the twenty-two-year-old traveler, disdaining a fare-charging taxi, set out on foot. He was accosted by a clean-shaven man of about forty, no bum, who asked if he might carry the bags for him. Knowing that comfortable salary checks would be coming his way before long, and sensitive to the petitioner's need for money, the traveler contributed his first-ever benevolence. He allowed the man to tote the bags, giving payment in silver, not folding money.

After a brief visit with his parents, Harold reclaimed his Davis automobile in Columbus, Ohio. His travel to Washington was interrupted only by a brief garage stop in one of the eastern suburbs that lined route 40 east of Wheeling, West Virginia. A break in the frame had to be welded. In Washington he lodged at the YMCA; and on a bright Monday morning he announced his arrival to Irene Hardaway, secretary to Elliott.

Elliott was out of town, as was Oris V. Wells, his lieutenant, who was to be young Breimyer's boss then and for many years to come. An

Illinois native, Elliott had made a name for himself by carrying out, for the Census of Agriculture, a "Type of Farming" project that produced a map of farming systems.

ORIS V. WELLS

Oris Wells was to be the dominant personality in Harold Breimyer's early professional career. Wells had studied farm management at New Mexico State College, where he had been recruited by Mordecai Ezekiel, then an economist with the Bureau of Agricultural Economics (BAE). Wells took graduate work at Minnesota and Harvard, and eventually shifted laterally out of the BAE into the AAA position he occupied when Breimyer joined him.

Oris Wells was destined to become the trusted counselor to successive Secretaries of Agriculture, as well as the favorite emissary from those Secretaries to Congress. He occupied various boxes on organization charts of the Department of Agriculture, none of which revealed how strategic was his role. That counseling role, though, carried its risks. Each new Secretary, wary of the influential status of Oris Wells, was poised to remove or isolate him. But repeatedly a familiar sequence took place. A decision crisis would arise, whereupon the almost omniscient Wells would shower a tenderfoot secretary with data including an assessment of the several options for action. Wells became instantly indispensable.

Wells was secure through several successive secretaryships until President Kennedy appointed Orville Freeman as his secretary of agriculture. Freeman, in turn, brought Willard Cochrane with him from Minnesota as his economic advisor. Cochrane had once been in Wells's employ and was terrorized by the Wells persuasive power. Wells was cashiered at once. He moved quickly to the Food and Agriculture Organization of the United Nations in Rome, where he soon ascended to the position of Deputy Director General.

One moral of this account of Harold Breimyer's first chief is simple. If escalation in a bureaucracy is aspired to, a primary rule is to latch on to a superior officer who is himself ticketed for advancement. Breimyer could not know that O. V. Wells would rise to prominence; he was just lucky. Serendipity is the mod word for it.

A second moral follows, relating to the qualities that attend a successful individual—one who climbs the ladder of private or public bureaucracy as fast as Wells did. Business schools have long looked for the revealing formula. In 1984 Lee Iacocca became a best selling author as he disclosed his supposedly secret formula for successes at Ford and especially Chrysler. A couple of years later authors Mark Potts and Peter Behr, in *The Leading Edge,* told one and all how chief executive officers (CEOs) turn their companies around—to the up side, invariably. Also in the 1980s TV evangelists treated their satellite communication flocks to weekly exhibitions of individuals who were glowing successes and, allegedly, devout Christians as well.

Oris Wells fit no one's stereotype. He was not the dapper man in gray flannel suit. He was big and ugly. His lower jaw protruded so badly as to impair his speech. He could dress shabbily and was indifferent to social amenities. How did he make himself so useful, even indispensable? He did it by out-knowledging everyone else. He had what is known as a trip-hammer mind, with almost instant recall. But, above all else, he came to a conference armed with newly compiled data that could be brought to bear on just about any question that might arise. For any formal session he prepared himself thoroughly.

He was meticulous about statistics. When his sharp-penciled statistician Lois Nelson put three too many zeros in an estimate of the cost of a tobacco program, his first warning to her, Wells said, should be regarded as also the last one. No one in his employ dared misposition a decimal point.

The Wells injunction was marvelously contemporary. If in medieval times a kingdom was lost for want of a horseshoe nail, in the modern day that enshrines the Arabic digital numbers system, a business or an economy can fold because of numerical error.

For Harold Breimyer the Wells model was fortunate. He, too, was mentally alert wherever data were involved. Champion cipherer that he was, he could calculate numbers mentally almost as fast as Wells could—although he found it discreet not to challenge his boss's display of dexterity.

The day had passed when he thought it necessary to excel at everything. At times, he learned, to mask one's skills is strategic. Like Wells, Breimyer lacked the arts of craftiness and eloquence. He could not charm, feint, palaver, story-tell, or swashbuckle. His lifelong attributes were confined to assembling factual information and conveying it in lucid language. O. V. Wells demonstrated that the ability was sufficient.

A HOME WITH THE WHITINGS

As is true of most virile twenty-two-year-old American boys, Harold Breimyer had only two needs. They were for a bed and for a new automobile.

He found the lodging first. Answering classified advertisements, he looked into a couple of rooming houses. At one, he could have bunked with two other young men for a ridiculously low rent. The two probably were scrounging to earn $100 monthly. Harold's emolument was a generous $217; he could afford better.

Although he knew that his new salary put him into what to him was affluence, he did not appreciate how far he was above the rank and file of other young people in Washington. Secretaries were classified at either $1,440 or $1,620 jobs. Statistical clerks were on the same scale, although a fortunate few were paid $1,800 annually. One of Breimyer's clerks, male, supported a wife and child on his $1,800. Other young men might have to crowd into a minimum-rent room. Harold no longer had to.

The homeless economist read more classified ads. Just how Nell Whiting phrased her willingness to accept a paying guest in her home is not remembered, but the language caught the eye of the young man eager to leave the YMCA. Mrs. Whiting proved to be a stately matron who spoke with a distinctive Tidewater Virginia inflection. Her landlord, she would observe later in self-depreciation, objected to her having "a cow in the garage." She, of course, referred to a car.

On that day in late May, Mrs. Whiting showed the inquirer a third-floor room, neatly furnished, that he could share with her son. What her powers of discernment may have been, by which she would regard Harold Breimyer as a suitable roommate for her son, was not known. Apparently something about his manner reassured her.

Sharing a room with Harry Whiting (Henry Clay Whiting, Jr.) turned out to be free of complications. Harry was affable and, as a member of the family, seldom appeared in the room other than during sleeping hours.

Nell Lee Whiting and her family were of a culture never before known to Harold Breimyer. They were of the genre of aristocrats whose hard times robbed them of neither pride nor poise. Nell Whiting was of the lineage of the famous Lees of Virginia, though connected more with the famous Light Horse Harry than the even more celebrated Robert. Separated, though not divorced, from her amiable but improvident husband, she rented a row house in northwest Washington, furnished it with fine antiques, made a bed for herself in the basement, engaged Gertrude

Cooper as her maid of all talents, and invited paying guests to share her hospitality. Any suggestion that she was a proprietor of a rooming house would have brought not only denial but indignation.

She presided at the dining table in the manner of, well, a Lee of Virginia. From time to time she welcomed guests of distinction including a few Congressmen, and did so in the manner of the lady of an estate. She was also one of the best bridge players in Washington.

Harold Breimyer, though in all respects a Midwest farm-boy alien, was invited warmly into the family. He remained five and one-half years, until he married. Daughter Betsy and her husband John Palmer invited him to Sunday afternoons at the beach at Annapolis Roads Country Club, and to horseback riding at Mr. Ridenour's farm (with its "panorama," he said) across the Potomac River in Virginia. Bridge games soon materialized, along with various other social activities. Association with the Whitings and the many interesting individuals who were guests during his stay there was one more instance of pure good luck in Harold Breimyer's life and career.

FIRST PROFESSIONAL EXPERIENCES

A young man ten days removed from graduate school can hardly expect that a profoundly important assignment will await him in his first professional job. Breimyer nevertheless was nonplussed by his initial reception. On the pleasant May morning when he walked into F. F. Elliott's office, Irene Hardaway guided him to a table in the corner of O. V. Wells's office. On it rested a stack of research bulletins, published by various state colleges (land-grant institutions had not yet attained the rarified status of universities). They were statistical price analyses for the major farm commodities. Wells had left word that young Breimyer was to read them. The assignment was only a time-filling stratagem but was a clue to the orientation of program making in agriculture in the New Deal 1930s.

The studies were aggregative. A price analysis for beef cattle, for example, had nothing to do with the trials of managing a cattle farm, or of the equally vexing ones in marketing and slaughtering cattle and in vending beef. The cattle analysis bulletin written by John Hopkins of Iowa State College employed the statistical techniques of multiple-correlation analysis that had been developed by Henry Moore and publicized by Henry Schultz, Mordecai Ezekiel, and other scholars as recently as the 1920s. Hopkins estimated how much various "economic variables" influenced the supply and price of beef cattle. By 1936 the correlation technique had been applied to most major farm products.

The aggregative nature of the studies told something about the orientation not only of the new farm programs but of the New Deal itself. The mission of the New Deal was aggregative; it was economy-wide. Impelled by the distress of the Great Depression and the mandate he believed citizens had given him, Franklin Roosevelt guided the New Deal to accept a considerable degree of responsibility for performance of the economy. It did so for the economy as a whole, and for major sectors such as agriculture.

The Agricultural Adjustment Administration, from which Harold Breimyer would get his paychecks for the next three years, was the central agency in the New Deal's farm programs. In 1936 it was in its fourth year of inducing farmers to retire or to divert acreages of major crops. Although the agency's name would change, it would continue indefinitely to monitor crop acreages, and in the next half century would pay out billions upon billions of dollars to eligible farmers.

Within the AAA of 1936, the seat of yeasty calculating, conjecturing, philosophizing about economics and political economy, and "planning," was its Program Planning Division. Breimyer was lucky to be a part of it.

Of the Division's salad bowl of personnel, the individual who would influence Harold Breimyer most was James P. Cavin. Cavin was an unlikely recruit to agricultural bureaucracy. Born and reared in the fishing city of Gloucester, Massachusetts, he lacked any familiarity with agriculture other than what he had learned from his esteemed professor, John D. Black, at Harvard University.

Almost ten years older than Breimyer, Cavin possessed all the intellectual sophistication that his younger associate lacked but strove for. He read every one (it seemed) of the books, fiction and nonfiction, reviewed by the *New York Times*. He had a sharp Irish perceptiveness and wit. Because his technical competence was in general economics, he complemented nicely the younger Breimyer, who was not only trained in agricultural economics but was so agricultural that the field dirt had been washed from his ears only a few months before (at the University of California, where school nurses marveled that his ear channel could hold so much of the Ohio silt loam).

Cavin was only one in the menagerie of bright but sometimes erratic minds who staffed the Program Planning Division. Carl Taeusch was an eminent philosopher who had been canned by the dean of the Harvard Business School on grounds that the times were too tough to ask young businessmen to bother with philosophy. Louis Bean brought his wildly tousled hair, slide rule, and French curves from the Bureau of Agricultural Economics; he was prepared to find recurring cyclical patterns in all natural and unnatural phenomena, including the weather and political elections. William T. Ham worried about farm labor. A little later arrived Paul Johnstone, a historian; and John Brewster, who would gain immortality as the most distinguished philosopher among agricultural economists. It was a beautiful spot in which a receptive, perceptive young mind could be exposed to the currents of intellectual thought about New Deal economic programs.

It's significant that the Program Planning Division included the word, "planning." For the nonce, the word was in good standing. Only a few critics charged it with statism. The Roosevelt administration, with Henry Wallace as head honcho for agriculture, was genuinely and sincerely trying to plan for a better agriculture and rural community.

As will be related later, the strategic position of the Program Planning Division would stay in place only a couple more years. Planning gradually came under ideological fire. The whole shootin' match would be banished to the Bureau of Agricultural Economics and allowed to survive there only a little longer.

THE COUNTY PLANNING PROJECT

The word "planning" was still in good enough standing in 1936 that the Program Planning Division saw fit to initiate a nationwide research project called "county planning." The objective was to get the forty-eight land grant colleges to estimate desirable patterns of land use, county by county. Harold Breimyer's first professional assignment was to supervise a cadre of statistical clerks in summarizing the data.

Although the project was not greatly different from the Regional Planning Project on which he had worked in Ohio the previous year, it arose from a major change in direction for the whole AAA program. The change was forced by the Supreme Court's decision of January 6, 1936, invalidating major portions of the Agricultural Adjustment Act of 1933.

That the law would be challenged in the courts was known to be inevitable. Also certain was that a majority of the nine justices sitting on the U.S. Supreme Court in those years would take a dim view of such radicalism.

The line of the Court's argument in the *Hoosac Mills* decision has been reported often and need not be restated here. More germane to this personal history is the coincidence that on the day the Court invalidated the AAA, Harold Breimyer was a guest, along with other graduate students, in the home of his California professor, Howard Tolley. On that day Mordecai Ezekiel had taken part in a farmers' meeting in Berkeley. He and Tolley were greatly disturbed by the day's Supreme Court action and wondered what course the farm program might then take. Disregarding Ezekiel's emotional state, Professor George Peterson, a graceless pedant, baited Ezekiel all evening. The whole federal farm program was an instance of stupidity, Peterson insisted. Ezekiel never lost his cool.

Harold Breimyer could not have guessed that ten years later he would be working with Ezekiel.

Soil Conservation. Within a few weeks — February 29 (it was a leap year) — Congress passed a new law, the Soil Conservation and Domestic Allotment Act. As the title indicates, it was built on the conservation theme.

From their beginning in 1933, the acreage programs had a double thrust. They invited farmers to reduce plantings of corn and cotton and similar crops, with the principal objective of reducing output and strengthening prices. But protection of soil was a second goal. As was noted previously, several of the program crops were cultivated row crops and therefore subject to erosion of soil. Thus, reducing their acreage also cut soil losses.

The decision after *Hoosac Mills* was to turn the whole scheme upside down. Farmers' contracts would thenceforth call for increasing the acreage of soil-conserving crops, principally grasses. A not-incidental result would be to reduce the acreage of the soil-depleting crops that were in surplus. The new law, which lasted only two years, gave a focus to soil conservation that was not to be repeated until forty-nine years later, with enactment of the Food Security Act of 1985.

Localization. Every activity of the federal government that is applied in the states runs into the federal-state controversy. From the hinterlands comes a call, always "clarion," to respect the grass roots. "Don't impose from Washington!"

If the conservation plank in the new 1936 program were to be taken seriously and not as a disguise for reducing the acreage of surplus crops, it had to be localized to some degree. Manifestly, soil damage varies by location; it is severe in some places and almost nonexistent in some others.

On that premise the county planning project was born. Data on desirable land use were to be compiled for all the country's 3,025 counties.

The project served a further purpose. It lubricated political relationships with the land grant colleges of the various states. Many of the classroom professors took stands as antagonistic as George Peterson's toward the acreage reduction programs. But all had graduate students who needed jobs and dollars. The Program Planning Division of the AAA could offer them both.

Prosaic Economics, Instructive Sociology. How many graduate students preparing to enter real-world employment have the illusion that they will be called on to use their highly intellectual knowledge to solve big, profound problems? Breimyer as a student was free of such an illusion—it's fortunate that he was! There was nothing scholarly about making sure the land-use numbers received from Nevada or Alabama added to the indicated totals. Nor was it hard to put summary data together. A capable corps of clerks had been recruited from the Bureau of the Census. Mary Grigg, Billie Hughes, Lois Nelson, Margaret McDermott, and Ted Miller would punch the comptometer and run the Marchant, Monroe, or Friden calculator all day long.

Breimyer and his team of numbers vendors completed the county planning project without incident. It offered no test of intellectuality. So it is, the young economist tentatively concluded, with most career jobs—what the Census Bureau calls gainful employment. The majority of jobs are humdrum, punctuated with neither debacle nor exciting reward.

Ever since leaving the farm, Harold Breimyer had associated only with other students and his professors. All were climbing ladders. The younger professors looked forward to higher scholarly attainment. Every student was grasping a higher rung as fast as he or she could, and dared to imagine that the top one would be as high as Jack's beanstalk.

Not so with the thousands of laborers in Uncle Sam's government vineyard in Washington. Some could hope to rise a few steps on the CAF or P scale. But the vast majority would punch the typewriters, keep clerical records, or perform any of hundreds of service operations without prospect of novelty or advancement. They would leave their homes at the appointed hour each day, ride the same streetcar (buses had not yet come to Washington's streets), greet the identical co-workers to whom they had bade goodbye the previous afternoon—in other words, go through essentially the same motions day after day, month after month, year after year.

Three reflections sank deep but also troubled Harold Breimyer. One was how dependent is the whole mutually supportive social mechanism—in this case, the government in Washington—on the dependable labors of scarcely noticed participant-contributors. Leaders of finance and industry are lauded, as are heads of state. But they would be powerless without the minions who make their systems work. This reflection ties back to the editorial Breimyer wrote as an undergraduate student at Ohio State, in which he asked respect not just for leaders but for the equally essential followers.

Second, Breimyer wondered where people who live plain lives get their kicks. He himself was taking on some of the marks of an intellectual and could enjoy reading, good music, the theater, playing bridge. What could a $1,620 secretary do? Perhaps go to an occasional movie . . . Listen to radio programs. . . . probably gossip with the neighbors. But the question would not stay out of mind: Does boredom invite the hallucinatory indulgences, spanning a range from the almost-innocent glass of beer to the hard drugs, on which society frowns? In the 1980s some social observers reported that hallucinatory drugs kept the worst sections of New York City's Harlem from erupting in violence—that they were socially tranquilizing. It may be so.

Third, when thousands of workers are mired in the same salary-schedule system, with little hope of individualized advancement, the ground is laid for political agitation to get across-the-board, automatic wage increases. In the Washington of the later 1930s and ever since, these have taken the form of routine seniority steps of increase, and of an annual general upward-factoring of the entire salary schedule. Because wage increases can be inflationary, it follows that throwing most workers, either industrial or governmental, into a single salary schedule contributes to a persistent tendency toward wage and salary inflation. It also invites organized action to press for across-the-board increments to a remuneration schedule. Unionization nevertheless was slow to come to the Depression-era federal bureaucracy, partly because Congress gave general raises often enough to mute any organized pressure.

CHAPTER 7

Reflections on the 1930s, after Fifty Years

ANYONE BORN BEFORE 1920 finds the most vivid recollections in two events, one of a decade and the other of a day. The decade was the Depression years and the early New Deal. The day was of the "infamy," as President Roosevelt called it, of Pearl Harbor.

Harold Breimyer's memories of the depressed 1930s are indeed vivid, but not graphic. They are like impressionistic art in oils: Their message is intense but not sharply outlined. If reflections and impressions swirl in his head, so do they, it seems, in the gray matter of most persons who remember that eventful decade, and try to sort out and tell what happened.

Scholars find it hard to divine the meaning of the 1930s from records of those years. Attempts are legion. Most are unconvincing.

No account of the 1930s has been written that equals Frederick Lewis Allen's idyll of the 1920s, his fondly perceptive *Only Yesterday*. Why is it so difficult to write about the 1930s—to report the happenings of those years and, even more, to interpret the subtle strains of the public temper?

Two answers come to mind. One is that each person lived those years within his or her grooved orbit. Few individuals had an opportunity to climb to a mountaintop to observe what was going on outside their own niche. Circumscribing of observations is a major cause of distorted views of a world that is bigger than one's own.

The second explanation for so much difference of opinion about the national experience of the Depression and the early New Deal is that it all was so different from anything that had been known before. Citizens of our still-young nation were, of course, familiar with adversity. There had been natural calamities such as droughts and the San Francisco earthquake and the Galveston flood. In the Civil War we had decimated ourselves. At various times the economy had gone into shock. Late in the 1800s the nation's heartland was wrenched by a monetary deflation that led to calls for relief via free coinage of silver. Periodic financial panics dot our history; the Federal Reserve Act of 1913 was designed to eliminate them, and in fact did so.

The Great Depression that began in 1930 was different. The industrial economy virtually collapsed. Farms and commercial non-farm businesses went bankrupt by the thousands. Financial institutions closed their doors. A fourth of the labor force was unemployed.

PERSONALIZING THE DISMAL EVENTS

We now would explain the debacle of the early 1930s in terms of a macroeconomic disequilibrium. Neither the idea nor the terminology was popular at the time.

Many of the first interpretations were personal — personal in self-accusation and defeat, and personal in accusing evildoers in the business world. It was not yet in fashion to explain economic malfunctioning in terms of general economic forces and, least of all, to put any burden on the government.

Lewis ("Studs") Terkel wrote in 1970 that the newly unemployed residents of his mother's hotel were conscious only of their own defeat: "The suddenly-idle hands blamed themselves, rather than society. . . . No matter that others suffered the same fate, the inner voice whispered, 'I'm a failure.'" To be sure, "outside forces . . . were in some vague way responsible, but not really. It was a personal guilt" (p.5).

But self-reproach soon turned into personal accusation. Samuel Insull, known for his manipulation of holding companies in public utilities, was symbol of all the harm done by grasping evil men. J. Pierpont Morgan was put on the carpet before a congressional investigating committee. His photograph with a midget lady on his lap made all the papers.

Religious fundamentalists took a somewhat different view. They said the Lord was punishing the evil, materialistic United States for its sins. Ella Breimyer, Harold's mother, was mildly of that persuasion.

CALDWELL, STEINBECK, AND TERKEL

Most Americans self-insulated themselves from the terrors of the early 1930s by looking the other way. Even Harold Breimyer, though sensitive and sympathetic, was not himself tormented by the times. He, too, stayed in his own circle. And he was never entirely destitute. If he had no money to be spent freely, that condition was not new for him. He and his family had never enjoyed even a touch of financial security. Not until later, when he had widened his orbit of observation, did he comprehend the magnitude, the intensity, of distress during the Depression, and what a threat it was to the nation's political stability.

How influential are men of letters? How much bearing have they had on the course of history? The question will stir debate until the sun burns itself out. Karl Marx stands as the foremost example of a penman whose words shaped the course of nations. In 1987, during the celebration of the 200th anniversary of the drafting of the U.S. Constitution, the contribution of James Madison to our country's history (his writings in *Federalist Papers)* was duly noted.

In the 1930s two writers were preeminent in arousing public consciousness of the distress of the time: Erskine Caldwell and John Steinbeck. Caldwell's novel, converted to a stage play, *Tobacco Road,* described not so much the cyclical crisis as the cultural depravity of a pocket of rural poverty. Steinbeck's *Grapes of Wrath,* with its depiction of the displaced Okies, was contemporary and explosive. Harold Breimyer remembers that other paying guests at Mrs. Whiting's home, on seeing a movie of *Grapes of Wrath,* conversed more soberly than ever before about the ravages of the Depression.

Thirty years later Studs Terkel compiled the oral history of Depression experiences referred to earlier. Veterans of the Depression years responded in interviews. The revelations, the filtrations of memory, published in *Hard Times,* constitute what may be the most sensitive of all chronicles of the Depression years.

PROTEST MOVEMENTS

The U.S. Depression of the 1930s was homegrown. It was a uniquely American experience. It is therefore not surprising that its resolution, clumsily pragmatic, was American to the core.

Most models of alternative economic systems were European— primarily English and French. Much of the extant literature about political relief of social distress was European-socialist. No American counterpart had yet appeared.

Nevertheless, the 1930s brought a swarm of protest and political agitations. Small, closely knit cells ranged from communist through socialist to fascist. Most Americans now regard the New Deal as the natural or inevitable path that would be taken in the setting of the 1930s. They are mistaken. The nation could have moved in a fascist direction, though patterning not after Nazi Germany so much as Mussolini's Italy.

Sinclair Lewis, the author known for his satirical novels *Main Street, Babbitt,* and others, warned of a fascist threat. His *It Can't Happen Here* carried the message that it (fascism) could indeed happen here. He probably thought it would.

Harold Breimyer never drifted into any of the political cells. In fact, he was never in close touch with any of the radical groups, left or right. But he learned something of the flavor of unconventional thinking from Jay Deiss, administrative assistant in the Division of Program Planning. Deiss, in his mid-twenties, was already frustrated on two counts—in getting a first novel published and in augmenting a moderately radical socialist movement. Deiss eventually earned a living with his pen. Whether he entered into political activism is not known. In 1936 he plied Breimyer each week with some new book that set forth unequivocally the proper course of economic action in a dangerously depressed Western world. Many of these books were British. He was attuned primarily to the English Fabians.

Breimyer was generously tolerant of the more radical movements because he saw them as born of intense desperation, and many of the participants—though not all—as innocents adrift. During the 1950s the McCarthy inquisition sought to punish anyone who had affiliated with a communist cell during the Depression years. In reality, many of the movements and alignments were amorphous, fluid, unspecified. Often, a communist link was loose and not disclosed. It was political goulash.

ANTI-RADICALISM; PRETENDING THAT ALL'S WELL

Not everyone took a radical stand, left or right. Memory of the Depression years limns them with a feature that was the opposite of radicalism. It was not political conservatism. It was denial, nondisclosure, almost a hush-hush tone.

During the years when a fourth of Americans were unemployed and many others were staying financially alive only by the skin of their teeth, there seemed almost to be a conspiracy of pretending that everything, or just about everything, was serene. Assurances heard so often, in the media or in drawing rooms, could have been taken from Robert Browning: "God's in his heaven — all's right with the world."

Or just about all. The hush-hushers did not call the Roosevelt New Deal all right, but an objectionable disruption.

In May 1936, when Harold Breimyer arrived in Washington, Franklin Roosevelt was still in his first term. The November election was six months distant. In those days the press media, particularly newspapers, saw themselves as guardian of public morality and molder of public opinion. By far the most papers were anti-Roosevelt. Some editors, and columnists such as Westbrook Pegler, were vituperatively so.

Roosevelt was to be elected three more times, but no such tenure in office was evident in 1936. The pundits called Roosevelt and his New Deal a passing aberration. In the fall of the year, the *Literary Digest* published its poll results indicating that Roosevelt would go down to an ignominious defeat. As things worked out, the *Digest* itself was the casualty.

Harold Breimyer learned about the prevailing sentiments when he undertook what any red-blooded American young man undertakes once paychecks start arriving. He shopped for his second imperative, a new automobile. (The first was a place to live, as stated earlier.) His choices were limited to the "big little three," Ford, Chevrolet, and Plymouth. For his lanky frame only the Plymouth had adequate leg room. Although he was a young bachelor who might be expected to choose a flashy sport model, he opted for the conventional four-door sedan, in black. The preference was consistent with a lifelong pattern: Harold Breimyer would be politically liberal but not libertarian, and traditionally conservative in personal tastes and behavior.

For the shiny showroom car with its irresistible lure, the dealer offered a discount price, a little more than $700. The eager would-be buyer had only the dollars he could spare from his first two paychecks. So he counted on the Chrysler Corporation's own credit financing, even though he did not like its high interest rate. His borrowing (and repaying) up to that time had been confined to his purchase of poultry feed from the Fort Recovery Equity, useless for getting a credit rating in Washington. He learned of the dilemma: without previous credit, no credit rating; without a credit rating, no new credit. Hence, for him, no new Plymouth.

Then, a glimmer of hope. The First City Bank was eager to make auto loans, a friend advised. At First City a youthful third assistant credit manager dutifully filled out a long form, then asked, "And who is your employer?" "The Agricultural Adjustment Administration," was the reply. Instantly, rudely, the man tore up the sheet and tossed it in the wastebasket. The Bank did not lend to New Deal employees, as their jobs would not last after the next election. The prospect was certain and the policy invariable, the applicant was told. Such was the business community's reading of the political situation in the summer of 1936.

Being denied a loan—first and only time ever—jarred the prospective car buyer doubly. He wanted a new car desperately, and moreover he wondered if indeed he had moved into a job that would prove temporary. His diary of July 23 notes that a new car was "on the brain" but also has the admission, "I am afraid, though, the New Deal will go out before I get it paid for."

Both fears turned out to be groundless. The young car-hungry economist would own several automobiles before the New Deal faded into the debacle of the Vietnam conflict and then the Reagan revolution. And the first one would be purchased without more contests with commercial finance people who misread the political signs. Harold's Uncle Dan (Breymaier), a vagabond bachelor, replied to a polite inquiry that surely he would lend the money. He lived so relaxed a life, however, that he delayed weeks in sending a check. Every day Harold scanned the incoming mail at Mrs. Whiting's home for a letter from Uncle Dan. Finally it arrived. Harold bought the Plymouth. Driving one's own first-ever new automobile is once-in-a-lifetime ecstasy. It was experienced by Harold Breimyer in September 1936.

THE FRANKLIN ROOSEVELT POSTURE

Probably no characterization of the Roosevelt era and the New Deal is more completely erroneous than to give it a specific ideological or political-system identity. Volumes have been written about how Franklin Roosevelt as a candidate dreamed up (or borrowed from others) a revolutionary change in our system of government, promised it to the voters, and then imposed it following his election.

Franklin Roosevelt only offered a posture; it was an activist posture. It's as though the electorate instructed, "Do *something!*" Roosevelt responded, "Can do!"

Political history is partly an accident of the personal characteristics ("personalities") of the individuals who hold high office. But how accidental is it? One thesis is that the sentiment of citizens is the motivational force, as it determines who will occupy the high places.

Be that as it may, Franklin Roosevelt's personal traits were a significant element in the history of the United States in the middle years of the twentieth century. Edmund Wilson, a noted columnist, offered a contemporary account that still strikes Harold Breimyer as valid. The comment was published in *The New Republic* April 5, 1933.

> Franklin Roosevelt will at least aim at a sort of justice different from that to which Hoover was inspired by his abject respect for big business. Public-utility magnates [cf., Samuel Insull] will not overawe him. Though the son of a railroad vice-president and director of corporations, and though himself once a corporation lawyer, he has still some of the democratic idealism of the days when Dutch merchants were rebels, and he has made some effort to see democratic problems from the point of view of changed conditions. He is at least superficially in touch with the enlightened thought of his time: there is a faint flavor of Charles A. Beard [a much-read historian] about him at moments. He understands that the American frontier has been exhausted and that economic crises can never again be relieved by sending the unemployed West.

The "something" that Roosevelt was about to do was not specified in advance but implicitly involved action by the federal government. Proposals as to what should be done ranged wildly, without a central theme, let alone consensus.

On the other hand, in all the agitation, the begging for action to bring relief, there was a strain of egalitarianism, of populism. Franklin Roosevelt sensed it and acted on it. The historian William Manchester has recounted an incident of October 31, 1936, a few days before the election date. Not only opposition candidates and bankers but also the Liberty League crowd and the *Literary Digest* had thrown epithets at Roosevelt and predicted his defeat. At the time of his campaign appearance at Madison Square Garden, Raymond Moley and Louis Howe were otherwise occupied and did not, writes Manchester, "soften wrathful presidential replies." The Manchester account reads as follows:

> Roosevelt . . . turned up that great organ of a voice, identifying his "old enemies": "business and financial monopoly, speculation, reckless banking, class antagonism," and "organized money," adding "Government by organized money is just as dangerous as Government by organized mob." The crowd, on its feet throughout, ringing cowbells, howled its approval. In an edged voice he said: "Never before in all our history have these forces been so united against one candidate as they stand today. They are unanimous in their hate for me — and I welcome their hatred. . . . I should like to have it said of my first Administra-

tion that in it the forces of selfishness met their match. . . . I should like to have it said of my second Administration that *in it these forces met their master."* (p.33)

UBIQUITOUS ADVERSITY

The bankers and "speculators" and other opponents of Roosevelt and the New Deal did not have a large enough head count to get their way. In the economic situation of the early and mid-1930s, distress and adversity were general. It caught people of all strata and stripes, even some of the bankers. Against their will they shared in the frustration.

Harold Breimyer has never credited the human moral balance with a big margin of benevolence over selfishness. During a few years of the 1930s, there was an uncommonly pervasive willingness to be charitable that is attributable almost solely to the ubiquitousness of insecurity.

In a 1987 book Robert Reich described the spirit of the times in these words:

> In fact altruism per se never figured prominently in the liberal public philosophy that dominated American political discourse from the start of the New Deal to the end of World War II. It was a precept of solidarity—a sentiment crucially distinct from altruism—born not of specific legislation or programs but of concrete, common experiences . . . that profoundly affected almost all Americans. The goals...were well understood and widely endorsed. The public was motivated less by altruism than by its direct and palpable stake in the outcome of what were ineluctably social changes.

If shared misery was a major instigating force, a feature of the moral sentiment of the time helps account for the first line of attack taken by Roosevelt's New Deal. Many citizens of the 1930s attributed the Depression to wrongdoing by persons in power, particularly those holding economic power. So it was that the regulatory arm of the government was brought to bear upon the perceived or suspected evildoers. The most conspicuous instance was the new policing of the financial world by the Securities Exchange Commission. It was a modern case of putting Jesus in the temple, to cleanse it. Trade practice regulation got a forward thrust. In agriculture, regulations reached even to requiring honest labeling of seeds. And where the Department of Agriculture did not itself levy and enforce rules, it authorized so-called marketing agreements and orders whereby commodity groups could impose uniform quality and container standards upon themselves.

In the 1980s this part of the New Deal revolution was brought under intense fire. Although the Reagan administration was advertised as overturning the New Deal lock, stock, and barrel, in fact it preserved the macroeconomic tools that came into being during the New Deal years and, further, manipulated them as never before. By contrast, much of the regulatory portion was dismembered, a true renunciation of the New Deal actions of a half-century before. The Reagan administration was intensely macroeconomic, but opposed to setting regulatory rules.

THREATS AND INSTANCES OF VIOLENCE

If the near-universality of economic distress in the Depression accounted for putting most shoulders to the wheel, a second incentive came from fear — fear that violence would break out here and there, and fear of general social unrest, too. The fears proved groundless. But instances of violence and threats of more of them were reported often enough to dispel the serenity that most of the nation's press was trying to cultivate. Some labor unions were turning militant. In 1932 the bonus-seeking veterans had demonstrated the depth of their despondence as they marched on Washington. Studs Terkel quotes a coal miner of southwestern Indiana, Joe Morrison, who told of his memories of the early 1930s.

> In '30 and '31, you'd see freight trains, you'd see hundreds of kids, young kids, lots of 'em, just wandering all over the country. Looking for jobs, looking for excitement. . . . The only thing that was unique was to see women riding freight trains. That was unheard of, never had been thought of before. But it happened during the Depression . . . .
> You'd find political discussions going on in a boxcar. . . . .
> Oh they was ready for revolution. A lot of businessmen expected it. The Government sent out monitors. They had 'em in these Hoovervilles, outside the town, along the railroads, along the highways. In monitoring these places they got a lot of information. The information was: revolution. People were talkin' revolution all over the place. (pp.122–23)

THE ROOSEVELT RADIO FIRESIDE CHATS

In modern times politics is a function not just of personality but also of the communication media. Franklin Roosevelt on a stump might have galvanized audiences of the city of Athens or Rome. Before a radio microphone he was an electrifying communicator to a nation. In a sense radio "made" Franklin Roosevelt, just as, a half century later, Ronald Reagan's adeptness in TV presentation contributed greatly to his political success.

One dramattic phrase, broadcast to millions of radio listeners as he delivered his first inaugural address, was almost enough to immortalize Franklin Roosevelt: "We have nothing to fear, but fear itself."

During World War II, aboard a Naval vessel in Manila Bay, Harold Breimyer viewed a movie in which the Roosevelt voice suddenly burst on his eardrums. Chiding anyone who did not respect the Nazi aggressions, including those north into Norway, Roosevelt preached, "Let him look to Norway." The eloquent voice sent chills up and down Lieutenant Breimyer's spine. It doubtless had the same effect on millions of other spines. Such was the Roosevelt magnetism.

AN ATTEMPT AT CATEGORIZATION

Remembering his classroom exercises at Ohio State and at the University of California, Harold Breimyer tried to fit the New Deal program into familiar categories. He had studied comparative economic systems with Bitterman at Ohio State. He had learned about Robert Owen and the Utopians, and remembered Proudhon and the Syndicalists. He had not studied much about Karl Marx. At Ohio State, and to lesser degree at California, it was acceptable to study the harmless socialists, but Marxist thought could only be whispered about.

It was easy to sense that Roosevelt's New Deal was not modeled after any of the European agitations. It wasn't modeled on anything. It was *ad hoc,* trial-and-error. It was nearly non-intellectual, though not anti-intellectual. Unemployed Americans were hungry. So the New Deal set up the FERA (Federal Emergency Relief Act) and WPA (Works Progress Administration). It put young men to work in CCC (Civilian Conservation Corps) camps.

Price deflation and vicious cutthroat competition were ruining the economy. The recourse was to ask Congress for a National Recovery Act (NRA). Let the indefatigable Hugh Johnson run it. Johnson was already famous in agriculture for his sharing with George Peek the advocacy of parity. Harold Breimyer as a student had watched with interest the slowness or quickness with which retailers displayed the blue eagle indicating adherence to the NRA code. The overriding objective was to stop price slashing—to arrest deflation. Before long, though, the Supreme Court invalidated the NRA.

In the later 1970s the nation had an opposite concern: inflation. Inflation was deplored in alarmist terms that helped put Ronald Reagan in office. Few persons knew, or would have believed, that forty years earlier the national effort was to reverse a demoralizing *de*flation.

TIMID STEPS TOWARD MACROECONOMIC POLICIES

Beyond question, the theories of the British John Maynard Keynes have dominated both economic thought and economic policy making during the last fifty years, in the United States and in many other countries. It has been easy to suppose that Franklin Roosevelt, who as candidate pledged to balance the federal budget, learned about Keynes and saw the light. The notion is attractive but groundless. It's doubtful that Roosevelt or any members of his kitchen cabinet of 1933 had even heard of Keynes, whose *General Theory* would not be published until 1936.

A more accurate reading of the first New Deal years is that the many new programs, including those in agriculture, were not funded fully by new revenue, and the budget deficit widened. Deficit financing was drifted into, rather than planned.

Nevertheless, counter-cyclical management of the budget was not a new idea, even in 1933. H. Gordon Hayes had called attention to it in his economics lectures at Ohio State. Its principal spokesmen were a pair of economists affiliated with the Pollack Foundation—William T. Foster and Waddill Catchings. Their ideas and writings were part of the economics instruction at Ohio State.

The two seminal thinkers suffered the fate that often befalls forerunners: They were given little credit for their path-breaking contribution. Few persons, including economists, knew of their names, or have learned them since. Immortality was denied them and given to Keynes. Keynes incorporated counter-cyclical budgeting in the comprehensive macrotheory that made him famous.

CHAPTER 8

Personal Tranquility, 1936–1941

IT SHOULD BE THE NORMAL LIFE PATTERN for every young man and woman to have a few years of comparative freedom between the end of formal schooling and the assumption of more mature responsibilities of marriage, parenthood, and dedicated attention to one's lifework, his or her career. Harold Breimyer had those years. They were not free of emotional stresses, particularly those of learning to be at ease in social relationships. But they were relatively tranquil.

Athletic and church-related activities proved to be two magic keys. Harold had always relished any opportunity to throw a baseball or to kick a football. Those opportunities had been few. Moreover, his confidence level was low. His emotional baggage had long included a judgment that his abilities were solely scholastic, that he lacked any other skills. So he had been led to believe.

In Washington the National Capital Park Service had left a grassed open area along the southern border of the reflection pool—a pool that mirrored the Washington Monument to an onlooker standing at the Lincoln Memorial. The area was laid out for softball diamonds and touch football.

Softball games were scheduled weekday evenings but not regularly on weekends. Saturday afternoon was a time for pick-up games. On wandering in the area one Saturday during his first summer in Washington, Harold Breimyer chanced upon two other relative newcomers to the city, Harold Horn and Charles Thornton. The two were to become his companions in athletic activities, and lifelong friends.

Later the three joined forces with an equally informal group composed of former college football players. They were led by Chester B. ("Buck") Snow, an attorney with the Federal Trade Commission. They played touch football during the fall and even on winter days that were free of snow.

And the Department of Agriculture had a dozen or more softball teams. They offered opportunity for summer play. Later Erwin Cort and Harold Breimyer organized a softball team that played in city leagues.

Harold discovered bowling, which he could now afford, to be not merely attractive but actually exciting. He first substituted on a team in the Department of Agriculture, then became a regular bowler. In 1990 he was still bowling.

To his amazement Breimyer found he could compete with other baseball and touch football players and bowlers. He could outrun the college stars and could throw a softball to the plate from center field with unerring accuracy. In bowling he was never a champion but could end each season with a respectable average.

Harold Horn and Charles Thornton were of Lutheran religious faith. They had affiliated with Luther Place Memorial Church at Thomas Circle in downtown Washington, to which they invited their new acquaintance. There he found a group of young men, many of them recent college graduates, under the tutelage of Irving Koch (pronounced *kosh*), an imaginative attorney on the staff of the Interstate Commerce Commission. Luther Place became a welcome haven throughout the prewar years.

For a brief period while an undergraduate at Ohio State, Harold Breimyer had swayed to a belief that science invalidated conventional religion. To this day he does not remember either what logic carried him to that stand or why he swung back slowly not so much to a strong religious faith, least of all one of fundamentalist variety, as to a distrust of the scientific alternative. Perhaps it's a matter of respecting the limits to human understanding of the universe and doubting all dogmas including iconoclastic ones.

SOCIAL AND INTELLECTUAL LIFE

To what extent is humankind hostage to technology and to all the physical trappings of living, including those for entertainment? One invention that was timed to accommodate Harold Breimyer's arrival at a paying job in Washington was electronic recording, which replaced the acoustical technique for phonograph records. The new record players, although still confined to 78 rpm, were a big improvement over the wind-up mechanism on which the acoustically-recorded records of

Kreisler and Schumann-Heinck had been played.

As fast as his income would allow, Harold built up a collection of records. Most were classical but some were the popular tunes of the day. They provided one of the enriching activities of the tranquil years.

Social life was always hard for Breimyer. He dated from time to time but never felt comfortable in his relationships. Yet he never was turned down when he asked for a date, likely because he always offered an attractive activity. He took Betsy Greene to the National Theater, where they saw a play or, maybe, Gilbert and Sullivan as performed by Martyn Green and the D'Oyly Carte troupe (if the spelling be remembered correctly). Betsy probably had not previously entered the doors of the National. He liked to go to the summer watergate concerts of the National Symphony Orchestra, sometimes renting a canoe for the occasion. Watergate in those pre-Nixon days meant the Potomac River at the Memorial Bridge leading away from Lincoln Memorial.

Never did Harold plan an evening at a nightclub. He did, however, accompany others to the Blue Room of the Shoreham Hotel, a posh place.

He read books. A number were histories, such as Arthur Schlesinger, Sr.'s *Political and Social History of the United States*. The one book that made an indelible impression was George Santayana's *Last Puritan*. Harold Breimyer saw himself as the flesh-and-blood embodiment of Oliver Alden. He reflected that every reader likely saw himself in the fictional depiction. "Not so," replied Jim Cavin, when asked if he also could be the Last Puritan. Harold did not trust the denial, but maybe Cavin was correct. Perhaps Puritans are few in our time.

FRANCES WALKER AND RACHEL STYLES

Only two ladies had a lasting influence on the life and personality of Harold Breimyer. Frances Walker, seven years his senior, was secretary to O. V. Wells. Essentially orphaned and cared for by an aunt, she was exceptionally bright and had developed superb secretarial skills. She contributed crucially to the rapid advancement of her chief. She, too, had never attained security in social relationships. Obviously, her dilemma paralleled Breimyer's and accounted in part for a bond that was established early. Their relationship, emotionally intimate but platonic, was confined to golf, in which both were inept; bowling, in which their skills were better; and long conversations after working hours in the drab setting of the South Agriculture Building.

Rachel Styles was a friend of Frances Walker who also appreciated Frances for her commendable personal qualities. Rachel had come from Atlanta to take a secretarial position in the office of the political commissar for the Department of Agriculture, Julien Friant. She moved later to the office of Sen. Richard B. Russell of Georgia. For several years Frances taunted Harold with urgings that he call Rachel and ask for a date. The young man was neither very much interested nor self-confident in such a relationship.

In the spring of 1941, he changed his mind. His cousin Paul Schulz asked him to come to New York City and be best man in his wedding. The two days of frolicking were so attractive that Harold decided courtship and marriage might not be so bad after all. Within a few days after returning, he called Rachel Styles. Three months later they had contracted to be married. When Harold notified Frances at the office the morning after Rachel's acceptance, his good friend burst into tears. She knew she would lose her best emotional and intellectual companion.

At a retirement dinner for Harold Breimyer, held June 29, 1984, a skit was presented that both revealed and lampooned the Breimyer/Styles courtship. Harold and Rachel's son Fred played the part of his father, and Sharon Schneeberger was Rachel. Charles Cramer presided.

Cramer: In the summer of 1941, Harold met Rachel Styles. They dated a number of times, often as a threesome with their mutual friend Frances Walker.

Fred: This is a new experience for me, pretending to be my father. But here goes. Rachel, I have enjoyed your company. Do you think we should give thought to making it a lasting relationship?

Sharon: Why, Harold! I am surprised. I just dated you because Frances Walker kept telling me about that young economist in her office.

Fred: Yes, Frances had urged me to ask you for a date.

Sharon: She started doing that three years ago. What took you so long?

Fred: I was busy playing softball and bridge, and bowling.

Sharon: Well, I'll think about it. We can discuss it later.

Fred: Let me know when you are ready to talk about it.

Cramer: A month or two later Rachel said she was ready to talk about it.

Sharon: Yes, I think I am ready to consider what you called a lasting relationship. But why do you think it might work out?

Fred: Because Frances said it would. And I trust Frances. Should we then plan to be married?

Sharon: I think maybe so.

Fred: Let me explain that my mother doubts it was she who reopened the subject of marriage. That doesn't fit with being a southern belle, she says. My father insists that this account embellishes only a little.

This memoir is only in part a personal story. It is also a chronicle of the times—of most of the twentieth century. The courtship account fits exactly with the atmosphere of the season the courtship took place—the summer of 1941. A shock wave of anticipation of military conflict was running through the nation. Defense industries were gearing up. The air was electric. Harold felt it, as did most of his friends. Everyone was thinking about and dreading what might lie ahead. The behavioral outcome took two forms. One was to abandon moral restraints and live self-indulgently ("Live it up; you may be in the army tomorrow"). The second was to speed up all sorts of personal decisions that otherwise would have languished. Marriage was one. Marriage rates increased. Marriage mills, as at Elkton, Maryland, became busy places.

In Harold Breimyer's experience the sense of impending disaster began on Labor Day, 1939. He was vacationing with members of the Whiting family at Buckroe Beach, Virginia. The radio news told of Hitler's invasion of Poland. Other holidayers were scarcely disturbed. Not so with the student of history. He too readily saw historic parallels and was uneasy with foreboding.

When Rachel almost nonchalantly promised to marry Harold, neither could have known that Pearl Harbor would mobilize the nation six days before their wedding. But so it proved to be. The storm signals of 1941 nevertheless might have told them that they would not live long together before their world, and everyone's world, would be convulsed.

CHAPTER 9

Farm Policy for Social Reform, 1936–1941

HOW DO HUMAN BEINGS, trapped in their limited vision and programmed for the original sin of selfishness, manage from time to time to improve their common lot? Especially, how do they find it possible to redesign their social and political institutions so that life need not be, in Thomas Hobbes's words, "solitary, poor, nasty, brutish, and short?"

COUNTERVAILING POWER

One answer often given to this perennial question is contained in the idea of countervailing action, or check and balance. It says that no interest group will be able to exercise sway over others, because its aggressions will be countervailed, not by defenses so much as by competing aggressions. The more naive interpretation goes a further step, offering an anomaly wherein various interest groups, though indifferent to the common welfare or even scornful of it, in their competitive strivings actually contribute to its improvement. Adam Smith pretty nearly built his *Wealth of Nations* on this neat thesis.

This view of the workings of the economy is essentially mechanistic. Economic forces are regarded as analogous to physical forces. They counterbalance each other to establish and maintain an equilibrium, just as the planets do in our solar system. Competition among business firms is the equivalent of the gravity that holds the planets in their place.

When teaching, Harold Breimyer has liked to point out that economists are attracted to the mechanistic model because it absolves them of any philosophical obligation. That way of explaining the economic system is the equivalent of Linus's security blanket. When economists only record and report the functioning of a self-regulating economy, they cannot be charged with peddling any upsetting or even dangerous social ideas.

In the Elysium of a self-regulating economy, government is not unnecessary, but it has only two roles. Each is specified exactly. The first is to set up the basic institutions and the rules that go with them. An example is the definition and legal protection of property and rights to it.

The second role is to monitor what goes on and to take corrective action as the need arises. In the 1980s it was popular to say that government has a "pragmatic" role. For eight years it was debated whether Ronald Reagan was an ideologue or a pragmatist. The Soviet arms-reduction treaties showed him to be primarily pragmatic.

In this second, pragmatic, role, government functions as a make-weight. If an established interest group gets the jump on others and wields exploitive power, government can itself act to restore balance. It serves as a counterforce. In the days of divine-right kings, the sovereign deftly pitted one noble against another. If one became too boisterous, the crowned monarch took to the field himself. The equivalent in the economy of modern democracies is antitrust action. If a business entity gets too big and insolent, the Department of Justice throws the antitrust book at it. The reluctance of the Reagan administration to enforce antitrust rules, with its merger mania companion, was one of the distinguishing marks of that administration and of its years.

SOCIAL ENLIGHTENMENT

The second answer to the question about how man's lot on Earth can be made less onerous is sharply different. It calls for elevating the sights and moral capacity of society's members. It defines common purpose and exhorts its pursuit.

Historically, the imagery and the maxims for socially unifying behavior began with tribal lore. In more modern times, religious instruction was legitimized for the purpose. Today, secular education is relied on almost universally.

Essential to ameliorating mankind's lot in this way is a cadre of enlightened and highly principled persons. They are not army generals or manipulating politicians but, anciently, tribal chiefs and religious prophets and, now, preachers and teachers but also individuals ranging from

CEOs of business firms to television personalities. They are the thought leaders, the role models, and the unifying agents in our society. The system is implicitly elitist.

When the framers of the U.S. Constitution drew up that document and thereby set the terms for exercise of government in their new nation, they incorporated both a check-and-balance mechanism and a mission for public-interest statesmanship. An example of the former is the House of Representatives, as its 435 members, elected by geographic districts, offer a geographic check and balance. As economic interest groups tend to cluster regionally, the House is their favorite medium for representation. By design and tradition the Senate's 100 members are regarded as less constituent-oriented and capable of some degree of statesmanship. The Executive Branch is receptive to interest-group pleadings but is intended to be primarily a coalescing, unifying force. The court system is regarded, among branches of the federal government, as the most exemplary in putting abstract principle above narrow backbiting rivalries.

COMMODITY INTERESTS, REGIONALISM, AND AGRARIAN DEMOCRACY

Policy making in agriculture during the later 1930s provided a marvelous example of both countervalence and a coalescing unity. From their beginning in the summer of 1933, acreage- and price-support programs were commodity-oriented. Commodity interest groups made their wishes known persistently and often effectively. But at the same time many leaders of the Department of Agriculture saw the money-grubbing commodity programs as secondary to uplift objectives for the rural community. Not a few visionaries conceptualized an agrarian democracy in which farmers collectively would use instruments dispensed by government to make the countryside a replica of the Garden of Eden.

The exceptional experience in which social welfare thinkers and planners had a visible, tangible effect on rural America has been described at length by the historian Richard Kirkendall in his *Social Scientists and Farm Politics in the Age of Roosevelt.* "In the 1930's," Kirkendall writes, "social scientists had become one of the influential groups in farm politics. Battling to promote change and to give farm policy a somewhat different shape than the rural pressure groups would give it, they altered American life" (p. 255).

The component parts of the thinkers' dream were delineated eloquently in the *Yearbook of Agriculture* for 1940, *Farmers in a Changing World.* The titles of the seven sections of the book tell something about what the authors had in mind: "The Farmer's Changing World"; "Agriculture and the National Welfare"; "The Farmer's Problems Today and the Efforts to Solve Them"; "Farm Organizations"; "What Some Social Scientists Have to Say"; "Democracy and Agricultural Policy"; and "Essentials of Agricultural Policy." It's a safe assumption that no *Yearbook of Agriculture* before or since has devoted pages to what social scientists have to say, or to the democratic aspects of agricultural policy.

The central theme was that old ideals for agriculture and the rural community had not changed greatly but that two powerful forces made it necessary to redesign institutions in order to preserve them. The stronger force was technology. In second place was urbanization. Together they brought an interdependence that had been almost absent in the earlier times of an isolated farming community of primitive practices. In the 1940 yearbook Paul Johnstone, the historian, put it in these words:

> The dynamic forces that are most profoundly affecting the nature of rural life today derive from the industrial city and the metropolitan community; and the most central characteristic of these forces is the economic interdependence that modern technology and industrialism have introduced into the country as well as the city. A situation has been created out of which new kinds of economic disparities and social dislocations have developed. Measures conceived in traditional terms, although helpful, have generally failed to achieve any substantial adjustment. . . . As a result . . . confidence and optimism . . . have been increasingly qualified by bewilderment and pessimism. . . . (pp. 166–67)

It seems incongruous today that the AAA's money-grubbing commodity programs of the 1930s should have been folded within a dedication to socially progressive rural communities. The explanation takes two forms, the one situational, the other personal. The kind of thinking and dreaming that fills the 1940 Yearbook fit the times. From its beginning in 1933, the New Deal, with its populist strain, had been hospitable to abstract thinking about social institutions and the manageable destiny of humankind. The atmosphere made it exciting to work in Washington during those years.

M. L. Wilson. The philosophical emphasis in USDA is accounted for also by happenstance of personalities. The dominant individual was Milburn L. Wilson, who from January 1937 to January 1940 was Under

Secretary of Agriculture. Previously he had held several posts in Roosevelt's executive branch, first in the Department of the Interior and then in Agriculture.

Wilson's personal history, wholly agrarian, was marked by venturesomeness, and by a philosophical bent that fit hand in glove with social thought about rural America as it evolved to its apex in New Deal farm programs. Born and reared on an Iowa farm, as a young man he homesteaded in Montana. Before long he became that state's first agricultural extension agent, and then its first director of Extension.

Within a few years Wilson chose to pursue graduate work. He studied under Henry Taylor and Richard Ely at the University of Wisconsin, and he became imbued with the ideas about social management of resources that Ely had learned in Germany. He returned to Montana and directed the Rockefeller-funded Fairway Farms, an experiment in tenant-purchase under modern technology.

Meanwhile, Wilson had made the acquaintance of John D. Black, William Spillman, Henry A. Wallace, and other persons who were due to influence farm legislation in the latter 1920s and the 1930s. In August 1932 Wilson and Wallace met with Franklin Roosevelt, urging upon the presidential candidate a domestic allotment plan and a program of subsistence homesteads. Wilson's influential role climbed steadily thereafter, according to Paul Conkin, in his 1976 book, *Tomorrow a New World* (pp. 73–89).

As under-secretary of agriculture, Wilson initiated a host of innovative activities. One example is the public opinion survey (commented on below). Also, he invited university scholars to give seminars for department personnel.

Further, Wilson made a habit of offering jobs to a variety of transient scholars. More than once he telephoned Howard Tolley, who remained as chief of the Bureau of Agricultural Economics from 1938 to 1946, in about these words, "I have just made the acquaintance of _____, an engaging (sociologist, anthropologist, _____) who knows the history of farming systems since the first days of foraging. Do you think you could find a spot for him?" Tolley usually managed to find or make a place for the stranger, all the while hoping that the appointee's habitual transiency would continue and that he would move quickly to a new host.

One Wilson venture did not work out at all. Wilson thought that the USDA could absorb some of the scholars who had fled Nazi Germany, many of whom were Jewish. A number of those refugees did in fact establish good careers. Years later Harold Breimyer, when studying for his Ph.D. degree, was an advisee of the splendid professor Simon

Naidel, and he worked for nearly two years with the distinguished Karl Brandt. But when Wilson brought in a cultural anthropologist named Ernst Harms, whose English was primitive guttural and whose dress anticipated the hippies of the 1960s, and who announced to second-tier USDA administrators that he would advise them on the cultural significance of what they were doing, Wilson had to back away. Dr. Harms was dispatched posthaste. Years later Brandt, who was not Jewish but intensely anti-Nazi, told Breimyer that Harms never found a niche and subsisted on the charity of other refugees.

The Wallace Saga. Wilson was in a position to operate so freely because he had the tacit support of Henry Wallace. Also an Iowan, Henry A. Wallace was the son of Henry C. Wallace, who had died while serving as secretary of agriculture. The younger Wallace had previously demonstrated a range of abilities. He was not only a successful publisher of a farm journal *(Wallaces' Farmer)* but also had contributed to the development of hybrid corn and had written a book on agricultural price analysis. As Roosevelt's Secretary, Wallace found it necessary to deal with, reconcile, and placate the many interest groups that kept pressure on him. At heart, though, he was a visionary idealist. Some critics called him a mystic. From time to time he expounded the thesis that the twentieth century would prove to be the "century of the common man."

After Wallace had completed his eight years as secretary, he was elected Vice-President. In 1944 Roosevelt dumped him in favor of Truman, who as President in turn dismissed him as Secretary of Commerce. Wallace then let his frustrations lead him into the 1948 debacle of candidacy for President on a Progressive ticket. Wallace later returned to the genetics field, working with poultry.

Wallace's agricultural rehabilitation came when he was invited to help commemorate, in 1962, the centennial of the founding of the U.S. Department of Agriculture. He delivered a lecture in USDA's Jefferson Auditorium. Probably to his surprise, his excellent talk was warmly received by a large audience, which included Harold Breimyer.

WILSON-SPONSORED ENTERPRISES

In the later 1930s Wallace gave the go-ahead sign to Wilson and to lesser lights among the USDA's crew of social thinkers, who collectively generated the enthusiasms that were recorded for the first and last time in the USDA's 1940 *Yearbook of Agriculture.*

Three of the activities of those years in which Harold Breimyer played at least a tangential part will be reviewed here. They are the farmer opinion polls, the experimental farm programs, and county land-use planning.

Farmer Opinion Polls. Polling of citizens' opinions, later to be so familiar, was new and not quite trusted in the 1930s. Farmers had never been polled about how they viewed the acreage- and price-support programs then in operation, and about what they would like to see in the future.

The polling project was undertaken not because of any nefarious ideas about manipulating farm policy but, rather, out of a faith in the democratic process, as testified to in the 1940 *Yearbook.* Learning farmers' opinions was seen as a part of that process.

Until that time the most conspicuous instance of national polling was the *Literary Digest's* voluntary mail vote for President in 1936. It was also a debacle, as it indicated a big win for Landon. The *Digest's* grand flub revealed to everyone that voluntary write-in polls are untrustworthy.

The leader in new, more scientific poll-taking was George Gallup. Invited to give a lecture to USDA in the Wilson seminar series, Gallup explained that the *Literary Digest* fiasco had taught one big lesson: the urgent necessity of using carefully designed, stratified samples. If that technique would be followed precisely, Gallup and others said, the findings of even small-sample polls could be highly accurate.

Chester Ellickson, one of Wilson's "please find a place" appointees, was put in charge of a cadre of pollsters. Of the half-dozen individuals sent out with unlimited budgets for personal-car mileage, only two ,ames remain in memory, John Scott and Gladys Baker. In personal interviews conducted face to face, the pollsters recorded farmers' answers to prescribed questions, then added their commentary. Most of the interviewing went smoothly, as farmers like to sound off about farm programs. One exceptional incident told more about policy in choosing interviewers than about farmers' willingness to be interviewed. One interviewer was a fair-skinned Easterner who spoke with a British accent. On a wheat farm in eastern Colorado, he found himself facing the barrel end of a farmer's shotgun. The unfortunate fellow did not try to complete the interview, or even to continue as poll-taker. He moved to other employment.

Gladys Baker was a petite, soft-spoken new Ph.D. whose dissertation was converted to a book, *The County Agent.* She interviewed farm wives. She faced no hostility but, instead, so much motherly responsiveness that she found it impossible to complete her daily quota of interviews.

Chester Ellickson was more resourceful than skilled in guiding the polling. Before long Rensis Likert took over. A highly trained statistician, he soon won respect for both the enterprise and himself. He moved to the University of Michigan, where he gained high standing in the field of surveying public opinion.

What was learned from all the costly poll-taking? Harold Breimyer, who conducted no interview but was closely associated with the project, arrived at two different conclusions. One is that the range of farmers' opinions about the acreage-reduction and price-support program traced a bell curve. The midpoint was a moderately favorable judgment. The majority of farmers were satisfied with the program.

Breimyer concluded that the political process was working. In later years when he polled Missouri farmers about farm programs, he got the same answer. Missouri farmers were reasonably satisfied with the program then in force, yet rarely enthusiastic. Hence, the Missouri polling affirmed the conclusion drawn in Washington in the late 1930s: When the making of farm policy is involved, the political process yields a product in which only a few farmers rejoice and only a few oppose strongly, but a sizable majority can accept without protest. The folklore that the democratic process leads to strong approval of action taken is just that — folklore. A more nearly correct judgment is that it minimizes disapproval, which itself is divided.

A second lesson learned relates to the polling process. Pollsters and their statisticians give great attention to design of the sample. Remembering the *Literary Digest,* Harold Breimyer did not discredit that concern. But he also noted how sensitive is the polling operation to the phrasing of questions and the skill of the interviewers. Keeping in mind this second lesson learned, he has since recoiled in indignation at many mailed questionnaires he has received, often from political organizations. The questions are selected and phrased (slanted) to yield the "findings" the pollsters want. The USDA's farmer polling of the later 1930s, it must be said, was done honestly.

Experimental Farm Programs. The Supreme Court's *Hoosac Mills* decision of January 1936, which invalidated the original Agricultural Adjustment Act, set all program makers back on their heels. The new law adopted two months later incorporated a soil conservation approach. It was only mildly successful. Had it not been for the 1936 drought, which reduced production, its inadequacy could have come to light quickly. It was replaced in 1938 by a law featuring supply management, explained a little later.

Throughout those years, a search for new or modified program design was carried on almost continuously. One form it took was to set up experimental programs in selected counties. The project, and the studies of their effectiveness, carried Breimyer into a new phase of his career. During the summer of 1938, he was dispatched to Iowa, Nebraska, and South Dakota, there to join with economists of the land-grant colleges of the respective states in studying effectiveness of the acreage-reduction and price-support program then in force, as matched against experiences in experimental programs of several designated counties.

Such was Harold Breimyer's baptism into collaborative work with land-grant college people. It was a relationship that he would continue until he himself moved to a land-grant university. The 1938 studies in the three states also inducted him into the taking of farmer surveys, which for him was emotionally traumatic but also maturing.

At Iowa State College, Walter Wilcox headed the research project, and Francis Kutish, who was completing his undergraduate studies, was Harold's fellow worker. Both were to become lifelong friends. Tama county, in eastern Iowa, was already recognized nationally for its innovative program. Its features are not recoverable from memory but may have combined a land-use capability with an historical approach in setting an individual farmer's acreage base. That program technique was being tried in several counties.

Beginning in 1933 and continuing until the time of this writing, issues in the design of acreage-reduction programs have been clouded by disputes about how to determine the number of acres a farmer must idle, or convert to non-program crops, to qualify for program benefits. The dreamers who wrote the 1940 *Yearbook* badly wanted to require that all land that is highly erodible or otherwise not suitable for cropping be eliminated from the program. If a farmer had been cropping that kind of land, the acreage would not be included in the base from which the permitted acreage would be calculated. If a corn-and-wheat farmer historically had seeded 200 acres of which 40 were highly erodible, and the program called for a 10 percent reduction, the farmer would be permitted to seed only 144 acres to qualify for program benefits.

Putting tight land-conservation rules into the program didn't prove possible — until 1985, when the Food Security Act was enacted. Even then, application of a rule denying program benefits where highly erodible land was cropped would be delayed until 1990, and full enforcement until 1995.

It is easy to pontificate that farmers ought not to receive program benefits for crops produced at cost of damage to land. Yet Harold Breimyer never forgot an observation from his interviewing in Iowa. At one farm a middle-aged farmer in tattered overalls was plowing a rather steep slope. The farmer's draft power was three horses; he apparently could not finance purchase of a tractor. Without being prodded he volunteered the comment that he knew he should not be plowing that soil, but he had only 100 acres and he just had to farm it.

It's fine and dandy to theorize about how all land ought to be used conservatively—to protect soil. But to disregard the human cost of changing past patterns is both inconsiderate and impolitic. If the year had been 1986, the Iowa farmer could have put his sloping land in the Conservation Reserve. In doing so he would have received a substantial rental payment plus a contribution toward the cost of seeding it to grass.

Experiences in the three states in the summer of 1938 were memorable. Talking with farmers in a number of communities revealed how high a quality of leadership had been discovered or developed as the New Deal farm programs went into effect. Farmers showed that their elected committeemen could administer the AAA's acreage reduction.

Iowa was getting electric lines but not many paved roads. Harold Breimyer learned about Iowa "gumbo." On a rainy day he tried to reach a farm located on a gumbo (mud) road. The wheels of his Plymouth became mired in the sticky stuff. He extricated the vehicle only by wading into the wet mud and putting on the chains that he carried for winter snows. He spent the weekend getting the muck off his shoes and out of his clothes. On inquiring how the rural mail carrier managed to get through, he was told that the man drove a Model T Ford, the tires (30" × 3 ½") of which were narrow enough to go through the wide ruts made by newer automobiles with their wide tires.

Field studies of experimental county programs brought Harold Breimyer face to face with a phobia that he could no longer escape dealing with. For some emotional reason he was frightened by the idea of field interviewing. At Ohio State some of his fellow students earned spending money by taking farm management surveys. But to Breimyer the thought of approaching a farmer and asking for so intimate a business revelation brought fear and trembling.

In the summer of 1938, working with Wilcox and Kutish in Iowa, immersion into field interviewing could be avoided no longer. After a near-sleepless night during which, in accordance with Lady Macbeth's injunction to her husband, he screwed up his courage to the sticking place, he set out. To his surprise, most of the interviews went smoothly. Some farmers were pleased for a break in their isolation. And Breimyer's aptitude for numbers helped him. Notebook hidden in pocket, he casually inquired about the farmer's acreage data and lodged the answers in memory until he could get back to his Plymouth and write everything down.

Only one farmer proved intransigent. He had read in the local newspaper that Walter Wilcox and Harold Breimyer would be interviewing farmers and was ready with his vituperative denunciation of the farm programs and just about everything else within his range of observation. He threatened no violence, only non-responsiveness. The young interviewer patiently purred the usual assurances of confidentiality and such, to no avail. The man remains to this day his one and only rejection in field interviewing.

Another farmer might have been a no-response man. Harold Breimyer came upon him in his farmyard, where he was trying to catch two hogs (shoats) that had escaped the chute for loading into a market-bound truck. The farmer was of slight build. He was frustrated. The lean and lanky interviewer grabbed each hog by the rear legs and marched it up the chute into the truck. The farmer allowed as how he had never had much respect for the local county extension agent and Iowa State College, and didn't approve of farm programs. But with his hogs in the truck, he was in no position to be uncooperative. He responded fully.

Upon completing one interview, a farmer asked if his next-farm neighbor would be questioned. Breimyer answered that yes, he was in the sample. Then, apprehensive and remembering his one rejection, he asked, "Will he talk?" The positive answer came with a chuckle. Breimyer spent the rest of the afternoon listening to the garrulous neighbor talk about every subject of past, present, and future.

In Nebraska the local cooperator was Frank Miller, who twenty-eight years later would be a colleague at the University of Missouri. Breimyer's lot was to interview ranchers in the vicinity of Benkelman in southwest Nebraska. Frank Miller made his Chevrolet available, with a stern warning to be sure the gasoline tank was full before starting out. It was possible to drive hundreds of miles to reach only a few ranchers. But Miller did not warn that driving on sandy roads in hot July sun would heat the motor. When the radiator boiled, the improvised solution was to use a cardboard chart tube as a makeshift bucket. Water dipped from an irrigation ditch cooled the motor.

Isolated ranchers were the most cooperative of interviewees. Their operations and their psychology were both a revelation to the farm boy from Ohio.

One observation in the Nebraska interviewing was the crucial dependence on windmills. In the center of a grassland, a mile or two from any habitation, a windmill would be seen pumping water for white-faced cattle that were getting grass-fat on the luxuriant meadow of the favorable summer of 1938. Every pupil of Ohio schools had read about how the windmill and barbed wire developed the Plains; for Harold Breimyer seeing was convincing.

In South Dakota he and Raymond Penn of the state's agricultural college conducted a field study in wretched, impoverished Ziebach County. South Dakota may have suffered more than any of the (then) forty-eight states from depression and dust-storm drought. Ziebach County in 1938 was barren. Only a handful of homesteaders was still to be found. They had taken up their 160 acres just before World War I. A few years of good crops and wartime high prices had offered a false hope that was extinguished with all the tragedy that James Michener describes in *Centennial.* In 1938 the largest source of income to the county may have been the grant money received by Indians (later to be called Native Americans) located there.

County Land-Use Planning. Perhaps no activity of the USDA exemplified the 1940 *Yearbook* philosophy more closely than its short-lived county land-use planning. From their beginning in 1933, various New Deal agricultural programs had a bearing on land use. The Agricultural Adjustment and Soil Conservation programs conspicuously did so, but a number of others were at least peripherally related. In 1937 an Office of Land Use Coordination was set up in the Office of the Secretary. Its head was Milton Eisenhower, brother of General Dwight.

As the USDA moved to make good land use more than a platitude, the state colleges and their Extension services began to worry about protecting their terrain. According to a 1963 account in *Century of Service,* a USDA publication, a committee of the Land-Grant College Association wanted to be sure that "the Land-Grant College be designated as the sole agency for leadership in research and extension education in all so-called action or other programs dealing with individual farmers" (p. 258). In July 1938, representatives of the Land-Grant College Association and USDA worked out a Mt. Weather Agreement. The essence of the agreement was as follows:

It provided that the Department was to continue administering action
programs from Washington, but was to cooperate with the colleges in
jointly setting up State and county land use planning committees in all
states and agricultural counties. Under this agreement, the State extension services were to take the initiative in setting up county land use
planning committees as subcommittees of their county agricultural program building committees. These committees were to be composed of
at least 10 farmers; of the representatives of the various action agencies
in the county; and of the county agents. (pp. 258–59)

As one outcome of the new agreement, a new Division of State and
Local Planning in the Bureau of Agricultural Economics got under way
quickly. Its director was Bushrod W. Allin, a Kentucky native (as the
first name suggests). Allin was a political liberal of the Wisconsin school
identified with John R. Commons and Henry Taylor. He enlisted lieutenants such as Dennis Fitzgerald, Harold Vogel, and Kenneth Nicholson.
In a flurry of excited evangelism the organizing of land use planning
committees county by county was set in motion.

Harold Breimyer was never assigned to the State and Local Planning Division but was made available for spot jobs. As one assignment,
late in 1940 he traveled to Minot, North Dakota, to work with the local
planning committee. As a stranger, he contributed almost nothing to the
planning process. As an observer, he learned that each county addressed
its assignment in so singular a fashion that the several county plans could
not be melded into a statewide composite. He learned that the primary
benefit of the planning operation was to bring the several local program
officials into communication. It is astonishing how quickly bureaucracy
can take on its characteristic pattern even in a rural county where, according to American folk wisdom, grass-roots democracy flourishes. In
Minot the heads of the local AAA office, the soil conservation people,
and others rarely got together—until the program planning committee
brought them together.

Harold Breimyer made a sociological observation also. Located in
western North Dakota, Minot is readily described as a trading center for
wheat farming and cattle ranching. The characterization is too chaste.
According to local lore, ranchers in particular came to Minot for
weekend holidays with the prettier among the city's high school girls,
who earned generous emoluments.

A question was asked earlier as to what materialized from the
AAA's farmer opinion polling. The judgment offered was not negative
but denied any earthshaking findings. The same question can be asked
about county land-use planning. The planning project was much more

elaborate and expensive than opinion polling. Its accomplishments, other than sponsoring inter-agency communication, were few. Hundreds of county land-use planning reports came to Washington. Each revealed the diligence with which a local planning committee had drawn maps, coloring the various soil types with crayons. The committee offered thoughtful suggestions about how the county's economy could be improved. It was Breimyer's lot to read many of them, writing pithy summaries that, presumably, would enable local leaders and the USDA bureaucracy to join hands in a glorious tableau fulfilling the dreams of the writers of the 1940 *Yearbook*.

It was never to be. It was all motion. Bushrod Allin and the other satraps of USDA had no idea how to crystallize some kind of operating program out of the elaborate planning documents. The entire planning thrust eventually would have fallen of its own weight.

Before that could happen, political opponents gave it a push, and they were preparing to unleash heavy artillery against it. The idea of farmer-led land-use planning was anathema to government agencies such as the AAA, which already were as firmly entrenched as though they had been established by George Washington. They brooked no interlopers. Farm organizations were equally indignant. Their reasons were similar. They, too, did not want any competitors.

By the time those two formidable adversaries could fire a barrage, the war clouds had become more ominous. Howard Tolley, chief of the Bureau of Agricultural Economics, knew he had a tiger by the tail. He almost welcomed an excuse to squelch his more enthusiastic planners, and he leaped to redirect his agency into defense preparation. Harold Breimyer stored the county land-use planning reports in USDA's spacious attic. He himself began to calculate food requirements in the event of hostilities, learned about the economics of long staple cotton, and otherwise made himself useful enough to justify one deferment from Selective Service. His boss, Dennis Fitzgerald, certified that he was needed for his contribution to a program for food and agriculture as our nation fought a war on both Atlantic and Pacific fronts.

As a footnote to the above, this negative report on the brief land-use planning episode is not intended to disparage either the conceptualization or the motivation that underlay it. If civilization is to continue its halting progress upward, human beings must find it within their collective capacity to set elevated targets for society and to pursue them. But the obstacles are formidable. Harold Breimyer learned in the later 1930s how quickly any interest group can coalesce and exercise whatever power it possesses, in defiance of social goals. The BAE was trying to establish goals for agriculture that transcended parochialism. It did so ineptly and became an easy target for pressure groups. Its intentions were unassailable, but its techniques were faulty, and the trend of the times vitiated any short-run successes.

The ultimate irony is that wartime forced agriculture's interest groups into a subservience to common purpose that they had reviled when BAE was attempting its idealistic heroics. They had to do so, of course, to provision waging of the war.

Fred and Ella Breimyer

College Hill School, 1924. Harold Breimyer is front and center, high kneeling

14.

VOL. V, No. 28 CIRCULAR Revised Dec., 1922
OF THE
OHIO STATE UNIVERSITY AGRICULTURAL EXTENSION SERVICE
H. C. RAMSOWER, Director

OHIO BOYS' AND GIRLS' CLUB WORK

MOTTO:—"To Make the Best Better"

PIG CLUB

RECORD BOOK

Pig Growing—Sow and Litter

Name _Harold F. Breimyer_

Address _Ft. Recovery O. R. R. 3_

County _Mercer_ Age _9_

Name of Club _Gibson Township Pig Club_

Project _Pig Growing_

(Pig Growing or Sow and Litter)

The Ohio State University, Cooperating with the United States Department of Agriculture
Agricultural College Extension Service
Department of Boys' and Girls' Club Work, W. H. Palmer, State Club Leader

Cover sheet of Harold Breimyer's Pig Club record book

Harold Breimyer (right), Ernest Heiby, and vocational agriculture teacher L. N. Geiger

Heiby and Breimyer at their prize-winning 4-H Club demonstration on producing clean milk

Ensign Harold F. Breimyer

Harold Breimyer (left), Joseph Ruwitch, and the LST 485, 1944

Milburn L. Wilson

Howard R. Tolley

Mordecai Ezekiel

Breimyer in his office at the University of Missouri

Harold F. and Rachel S. Breimyer

Harold F. Breimyer on the occasion of receiving the Thomas Jefferson Award, University of Missouri

CHAPTER 10

Commodity Interests
and Supply Management

THE MORE AGGRESSIVE INTEREST GROUPS in society typically tolerate social dreamers and planners in proportion to the latters' ineffectuality. When the planners pose no threat, the live-and-let-live rule applies. Occasionally, though, the planners' formulations provide a convenient facade for pressure groups' activities. Big cotton planters, for example, may find it expedient to ask endorsement of price supports for the fiber on grounds that the price aid is consistent with agrarian democracy.

During the years when M. L. Wilson's small band of intellectuals was holding seminars, taking field opinion surveys, and writing essays for the 1940 Yearbook, commodity interest groups were growing more assertive and influential. They flexed their muscle in the fall of 1938 when they forced Howard Tolley out of the office of administrator of the AAA and banished him to the position of chief of the Bureau of Agricultural Economics. In the reorganization of the Department of Agriculture that Secretary Wallace announced in October, Tolley was told to take with him the Program Planning Division. "Practical" farm leaders did not want a professor in the top spot of the AAA, or professional economists and social thinkers close at hand giving advice.

Tolley was replaced by R. M. ("Spike") Evans. Evans was Tolley's opposite. Tolley was a mathematician who had learned the economics of agriculture on the job during the 1920s, first in the Office of Farm Management of USDA; he was a squat, ugly Irishman of irrepressible good humor. In contrast, Evans was a salty Iowa farmer. He had been chairman of his local corn-hog committee and then of the Iowa Agricultural Conservation Committee. As recounted by Theodore Saloutos, in *The American Farmer and the New Deal,* Wallace brought his fellow Iowan to Washington to serve as his leg man, prior to moving him into Tolley's AAA spot (p.249).

PERMANENT PLANNING FOR A TEMPORARY TRIPLE A

Events of the momentous year 1938 were packed with irony. The upheaval in October of that year and the sacking of Tolley may have been a crowning success of commodity interests, but those skilled operatives had already succeeded in getting a new farm law that was to their liking. It was the Agricultural Adjustment Act of 1938, signed into law in February 1938.

Moreover, although commodity spokesmen had a voice in drafting it, the new law essentially came out of the AAA's Program Planning Division, which the commodity people disliked, and was the handiwork principally of a theoretical economist, Oris Wells.

An even more outstanding irony is that a major new law should have come into being, carrying all the marks of permanence, in defiance of the "temporary" tag the programs had carried. From their beginning in 1933, the AAA and its programs were announced and advocated as being short-term, provisional. They were an expediency resorted to in order to deal with an emergency— aspirin for a passing headache. So went the liturgy.

Nor did the emergency label fade fast. Traces of it remained in the 1980s!

Calling the AAA an emergency expedient was in part a political ploy. A costly public program can always be defended more easily if its early demise can be promised—if it has a sunset clause. It's not too farfetched to say that over the years, farm programs have accumulated a dozen sunset clauses.

To be sure, authors of *Farmers in a Changing World,* the 1940 *Yearbook,* saw the changes under way as irreversible. They regarded their own prescriptions as enduring and were certain that farm programs would continue. They wanted to help craft them.

The consensus, though, was the opposite. Academicians, politicians, and even many farm leaders joined in a chorus that the all-enveloping acreage controls of the Depression years were an accommodation that would be dismantled as soon as the farm economy would recover.

The farm economy was truly expected to recover, although optimists were divided as to where a restored prosperity would come from. One school of thought said domestic economic recovery would generate consumer demand for food that would be strong enough to eliminate all need for acreage programs. A second school put almost unbounded faith in expanded export markets. Leslie Wheeler, who for a decade was head of the Office of Foreign Agricultural Relations, had endorsed Cordell Hull's trade agreement initiative on the grounds that inasmuch as those agreements "opened up the channels of world trade and permitted a larger flow of agricultural exports," the domestic farm program "could be gradually abandoned" (p.806).

As recently as the 1980s it could be asked whether old ideas, even as old soldiers, never die. A hallmark of that decade was an inextinguishable confidence that export demand would erase agriculture's economic problems. It did not do so.

AGRICULTURAL ADJUSTMENT ACT OF 1938

Even as farm politicians tut-tutted that acreage programs were a passing improvisation, they took steps to draw up a more comprehensive statute. Why did they do so? One reason is that it had become clear, by the fall of 1937, that the conservation-linked program of the 1936 law was ineffective. Something stronger was sought. It's also likely that some of the commodity leaders had decided that acreage and price-support programs, though clumsy, were a good thing.

Whatever the rationale, political agitations in 1937 led to a comprehensive mechanism to match productive capacity with prospective demand at a price that farmers could regard as acceptable. The mechanism was incorporated in the Agricultural Adjustment Act of 1938.

As principal architect drafting the 1938 law, Oris Wells worked closely with Carl Farrington of the Western Division of the AAA. Wells's technique could have come straight out of the boardrooms of General Motors. Lois Nelson, Bertha Burnett, and other clerk-statisticians assembled voluminous data on the U.S. farm and food economy. Using $8 \times 10\frac{1}{2}$-inch ruled cards that Wells had ordered to be printed for the purpose, they collected time series data on food consumption, livestock feeding, export trade, price, income—not to mention national income and other macroeconomic measures that bore on demand. Meanwhile, James Cavin and Harold Breimyer sorted through price analyses for major farm products. Where good studies were lacking, they made their own. U.S. agriculture was treated as one huge conglomerate, to be planned for and managed in the same manner as a large industrial corporation.

Breimyer did not himself contribute to writing the language of the new law. He only fueled the process statistically and analytically. But he learned lessons about both program design and the policy-making exercise that he was never to forget.

To this day, the 1938 law stands as the most innovative and precedent-setting farm law of this century. It was far more comprehensive than the timidly venturesome original 1933 law. It divided farm products into categories, separating those for which production control was mandatory (following a farmers' vote) from those for which control was discretionary with the secretary of agriculture. The five commodities of the first category, designated for acreage allotments and marketing quotas, were cotton, wheat, corn, tobacco, and rice.

Farm programs of the 1980s were often said to trace back to the Agricultural Act of 1949. Legalistically, the statement is not wrong. But the basic principles were first incorporated in the landmark legislation of 1938. Only one really big change has been made since 1938. It was the ending of authority for mandatory acreage controls on all commodities except tobacco. Programs were converted to voluntary form progressively in the 1960s. Otherwise, the 1938 law remains the prototype.

Ever-Normal Granary. The 1938 law continued the non-recourse loans that enabled farmers taking part in acreage reduction to put their crops under loan, thereby being assured of netting at least the support price. Farmers were not required to redeem the commodity and to pay the loan; they were likely to do so only if market prices strengthened.

This feature of programs had the secondary effect of building up, in a year of large harvests or weak demand, a reserve stock in the hands of the Commodity Credit Corporation (CCC). That stock then was available to be drawn on in a year of small harvests or big demand.

The arrangement was dear to the heart of Henry Wallace, who had espoused it fervently under the rubric of an Ever-Normal Granary. He had advanced the idea when he was editor of *Wallaces' Farmer.* As secretary he revived it in an address delivered in Bismarck, North Dakota, in June 1935, reported in Saloutos's *The American Farmers and the New Deal* (p.203). Throughout his tenure as Secretary of Agriculture, Wallace proclaimed the stabilization features of government commodity programs.

Big Influence of Small Commodities. The growing influence of farm politicians, and increasingly those associated with commodity organizations, helped account for the onset of supply management in the Agricultural Adjustment Act of 1938.

But writing a law is a minor part of the influence story. Every law accords the Secretary of Agriculture a wide range of discretion in administration. Commodity organizations invariably provide a corps of volunteer helpers, who stay in close touch with USDA officialdom. Often, they work even more effectively via committees, or subcommittees, of the Congress. They induce congressmen to put pressure on the Department of Agriculture. The telephone and open hearing are effective channels for congressional persuasion.

All this is a secret to no one. More than any other economist, James Bonnen of Michigan State University has written about the locus of power in administering farm laws.

What Harold Breimyer learned during his AAA years is that the amount of power a commodity group can exercise is inverse to the size and importance of the commodity. The one exception is cotton. Southern senators and congressmen have been so strategically placed that they have long won generous concessions for their favorite farm commodity. Francis Kutish once told a Missouri audience that enacting any commodity legislation is impossible unless it contains something extra for cotton. At the time, Kutish was an aide to Congressman Neal Smith of Iowa.

Except for cotton, the rule holds: The more prominent the commodity, the less the chance of slipping concessions past budgetary and other eagle eyes. And vice versa.

Corn and wheat are so exposed to public view and have so many constituencies that it is almost impossible for their emissaries to get special privilege legislation. Not so with tobacco or sugar, or even wool with its incentive payments, or honey with its generous price supports. "Are bees a species of livestock?" wags ask.

During the early 1960s, as will be reported later, Harold Breimyer was economist to the administrator of the Agricultural Marketing Service. Personnel in the tobacco division were pleasant, agreeable, and almost silent. Not until later did Breimyer learn that Si Smith, the administrator, was almost powerless with regard to tobacco marketing. A couple of tobacco congressmen surreptitiously called the shots.

Sugar offers an even clearer case. In the 1930s a reputable economist named Joshua Bernhardt brought order out of the helter-skelter sugar operations, making sugar the most protected and sheltered of all farm commodities. Thereupon a series of sugar czars in USDA ran their programs in defiance of any outside principle or authority. Harold Breimyer watched Tom Murphy control the sugar operations of the Agricultural Stabilization and Conservation Service without any apparent awareness of public interest.

The axiom is alternatively stated. The more obscure the commodity, the more paternalistically generous are the government programs available to it.

FINAL VANQUISHING OF THE BAE'S PLANNING.

Conservative farm politicians saw it as a victory when all so-called planning within the USDA was pushed one agency distant from action agencies such as the AAA. They nevertheless should not have been surprised when Tolley and his newly reconstituted BAE took the planning assignment seriously. The BAE assigned individual staff members, often newly employed, to work with various action agencies in a liaison capacity. William F. Watkins, for example, worked with the Soil Conservation Service. Because he was highly competent, he did so without serious difficulty.

Pearl Harbor redirected the BAE into wartime food concerns, but not for long. As war's end came into view, the agency offered its prognostications as to what U.S. agriculture would face after the war, and the policy steps that might be appropriate. Conservative opposition mounted once more. When a Southern congressman was tipped off that a sociologist in BAE had drafted a report — unpublished — alleging discrimination against Negroes in a Mississippi county, Howard Tolley was subjected to congressional impalement. The weapon used against him, in addition to grilling at hearings, was reduction in the BAE appropriation. Tolley once again made a career change, this time to the Food and Agriculture Organization of the United Nations, in Rome, Italy.

During all the hubbub Harold Breimyer was serving in the U.S. Navy in Pacific waters. The sequence of events decapitating the BAE has been reported with insight by Charles Hardin in the *Journal of Farm Economics* and will not be commented on further here. It suffices to be said that the Bureau of Agricultural Economics, itself to be liquidated under the ax of Earl Coke, Ezra Taft Benson's Assistant Secretary, never again sought to cultivate its own version of an uplifting rural democracy.

In the years to come, the warring factionalism among agriculture's internal interest groups would be interrupted and modified in the direction of the national welfare only by consumer organizations. Such was to be the case until, in the 1970s and especially the 1980s, a new entrant would bring a pressure not known before. The several environmental activists of the 1980s were in some respects the ideological successors to the BAE dreamers and planners of the later 1930s.

CHAPTER 11

Wartime Interlude

To call the world war ii years of conflict and destruction an interlude may seem inappropriate and even unfeeling. Yet, in terms of Harold Breimyer's lifetime experiences and professional career, they were that. They were the same for millions of young Americans, male and female, who did not hesitate to enter the armed forces, particularly after the December 7, 1941, bombing of Pearl Harbor, but who had every intention of resuming civilian status at the first postwar opportunity.

Even though an interlude, the war years were for Harold Breimyer educational and maturing. His experience doubtless paralleled that of many other persons who shed the mufti in favor of—as it turned out in Harold's case—the navy blue.

This book is a memoir of an Ohio farm boy who found himself in a lifetime engagement of studying the economics of agriculture—a lifetime, that is, except for the three-and-a-half war years. The exceptional experiences of those years could readily be narrated at length. What a saga it is, indeed, for a young man who could not distinguish a destroyer from a battleship to find himself the commanding officer of a ship of the fleet, and later the personal aide to a vice-admiral.

INDOCTRINATION INTO WORLD WAR II

An account of the wartime experiences could fill many pages, but it will be telescoped into a chapter. It begins December 7, 1941.

All Americans born before 1935 who have retained their mental faculties know precisely where they were on that historic day, and how they were engaged. Harold Breimyer and Rachel Styles were in an apartment on the third floor of 906 North Wayne Street in Arlington, Virginia, busy with broom and brush as they prepared it for their occupancy. They were to be married December 13. They had no radio in the apartment, but through the walls they heard a crescendo of emotionally pitched announcements. Only in the evening did they learn of the Japanese bombing of Pearl Harbor in the Hawaiian Islands.

Harold had received a low number in the draft lottery of the previous year. Within the first week after Pearl Harbor, he received "greetings" from General Hershey, instructing him to report for induction a couple of days before Christmas. But Dennis Fitzgerald, Harold's division chief, won from the draft board a six-months' deferment. Before that time expired, Harold applied for and received an Ensign commission in the navy. So Harold Breimyer, ignorant of the profile of a destroyer and a stranger to words such as "port" and "starboard," became a naval officer. On July 1 he entered indoctrination training at Cornell University on the beautiful Ithaca campus.

The school was a model of efficiency. Within two months the erstwhile USDA economist, always the bright student, had learned the movement of the stars (for celestial navigation), the meaning of "rules of the road" at sea, the organization of the navy, and the profile of a destroyer. He also attained an unexcelled degree of physical fitness as he and his fellow officers were marched up and down Cornell's hills. Life at the school was tightly cloistered except for three weekends. He met Rachel once in New York City and one time in Bethlehem, Pennsylvania; she came to Ithaca on one occasion.

Harold left Cornell with orders not to a prestigious destroyer or even a baby flattop (aircraft carrier), but instead to the amphibious service. His next stop was Solomons Island, southeast of Washington, a sinkhole that had the one merit of being within weekend commuting distance of his home in Arlington. At Solomons the young Ensign learned about communication, including how to signal with flashing light and semaphore. At those skills he outshone everyone.

Before long, orders were received assigning him to the U.S.S. LST 448, then under construction. A cross-country train trip took officers and men to Portland, Oregon, there to prepare to receive their vessel from yards in Vancouver, Washington. Ensign Breimyer was to be communications officer. He journeyed to Bremerton, Washington, to get the required documents, arriving there without an authorization signed by his commanding officer—a piece of paper the U.S. Navy said to be essential to release of classified material.

The young Ensign then got his first inkling of how the U.S. Navy managed to win a Pacific war. The wartime navy was an immense bureaucracy, working its mimeographing machines incessantly. It turned out mountains of official papers conveying regulations and instructions. Rules were followed to the letter—except when they interfered with getting a job done. When that was the case, they were disregarded. At Bremerton the official guarding the precious communications books gazed out over Puget Sound, let Harold Breimyer sign as his own commanding officer, and handed over the documents.

The pattern of experience would be repeated many times. Even at sea the captain of a ship could violate instructions as necessary to protect the ship—except, of course, if the ship's mission were to be defaulted thereby.

RUB-A-DUB-DUB, 115 MEN IN A TUB

An LST (Landing Ship-Tank) in 1942 stood near the bottom of the U.S. Navy's social register. It probably still does so. The 1942 model was 330 feet in length and 50 feet abeam. The 448 had seven officers and 108 crewmen. A relatively flat-bottomed vessel, the LST could, supposedly, push its bow far enough up on a sandy beach to permit opening its big bow doors and dropping a ramp on dry land. The cavernous tank deck, accessible via the ramp and doors, would hold vehicles of many categories, even, sometimes, the automobile of the flotilla's commanding officer. The ship was a slowpoke. It could make 10 knots only when a current helped the diesel engines.

The 448 was commanded by a veteran of World War I. Lieutenant Zitenfield was a bachelor who had made it big in business and succumbed to social pressure to lend his talents in the new conflict. He had the good sense first to confine himself to his deck chair, reading a book, as he let Charles Roeschke, his executive officer, run the ship; and then, after enough delay to avoid seeming impulsive, to retreat back to his stocks and bonds.

Roeschke was a Mustang. A former chief quartermaster, he, like many of his fellows, had been elevated to officer status. He proved to be one of the Navy's noblemen, extremely competent. He also was patient tutor to young Ensign Breimyer. L.E. Sliffe, also a former chief petty officer, was engineering officer and, like Roeschke, highly capable. The third former chief petty officer, John Leonard, was first lieutenant. He kept the ship's shell and gear, other than the engines, in working order.

Leonard, less astute than Roeschke and Sliffe, would soon show some of the unattractive qualities of Captain Queeg, whom Herman Wouk immortalized in *The Caine Mutiny*. Other officers were as green as Breimyer: Norman ("Butch") Martin, John deGottrau LaMontagne, and Albert Harvey Hayes.

The ship steamed down the Columbia River on New Year's Eve 1942. The few miles of the river were smooth sailing, but off the mouth the LST, a skow of a naval vessel, bobbed and rolled in the manner of the tub it resembled. Thereupon class distinctions were revealed. Until that time many of the sailors, and even one or two of the officers, had told tall tales of what tars they were. Ensign Breimyer could not join in. He had never been on water in anything larger than a racing shell at Cornell. He wondered how well he would respond.

The noon meal consisted of sandwiches, because the ship rolled so hard that anything put on a table would become a flying missile. Various of the chest-beating tars were not hungry. More than a few ran for the rail. They gulped, futilely, the Mother Sill's Seasick Pills they had brought with them. Dramamine was not yet known. Harold Breimyer, gratified and a little surprised by a newly discovered seaworthiness, enjoyed his sandwich. In three-and-a-half wartime years, two of them at sea, he was never to be seasick.

The U.S.S. LST 448 cruised to San Diego and to Mare Island in San Francisco Bay, then set sail (an ancient nautical expression that survived conversion to motor-powered ships) for the South Pacific, via Hawaii. Breimyer found himself fully occupied. He took his turn on officer-of-the-deck watches. Only the mid-watch bothered him; the hours from midnight to four o'clock dragged interminably. Conversation with the seaman who shared the watch was the only relief to tedium.

A second major responsibility was to decode radio messages. Three radiomen stood their four-hour watches in the cramped radio shack, punching the typewriter to record the messages to the fleet that were broadcast in Morse code from Honolulu. The message had to be decoded using heavy-paper code strips, as the low-ranking LST was allowed only the strip cipher. Breimyer did some of the deciphering himself, but the practice was to put guest passengers to work at the task.

The LST was a commodious vessel and served also as a transport. The 448 often carried among its passengers a half-dozen or more officers, often of the U.S. Army. Pressed to play the game of extracting sensible messages from the radio code, most were incapable of doing it. They lacked imagination in correcting for the radioman's errors. Breimyer knew how hard it is when listening to the radio signal to distinguish between a four-dot h and a three-dot s. To unscramble a message, he would try interchanging the two letters. Not so the lieutenants and colonels of the U.S. Army. That was too much for their non-nimble minds. What a dull-witted lot they were, Breimyer reflected. The Pacific navy loved the marines and excoriated the army.

THE SOUTH PACIFIC

Years before, a fellow graduate student at the University of California, Ely York, had sung the ditty, "I joined the Navy, to see the world; and what did I see? I saw the sea." York himself also got an Ensign's commission from Washington's Gun Factory, then lost his life aboard an aircraft carrier in the western Pacific. Harold Breimyer, for weeks on end after the LST 448 left Pearl Harbor, saw the sea, only the sea. He saw the southern waters of the Pacific, which, in the absence of high winds, were as calm as a mill pond. Among his memories of tranquility are those of plowing the LST's broad bow through waters that scarcely showed a ripple. Only the arching dives of the dolphins disquieted the water.

On a sunny Sunday morning following brief worship services, Breimyer would watch the signalmen practice their semaphore, and boatswain's mates mend a line (rope), while he listened to the concert of the Mormon Tabernacle Choir projected by the ship's loudspeaker. He was joined in appreciation by a superb coxswain named Malloy, a devout Mormon from Nephi, Utah, who later lost his life.

The first destination was Noumea, New Caledonia, a French colony. The LST reached it following a one-day stop at Espiritu Santo, remembered only for a mounted sign reading, "Los Angeles City Limits." Sailors have an unquenchable sense of the bizarre as humor.

The ship's duty was to begin in the Solomons Islands. For several months all went well. Then came disaster. On November 1 a squadron of LSTs including the 448 moved forward to Vella Lavella with provisions for the troops on the island. The beach was nicely sloped, and its white sands smooth, so the clumsy LST had no trouble pointing its nose on it and disgorging cargo. Precisely at twelve o'clock noon several Japanese Zero bombers swarmed on the ship and dropped their deadly explosives. One hit aft, and one amidships. A third was targeted for the forecastle, where Lieutenant (j.g.) Breimyer had gun control duty, but it was errant and exploded in the water fifteen feet from the ship's side. Breimyer and a half dozen crewmen were spared their lives because of that error. The gusher of water drenched them. When their eyes could open again, they saw the midships and stern to be in flames. Cut off by the flames, Breimyer and his crewmen climbed down to the beach via the ladder on the bow doors.

Only the 448 was hit that day.

Rumor spread fast that the enemy had come in exactly at noon because the Japanese had observed that pilots of the U.S. Army Air Force who were charged with providing morning air cover made a practice of returning to base a few minutes before they were relieved—that is, before noon. They wanted to get to the noon meal on time!

Two years later, when Lieutenant Breimyer was serving with Admiral Wilkinson, he read of investigations into that charge but never learned whether anyone was court-martialed for the dereliction. All he knows is that more than fifty persons lost their lives because of it—nineteen from the ship's crew and the rest from the U.S. Marines and the New Zealand army. The 448 had carried the Marines and New Zealanders to Vella Lavella so they could garrison the allies' operations there. They were caught in the bombing as they were unloading cargo.

The bombing at Vella Lavella was to be Harold Breimyer's only direct exposure to the horrors of war. The death of the nineteen crewmen and injuries to others were to be engraved permanently in his memory. Among the dead were Martin, a nervous seaman who was perpetually frightened even during the tranquil cruise across the South Pacific; and Burgess, older than most and pillar of his Louisiana family. The stupid Lieutenant Leonard, who had been elevated to Executive Officer, had ordered Burgess to the emergency steering gear post in the bowels of the ship even though a ship in port requires no steering. Hall, a fireman on engine-room duty, doubtless was scalded to death. Another fireman, Loop, miraculously found his way from the engine-room via an escape ladder. He was so emotionally scarred that he had to be sent back for hospitalization at once.

Shanahan, a wisp of a youthful radioman from Philadelphia, perished. Also lost was a man named Lawicki, who had arrived in the Pacific and come on board the 448 only a few weeks earlier. What a shock his quick death must have been to his family. A red-headed older man, Fallon, finding himself mortally wounded, whispered to Lt. Sliffe that it was okay; he could rejoin his first wife, deceased, whom he loved. Also among the dead was Malloy, the coxswain already mentioned; Cazaubon, an Acadian from Louisiana; Adams, a postal clerk in civilian life who was aghast at the Navy's casual handling of mail. Another Martin was the ship's chief steward. He was regular Navy, and exceptional in that he had no family; there was no one to be notified of his death, or to mourn it.

In March of the next year, Breimyer wrote to the next of kin of the men who were lost—of all, that is, except Martin, the steward. About half responded, and did so graciously.

Harold Breimyer could not know if every wartime casualty list inscribes itself so deeply on the memory of survivors. But the 448's dead, who perished because a couple of flyboys chose to go to lunch early, will stay on his mind so long as his mental processes function.

A NEW SHIP AND THE SAIPAN INVASION

From Vella Lavella, Lieutenant (j.g.) Breimyer was sent back to Florida, an island in the Solomons, where he got the message that a son, Frederick, had been born November 13. By counting backward, he could know that the baby had been conceived when Rachel was following her husband up and down the West Coast, meeting him at each port at which the LST 448 landed. The baby's name was quickly converted to the diminutive Freddie, which gave way later, when the boy insisted on Fred.

Before long new orders arrived. "Smokey" Stover, commanding officer of the LST 485, wanted an executive officer. Roeschke, who also survived the bombing of the 448, had recommended his former communications officer. After several months of duty in the Solomons, which had become increasingly secure, the 485 was sent back to Hawaii in preparation for invasion of the Marianas Islands. The Marianas (Saipan, Tinian, Guam) were a leg closer to Japan.

At Pearl Harbor, Stover left the ship and was returned home for leave and reassignment. He had asked that his executive officer replace him. In fact, the crusty, taciturn Stover, a Mustang, had once given Breimyer a most appreciated compliment. Learning that his exec had been forehanded in pressing all officers to get their paperwork done before the ship arrived in port, Stover told him, "You are the most capable Naval Reserve officer I have ever seen."

So Harold Breimyer, who twenty months previously had not known of the existence of an amphibious force, became captain of a ship of the United States Navy.

The only major engagement of the LST 485 was the invasion of Saipan. The ship led a column of LSTs toward the island on June 6, 1944, which was the date also of the invasion of Normandy in Europe. At Saipan the LSTs did not stick their noses up on beaches. The shoreline consisted of too many bluffs. Instead, they dropped into the water near shore the amphibious vehicles called amphtracks, carried on the ship's tank deck, which were packed full with marine foot soldiers. On reaching the shore the marines moved into attack against the island's defenders.

The 485 was designated to remain in place to provide emergency medical treatment. Mainly, the physicians on board gave plasma to wounded who were brought by. They then dispatched these wounded to vessels equipped for hospital service. For one marine, the 485 could do nothing but provide burial. Lt. Breimyer performed his one and only burial service at sea.

BACK HOME

After spending a number of weeks in the waters of the Marianas, the 485 was ordered back to Hawaii. Once more, the 485 while berthed in Pearl Harbor lost her commanding officer to reassignment. After twenty months at sea, Harold Breimyer, tired and gaunt, was given orders to go back to stateside. At the time, he gave little thought to his experiences during those twenty months at sea on two LSTs. Later, though, he had thoughts aplenty. His memory of his fellow Reserve officers has been sharpest regarding those of his first LST, the 448. John LaMontagne, handsome, debonair, and Harold Breimyer's lifetime friend, was a good seaman but had trouble keeping the ship's business accounts straight. After the 448 went down, Breimyer spent several months cleaning up the records. Albert Harvey Hayes, exceptionally bright and competent, was frustrated in trying to find card players skillful enough to give him competition. Breimyer could not match the Hayes skill at gin rummy, but he tried. Roeschke and Sliffe, Mustangs, were truly exceptional officers.

Most of the thoughts Breimyer would mull over later related to the polyglot collection of enlisted men. They were a cross-section of the America of the early 1940s. A few had attended college, but some others were scarcely literate. Harold Breimyer was astonished to learn how few of the more than 100 men on board the 448 had completed high school. Three men who had been pulled out of the hills of West Virginia wrote letters home that required little censoring because they contained barely more than three sentences of pidgin English. The three couldn't write, but they could drink hard liquor. Yet they were responsible sailors. And when the Japanese bomb blew a man off the side of the LST, the oldest of the three West Virginians, James Repass, jumped in the water and dragged him to shore. Lieutenant Breimyer tried to make certain that the man would receive a life-saving award.

The most irresponsible of the crewmen of the two LSTs was a dour man named Fletcher, who indifferently performed minimum duties aboard the 485. Breimyer as commanding officer noted that Fletcher could fall asleep at his gun station. One day other seamen announced to him that Fletcher had turned on the fresh water for his shower. That, the seamen knew, was ticket to disaster. The LST had no evaporator, and when at sea had to draw sparingly on the tanks of fresh water it carried. In the warm Pacific all showers were connected to sea water. Fletcher decided he wanted fresh water, and he drew on it without regard for the ship's water supply. The peril of running out of fresh water was engraved on every seaman, and officer too, except the miscreant Fletcher.

One day when the LST was anchored in port, Fletcher was reported missing. Also anchored in the harbor was a transport, the converted prewar Lurline, which had ferried holidayers between California and Hawaii. Fletcher swam to her and climbed her anchor chain. He must have stayed under cover until she got underway for the United States. He preferred stateside incarceration to the hazards of duty in Pacific waters. Fletcher's brig time proved brief and was followed by assignment to duty at a United States base. He reported his good fortune in a letter written to a friend on the 485 who, indignant, told his commanding officer— (who still was Lieutenant Breimyer). That officer wrote his once-in-a-lifetime letter to the Chief of Naval Operations, expressing resentment that a man who jumped ship would be rewarded with stateside duty.

A few months later a general directive came out of the CNO's office, instructing that any man who had jumped ship and had completed his prison time should be assigned to sea duty. Harold Breimyer wondered if his letter had influenced a Naval policy. He soberly reasoned that dozens of protests had reached the chief of naval operations, and his would hardly have been instrumental. Correct reasoning, doubtless. But Lt. Cdr. Harold F. Breimyer, USNR (retired), still wonders: Did he help make navy policy?

NAVAL WAR COLLEGE

Harold Breimyer read his orders to his officers and men and booked passage on a transport headed for San Francisco. Sick and exhausted, he arrived in Atlanta, where Rachel and son Freddie were living. Still only thirty years old, he regained vitality rapidly. He was overjoyed when his application for the Naval War College in Newport, Rhode Island, was acted on favorably. He, Rachel, and Freddie took off for the cold north.

The five months at Naval War College were a welcome respite from wartime duty at sea. Above all other considerations, the duty was safe! At the War College instruction was of high quality. A few naval reserve scholars joined with veteran USN officers to present a good dose of naval thinking about strategy and the planning of campaigns. Instructors quoted incessantly from Mahan, the Navy's most revered strategist. Harold Breimyer was struck by the analytical discipline whereby an inquiry into any course of action invariably began with an "estimate of the situation." Years later, when he was a civilian agricultural economist once more, he declared often that any thinking about a desirable agricultural policy should begin with an estimate of the situation. It proved surprising to note how often a careful empirical review would modify or change what had been presupposed to be a proper course. The disciplined reasoning was an instance in which military training was transferable to civilian professional life.

Next after becoming addicted to making an estimate of any situation, the experience at the War College that stayed longest with Harold Breimyer was that of the war games. The floor of a classroom was a huge world map in which the water area was a checkerboard of black and white tiles. Lines between the tiles were parallels and meridians. On this big floor war games were played, by means of models of ships that could be pushed around to carry out fleet or ship orders. As a pedagogic device the prop was superb. What struck Breimyer, who was (and is) more moral philosopher than either economist or naval officer, was that a battle was always engaged in between the good-guy U.S. fleet and the evil enemy. There always had to be an enemy!

It seems strange or even shocking now, but historically the enemy fleet on Naval War College simulated waters had long been the British. At the time of World War I it became the German. It's interesting to wonder about what navy was so designated during the 1920s. In 1945, when Harold Breimyer was learning about naval wars, the enemy was, naturally, the Japanese. We can suppose that early in the postwar Cold War, the fleet's colors were changed to those of the Soviet Union.

In the later 1980s, when some citizens were tiring of the Cold War with the USSR, even as others wanted to heat it up, a few thinkers advanced the there's-always-an-enemy hypothesis. They said that human beings find it a routine practice to declare someone, or some entity, as antagonistic and threatening to their position. Certainly at the Naval War College of 1945, and doubtless that of the 1990s too, it was necessary to designate some nation's navy as the opponent of ours. College instructors were unable to conceive of an anonymous opponent, one without an identifying name. Some foreign flag had to be regarded as our enemy.

The observation of 1945 has haunted Harold Breimyer ever since. Maybe, in naval thinking, if we don't have an enemy, we must designate (or make) one. Is our civilian thinking similar?

In his five months at the War College, Harold Breimyer was thrown in with yet another category of individuals with whom he had never previously been acquainted. In the parlance of the 1980–1990s, they would be called Yuppies or, more narrowly, business-world Yuppies. When Breimyer entered the navy, he found himself competing with officers from business and the professions whom he could readily out-compete. The officers of similar background who were his classmates at Newport were a much more select group; all were highly capable. Among them were officers who had just finished college at war's beginning and in 1945 were only twenty-three to twenty-five years old. They came from established families that had never lacked for a dollar or a thousand.

Shielded as they were from the rigors of the Great Depression, these young officers saw the New Deal as an alien dogma. They regarded the columnist Westbrook Pegler as too liberal. (Pegler was an erstwhile sports reporter who especially castigated Eleanor Roosevelt.) Harold Breimyer was unable even to discuss political or national policy topics with his fellow officers. There was no intellectual meeting ground. In the 1980s he conjectured reflectively that those bright and capable but totally sheltered young men of 1945 became bastions of the Reagan Revolution.

ORDERS TO THE THIRD AMPHIBIOUS FORCE, A MISASSIGNMENT

In June 1945, at the end of the five months' schooling, all officers received orders to new assignments. One boot-licking sycophant was retained to serve on the college faculty, but the others were directed to destinations scattered over the globe.

During the five months of the Naval War College term, the war scene had changed materially. President Roosevelt had died, V-E day had been celebrated, and the Pacific war against Japan was moving toward its end. All graduates moving to new posts sensed a letdown.

Harold Breimyer's good classroom record led to his receiving orders that were regarded as enviable but proved to be a blunder. He was told to report to the Third Amphibious Force, where he would be Aide and Flag Lieutenant to Vice-Admiral Theodore Wilkinson. Admiral Wilkinson, he learned from old navy hands, was regarded as one of the most astute officers of the U.S. Navy. His Third Amphibious Force would mount the central portion of the planned invasion of Japan.

Breimyer flew at once to Hawaii to report to his admiral on board the U.S.S. Mount Olympus, a ship that had been specially outfitted to be a command ship. From Hawaii the Mt. Olympus cruised to Guam and to Samar-Leyte in the Philippines, and then to Manila Bay. At Manila, preparations were under way for an invasion of Japan. The preparing was done halfheartedly. Expectation of a Japanese surrender made it all seem an empty exercise. The hunches were to prove correct. After atomic bombs were dropped on Nagasaki and Hiroshima, Japan screamed her surrender.

Some events in history are destined to stir debate eternally. One such event was the decision by President Truman to drop the A-bombs. Disclosures made later virtually prove that Japan had already asked for an armistice, but garbled translation of the subtle language of diplomacy led to misinterpretation. Some military leaders wanted to "try out" the A-bomb. At the same time, Admiral Wilkinson's staff had concluded, even prior to the A-bombing, that the fight was out of the Japanese.

Harold Breimyer's doubts about the wisdom of the A-bombing have been reinforced by the observation, often expressed, that if the Japanese had been a white race instead of a yellow one, the bombs would not have been dropped.

On surrender day Admiral Wilkinson and his staff moved into Yokosuka and began the occupation. The admiral worked closely with General MacArthur, who would direct the occupation. The general had in fact traveled into Japan aboard a ship in Admiral Wilkinson's convoy.

Douglas MacArthur may have been a hero popularly but was not that among naval officers, who ridiculed him. They thought him to be pompous, a stuffed shirt. Admiral Wilkinson liked to recount the exchange of messages when MacArthur's ship joined Wilkinson's large entourage of ships. The general sent Wilkinson a long message in flowery language about the majesty of the joining of naval and army forces. The red-headed admiral, chuckling, told how he replied: "Your message received. Take second station third column."

Either the day of the surrender or the next one, there occurred a remarkable display of Japanese receptiveness toward the Americans. It doubtless was reflective of relief in the war's ending but perhaps also of antagonism toward the Tojo leadership. Admiral Wilkinson, his Flag Lieutenant, and many members of his staff joined in taking a jeep tour of villages in the vicinity of Tokyo. Citizens lined the route and flew U.S. flags; and the air was not of despondency but of rejoicing. Surely the attitude the conquered Japanese displayed toward the conquering Americans will stand as unique in the history of mankind.

The devastation found in Tokyo and neighboring cities such as Yokohama and Yokosuka has been reported often and will not be described here. Also told in story and pictures is the resilience of the Japanese as they propped up pieces of corrugated roofing to form a kiosk at which they could display trinkets for sale. It's a mystery where the knickknacks had been stashed during the war years, and how they were unearthed and transported for sale in the improvised bazaars in the wastelands of the port cities.

Equally revealing of the Japanese character and resilience was a merchandising venture on board the Mt. Olympus. The ship with so majestic a name had been tied up at a pier in Yokosuka only a few days when, one sunny morning, a middle-aged Japanese man of small stature, dressed in a well-pressed worsted Western-design suit, approached the ladder of the ship. Could he come on board and show the officers his pearls? Those of the ship's officers who had visited Japan before the war knew that Mr. Mikimoto was always welcome on board. The prewar practice was reinstituted, and the pearl salesman found an eager corps of buyers among both the old hands and the wartime Naval Reservists. Apparently every representative of the jewelry firm was addressed as Mr. Mikimoto.

Sequel to the two months' duty in Japan was a final cruise eastward, and receipt of orders to inactive status. The six months' duty as an admiral's aide had been instructive but not really satisfactory to Breimyer or his respected admiral. Harold Breimyer never could find an acceptable way to carry out his protocol duties within an oversized staff of hangers-on.

So a three-and-a-half year divertissement in Harold Breimyer's life and professional career, in retrospect not an unpleasant one, came to an end.

REFLECTIONS

To a landlubber previously innocent of acquaintance with the regime of the U.S. Navy, wartime active naval duty is equivalent to the science fiction of living on another planet. It's a world apart. During his duty years, Harold Breimyer learned something about himself, about other persons, and about the sociology of the naval establishment.

The first three years of duty were confidence-building. To begin from total ignorance of naval matters and to become within twenty months commanding officer of a ship of the fleet would instill a degree of confidence in any insecure individual. Harold Breimyer was never that lacking in self-assurance. Nevertheless, he found gratification in his mastery of a new endeavor.

A naval lesson learned was that individuals brought together for wartime duty vary widely in their competency. In graduate school and in his circumscribed government experience, he had associated with fellows of a relatively narrow stratum. The selection process that had landed him in both places had positioned persons of similar character and ability there.

Not so in the hastily recruited wartime corps of naval reserve officers. A few were of outstanding qualifications. Wartime stress sorted them out fairly efficiently, and they contributed much to the wartime Navy. Others were duds. A few were so incompetent that they could not be trusted to stand a deck officer watch. A Maryland legislator aboard an LST sister to the 448 spent all his time reading Baltimore newspapers. He provided an instance also of the wide range of morality. He boasted of giving statewide examinations for appointment to the U.S. Naval Academy, and then naming his political friends. A few years later, following return to the Maryland legislature, he was convicted of embezzlement and sent to prison.

Harold Breimyer's fellow officer on the LST 448, Norman Martin, revealed openly an amorality that Breimyer had never witnessed before. He unhesitatingly declared his scorn for human beings generally. They are dolts, he said, who deserve to be fleeced. He may have applied that philosophy to his fellow officers, as he was suspected of diverting officers' mess money to his own pocket. Martin probably has a purple heart, the decoration given to personnel injured in military duty. After the 448 was bombed, he told the ship's physician that he needed treatment for a back sprain sustained in the bombing. The sailors guffawed that the only way he could have hurt his back was by diving for cover instead of staying at his post. Sailors are adept at reading the character of their officers.

When Martin, along with other survivors of the 448, submitted claims for reimbursement for personal possessions lost, Martin borrowed a Sears, Roebuck catalog to remind himself of items for which he might ask payment. He had not possessed them, but that was, to Butch Martin, an irrelevant consideration. Ever since knowing Martin, Harold

Breimyer has been convinced that evil, and evil persons, are not rare in the world.

Variable competency was a mark of officers of the regular navy too. Wartime exigency proved as efficient a selection process for them as for reservists. The best among them rose to the top, and on their skill and dedication rested, in large measure, the success of the naval expeditions in the Pacific. Lieutenant Breimyer had no occasion to meet Admiral Nimitz, commander-in-chief of the Pacific fleet, who will be immortalized as a truly outstanding officer and person. Vice-Admiral Wilkinson proved to possess all the wisdom that had been attributed to him at the Naval War College. Admiral Halsey was pretty much a bust, but Admiral Spruance, whom Breimyer met once, enjoyed high repute.

A number of the members of Admiral Wilkinson's staff were outstanding. This was true of Cdr. Burt Hanson, USN, and of Lt. Cdr. Hugh Scott, USNR. Already a member of the House of Representatives, in later years Scott became a distinguished U.S. senator from Pennsylvania. But Breimyer wondered what qualifications could be attached to Armistead Peter III, who seemed to think that his family name relieved him of obligations, and to a number of others whose count of stripes on shoulder or sleeve overstated their worth to the navy.

THE MILITARY MENTALITY

Harold Breimyer, whose every sinew was civilian, received as a by-product of his naval experience an intimate instruction in the nature of the military mind. To this day his evaluation is dual, part respectful and part skeptical or even scornful. Naval reserve officers called the Annapolis USNs "trade school boys." The Annapolis curriculum was highly oriented toward physical sciences and engineering. Social sciences and the arts and letters were given short shrift. The Naval Academy regime established close fraternal bonds that probably are essential in a military service but also contribute to a singleness of purpose and narrowness of vision that Harold Breimyer sensed as marking the military mind.

As is true of any assemblage, some individuals rose above the limits of their clan. Generally, though, the regular navy veterans with whom Lieutenant Breimyer was associated were highly programmed in their life pattern and their practices in carrying out their professional duties. Breimyer, almost a teetotaler, was struck by the importance nearly every USN officer attached to liquor and the daily drinking bout that began at a prescribed time. At each new island base an officers' club was established almost, it seemed, before the territory was secure. Yet, with very few exceptions, the Annapolis-trained officers were meticulous about keeping liquor off the ship.

Living as they did in a social support system of their own making, officers of the regular navy had a distorted mental picture of the civilian world. Many of them had self-images as the counterparts of the heads of corporate business. Having heard of the astronomical salaries received by corporate executives, they believed themselves to be sacrificial victims of their dedication to the public service.

The USN officers aboard the U.S.S. Mt. Olympus were contemptuous of civilian authority. When a small subcommittee of U.S. congressmen paid a routine visit, Admiral Wilkinson's minions were formally polite but silently disdainful.

Politically, the gold-braided gang was far to the right. Perhaps a Democrat was to be found among them, but, if so, he kept his leanings to himself. Harold Breimyer had always been skeptical of a military role in civilian government, and after three-and-a-half naval years, he was convinced of the necessity of keeping a strong civilian hand on the military component of government.

CHAPTER 12

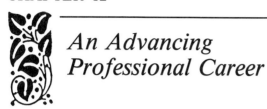

An Advancing
Professional Career

IN HUMAN AFFAIRS, crisis brings forth, first, cooperation to resolve it or at least to minimize its damaging consequences, and then action to prevent its recurrence. For the United States, World War II was a crisis. The nation's response was magnificent. When Harold Breimyer returned from naval duty, he found his homeland proud of its achievement and even basking in its glory. Yet it was also unsure whether it could manage the conversion to a peacetime economy and uneasy about its new world dominance.

The war had followed on the heels of an economic cataclysm that was itself a crisis. Memory of the Great Depression of the 1930s was much on the mind of adult citizens of 1946 other than, among Breimyer's wartime associates, the Yuppies of the Naval War College and the officer corps of the regular navy. Both groups were shielded for a lifetime against economic insecurity.

Awareness of the two crises that were survived by virtue of the nation's heroic efforts engendered a liberal public spiritedness not before known in the century. It was destined to continue a number of years, although interrupted by the McCarthy inquisition of the early 1950s. Eventually, it would be lost in a nasty factionalism that began in public opposition to the Vietnam conflict and picked up intensity in the turbulent 1970s.

Internationally, postwar America placed its faith in the newly formed United Nations. It also endorsed the new international monetary institutions crafted at a Bretton Woods conference. Before long, the Marshall Plan, reviving a prostrate Europe, would give further cause for pride.

Domestically, the preoccupation was with avoiding another severe depression. In 1946 the U.S. Congress enacted, and President Truman signed, an Employment Act that declared it not only the goal but also the considerable responsibility of the national government to attain a high level of economic activity. A Council of Economic Advisers would advise the president how to avoid repeating the Great Depression of the 1930s.

By this time John Maynard Keynes had become the patron saint of economists, who were confident that deft management of monetary and fiscal policy would keep the economy on an even keel. Keynesianism was made to order for the postwar era of the nation-state when national governments everywhere assumed more authority than previously over the economic welfare of their citizens.

The Keynesian contribution to both theory and practice in economics was the concept of macroeconomics, the thesis that economic forces are observable and can be managed not only in the individual business enterprise but also for an entity as large as a nation. The thesis became a creed, one to be invoked as a rationale for central government manipulation of fiscal, monetary, tax, international trade, and other economy-wide policies.

ECONOMIC GROWTH

Very soon a new catchword caught on: "economic growth." This was destined to be the term of infinite citations, and the talisman for economic policies the rest of the century.

Economic growth is indeed the supreme elixir of society. When the economy is expanding and national income is increasing faster than the population is, many of the disaffections that can foment social unrest are absent or dampened. An expanding economy offers new opportunities for jobs, careers, a place in the sun. In prewar years Oris Wells had dinned these observations into Harold Breimyer's ears. Even the agricultural programs would have led to more friction among farm groups were it not that all agriculture was enjoying a rising income, Wells said.

Even though he listened to Wells with respect and did not disagree, not until many years later, when he became more globally reflective, did Breimyer appreciate how much economic growth had meant in the history of the United States and, beyond that, the entire Western world.

About the time he had these thoughts, our nation's growth began to ebb. In the 1970s the genuine economic growth of the previous quarter-century was converted into a fraudulent substitute— inflation. Even in the 1980s, after rapid inflation had been arrested, statistical evidence of a resumed slow growth was a chimera. It primarily reflected the fast entry of women into the labor force. Employment of women had the effect of putting dollar values on economic activity that previously had been carried out, unpaid, in homes. Taking in each other's laundry, or cooking each other's dinner, does not add to real national product but makes the national income figures look better.

Rapid, sustained national economic growth was the mark of the quarter-century that began with the first peacetime years after World War II. It became a casualty of Vietnam and was interred by the oil price rises of the middle 1970s. A thousand incantations lifted to heaven since then have not restored a solid, continuing growth, nor will they do so.

SEARCHING FOR, AND FINDING, A SPOT

So it was that Harold Breimyer, released from active naval duty, returned to Washington to resume civilian employment at a time when the majority of citizens truly wanted to make ours a better nation. Almost as many hoped for a better world. He went back to the Bureau of Agricultural Economics, where his prewar job had vanished. He wandered footloose.

Breimyer also became self-aware that just as his native land was different in 1946 from what it had been in 1942, so was he. As was true of so many veterans, he found himself more soberly sensitive to his responsibilities, and more concerned to advance his career. To be sure, he had acquired a wife and son, and he hoped to put them in a home of their own. In addition, he had taken on a maturity of outlook and a self-confidence, also characteristic of the majority of persons returning from service, that were to influence his professional and private life from then on.

Before long Mordecai Ezekiel asked the wandering Breimyer if he would join in a project to promote and aid rural economic development. The field was new and strange to Breimyer, and not very appealing. But he was not besieged with counter offers, and he accepted.

Ezekiel had been known as the brilliant economist of the BAE of the 1920s who had published an already-classic book on correlation analysis. He had contributed much of the brainpower behind Secretary Wallace's programs. But Wallace had been replaced first by an Indiana farmer, the well-meaning but bumbling Claude Wickard, who was then followed by the adroit, urbane Clinton Anderson. Ezekiel had lost status, yet he retained enough to be a gadfly. Futurist in his thinking, he had pronounced upon a largely hostile South the inevitable decline of the cotton economy and the urgent need for rural industrial development as a replacement. The Tennessee Valley Authority's demonstration of what local industry could do made his task slightly easier.

In his cotton study of early 1942, Breimyer had had his baptism into southern issues and thinking. To his surprise, soon after joining Ezekiel, he was assigned to Project VII of a study commissioned by the Committee on Agriculture of the House of Representatives, "Industrialization and the South," of which the hearings were held in 1947. The committee writing the Project VII report was heartless in its listing of deficiencies in the southern economy, and firm in its recommendation for industrial development. The latter would require "time, patience, inventiveness, and harmonious collaboration between individuals, groups, and government at the Federal, State, and local levels" (p.7).

Harold Breimyer's second and last project with Ezekiel was to make a study of the manufacture of brick. Brick kilns could be located wherever suitable clay could be found. Hence, they could contribute to rural development. Breimyer worked with an old ceramic hand in the Department of Commerce named Brooke Gunsallus. The two visited brick manufacturers such as Belden in Ohio and the imaginative designer of a tunnel kiln in North Carolina, whose name has been forgotten. When Gunsallus's name was put on a bulletin, *Manufacturing Brick and Tile to Serve Your Community,* the man's self-esteem was lifted heavenward. Breimyer, too, found satisfaction in successfully completing an assignment that was initially as foreign to him as his naval officer duties had been when he first boarded an LST.

Ezekiel, it was now obvious, had been eminently correct in his assessment of the urgent needs and of the potential for the Southeast. His short-term assistant was glad to learn some of his insights and to get his own feet wet in yet another endeavor.

The S&HR Division. In the BAE, the Division of Statistical and Historical Research had long been noted for its straightforward, objective, and dull reporting of the state of economic affairs in the United States and internationally. Among the division's publications was a series of so-called situation reports written by individual specialists but reviewed, and sometimes torn to pieces, by an Outlook and Situation Board. It would have been logical to reverse the word order in the board's name, as a review of the existing situation (the navy's "Estimate . . .") necessarily precedes arriving at an outlook. But the Board rebelled at SOB, so it became the OSB.

Jim Cavin, Harold Breimyer's prewar fellow worker, had moved up to director of the S&HR Division. He invited his old friend to edit — actually, write — the *Demand and Price Situation.* Once monthly the state of the economy and of agriculture would be sketched and its prospects predicted.

The new editor was less than enthusiastic. He knew that a hundred or more economists in the business world and a fourth that many in various agencies of government were playing the business forecasting game. Some were earning big salaries as they wrote the "letters" of National City and dozens of other banks. Harold Breimyer's countryman instincts made him skeptical of those seers and necromancers. Even though he, too, would do lots of "seer-ing" and necromancing during his career, his native doubts never left him.

He chuckled when he read, in 1987, of a study by Jim Eggert of his father's Blue Chip economic forecasts. For predicting inflation, it was more accurate just to project a trend than to take the consensus of the prestigious, over-salaried friends of Bob Eggert. Bob was a friend of Harold Breimyer of many years before and was the man who, as economist for Ford Motor Company, gave the name to the Mustang model of Ford car.

For a year Harold Breimyer plugged at writing the *Demand and Price Situation.* He dutifully reported conventional data and made forecasts so vague they could not be proved right or wrong.

Editing the Livestock and Meat Situation. Jim Cavin sensed that his old friend was not really at home doing the Demand and Price Situation. He thoughtfully — mercifully — transferred him to writing the *Livestock and Meat Situation.*

In the life of every human being is there an episode that is exceptionally developmental, that projects into sustained achievement? Is it likely to occur at a particular age, or might it be random as to both the impelling circumstances and the age at which it takes place?

Either Harold Breimyer's genes called for delay in maturity, or the gods of chance willed or so arranged it. In 1948 he was already thirty-four years old but still tentative socially and professionally. His wartime experience had revealed some leadership capacity, but during the first two postwar years he wandered.

Forty years later it is still hard to explain why assuming responsibility for an obscure government publication would light a fuse for personal and professional self-realization. To report once monthly that the nation's cow herd was being expanded, thereby creating a shortfall in animals currently marketed for slaughter and, likewise, a brief and unsustainable price boom, could not be construed as dramatic or even highly impressive. Yet that is what Harold Breimyer did for eleven years. At the end of the period, he had gained standing as one of the nation's best agricultural economists.

The feed and livestock sector of agriculture has long been a splendid exhibit area for the theories of partial equilibrium, and the multiple correlation statistical exercise, that are the economist's stock in trade. Harold Breimyer was steeped in both; he was as comfortably at home with them as he was alien to macroeconomics. Moreover, prognoses of trends in the livestock industry found a large and eager audience. An army of extension economists in the (then) forty-eight states were vigorous purveyors of Breimyer's forecasts. Livestock producers and meat processors everywhere wanted to know what the stars, crystal ball, or economic analysis could reveal.

The new editor of the *Livestock and Meat Situation* publicized the statistic of the percent of consumers' income spent for meat as an index to the steady uptrend in demand during the first two postwar decades. Breimyer charted the cycle in cattle numbers. When he predicted that the nation's cattle herd would expand to 100 million head, he won acclaim for his intrepidity. He wrote many livestock-outlook articles and eventually wrote a major USDA bulletin, *Demand and Prices for Meat: Factors Influencing their Historical Development,* published in 1961.

Meanwhile, he received invitations to reveal his divinations to livestock organizations. The first came from nearby West Virginia. The suddenly-recognized expert prognosticator had no trouble deciding what to say, but he still had his old emotional block about appearing before an audience. How he conquered that is a story in itself, but the telling must await an account of another episode.

A TWO-YEAR HIATUS

Prior to the war Harold Breimyer had been almost lackadaisical about his professional career. He carried out his office duties responsibly but felt no surge of ambition. He did not enroll as a member of the American Farm Economic Association or attend any of its annual meetings.

On returning from naval service, he had done what the navy would call a "turn-one-eight," a complete reversal. He became career-conscious. When he moved into the livestock forecasting assignment, he did so with high emotional intensity. He began to spread his professional wings. He paid his dues to the American Farm Economic Association and started submitting articles to the association's journal.

Meanwhile, he and Rachel had bought their first home, a small brick Cape Cod in Kensington, Maryland. Harold then tried to play the role all members of the preceding generation of his family had played. He attempted to be a craftsman. He constructed a porch, learning how to lay brick, pour concrete, and install electric wiring. Every hour, seven days a week, was filled with productive activity.

He found himself also drawn into roles of church and community service—which, too, carried a high approval rating in both his father's and his mother's family. He was elected to the governing council of Luther Place Memorial Church in Washington, and to an office in the newly formed Parent-Teacher Association in his new community of Kensington.

He retained his naval commission and became executive officer of a reserve unit that met once weekly at the Naval Gun Factory. He decided to pursue a Ph.D. degree. The first step was to enroll in a class in French taught in the graduate school of the U.S. Department of Agriculture. French would be needed for the language examination.

The intensity with which he undertook his new program presented some risk. Then in 1948 came an emotional jolt. Rachel and Harold had wanted a second child. Finally, late in 1947 Rachel could announce that one was on the way. On July 30, 1948, Neal Raymond was born, a beautiful baby. He grew fast—too fast, as events were to prove. At a couple of months, he was diagnosed as having an abdominal blastoma. After weeks in and out of Children's Hospital, he died on December 13.

Harold Breimyer had experienced periods of fatigue, but the illness of his baby kept his energies from flagging for long. In 1949 his difficulties mounted. One day while at his office in the Department of Agriculture, he broke into hysteria. His physician, Thomas Hindman, admitting officer at the Veterans Administration hospital, put his patient through the round of GI and other tests that, then as now, are routine for anyone with an undiagnosed illness. "Ah," Hindman reported, "the laboratory found bacilli for amoebic dysentery." Remembering a dysentery bout he had when the Mt. Olympus was anchored in Manila Bay, Breimyer found the diagnosis credible. The course of treatment was innocuous. After a couple of weeks, he returned to his desk.

But the fatigue reappeared, and once again he collapsed. Hindman was perplexed, as his patient's symptoms did not conform to the pattern of a nervous breakdown. Exploratory abdominal surgery revealed nothing. The only course left, Hindman instructed, was psychiatric counseling. Dr. Klein, whom Breimyer surmised to be Hindman's own psychiatrist, pooh-poohed all concerns other than some difficulty in domestic relationships and a lack of confidence. Go back to work a few hours a day, he advised, and take as many phenobarbital tablets as needed. Finally, after two distressing years, Breimyer assumed full-time work without insecurity. Periods of fatigue, with their limited attention span, recurred but at diminishing frequency. They eventually disappeared.

The two-year episode taught Harold Breimyer something about himself and fully as much about others. He learned that the limitless energy reserves with which youth are blessed come to an end. Thereafter it is necessary to manage the employment of one's resources. The second lesson was really a discovery—that emotional distress is not rare but is commonplace.

Having himself dipped to a low point of discouragement and then regained his equanimity, Harold Breimyer found himself playing a role new to him. He became father confessor to persons going through a trauma similar to his own. Sidney Gubin, a brilliant economist, suddenly found himself in intense emotional distress. Robert Masucci likewise suffered a breakdown; he would enter Breimyer's office plaintively asking, "Tell me again how it all eventually passes over." Masucci's cloud had passed only part-way when, still in his thirties, he succumbed to a massive heart attack.

"WHAT ONE FOOL CAN DO . . ."

For years two livestock producer organizations in West Virginia had invited Charles Burmeister, crusty veteran livestock analyst, to present his forecast of livestock markets. When Burmeister retired, he steered the invitation to the younger Harold Breimyer.

Meetings were held in late April each year at Jackson's Mill State Park, not far from Clarksburg. In some years the mountains would be sun-filled and green. Other times they would be covered with snow, and the heaters in the rude huts would hardly vanquish the chill. The usual practice was for the guru from Washington to present a complete review at an evening session of one organization, then to repeat it in summary form the next day as members of the second producer group assembled.

Harold Breimyer has never been swayed by the born-again-Christian charade of fundamentalist churchmen. Yet, in struggling with his fear of audiences, he went through something akin to born-again conversion. If a "scriptural" passage be chosen for it, it would be an opening line from a book on calculus, *Calculus Made Easy*. The author, Thompson, wrote, "What one fool can do, another can." Breimyer declared himself to be the "another."

Harold Breimyer could readily acknowledge as irrational his fear of audiences. He observed that a lot of other fools were speaking their pieces without emotional blocks. One evening at Jackson's Mill Park, he hesitantly reviewed the livestock outlook, staying close to his prepared text. The next morning, asked to present a digest, he rose to his feet, announced that five factors were framing the prospects, explained what they were, and sat down. Immediately he reflected, "Why, that's not hard." Never again did he shrink before an audience. Before long he was abandoning his written text, speaking casually from notes.

What one fool can do, Harold Breimyer can.

SOURCES OF INCREASING FOOD

As he became secure in his livestock and meat field, Harold Breimyer reached out into other topics. By the middle of the 1950s, he was gaining national status and recognition in agricultural economics. His standing leaped higher when he published an article in the *Journal of Farm Economics,* "Sources of Our Increasing Food Supply," and then received an award as it was judged the best article in that journal for 1954.

A table and a beautifully drawn chart (contribution of the artists of the BAE's chart-making office) showed that of the increase in food consumption since 1910–1914, almost half was attributable to gains in average yield of crops per acre. The two factors next in rank were of about equal importance: (1) the reduction in number of horses and mules, and (2) improvements in efficiency of converting feedstuffs to meat, milk, and eggs. Only a tenth of the gain in total food supply was credited to addition of new cropland acreage. Foreign trade in foodstuffs was neutral, as the export-import balance was the same in 1947–1950 as it had been in 1910–1914.

A second article published in the same journal gave another boost to Breimyer's professional ranking. "On Price Determination and Aggregate Price Theory" appeared in August 1957. It, too, was adjudged the best article of the year. The award told less, though, about the intrinsic quality of the article than about its author's alertness to the trend of events in agriculture at the time. Harold Breimyer always has had a knack of sensing emerging issues, often addressing them in advance of his fellows. Marketing and price making was very much an issue in the 1950s. Harold Breimyer not only joined in examining it from all angles, but he made his distinctive contribution as well. The 1957 award is evidence.

MARKETING AS THE GREAT POSTWAR HOPE

Marketing was one of several landmarks, or decade-marks, of the 1950s. The decade itself, the Eisenhower years, usually has been regarded as drab, unexciting. The good general who became president was seen as a father figure. Except for the marauding by Senator McCarthy, who ruined the reputations of many honorable public servants, the times were tranquil. In agriculture Ezra Taft Benson, Eisenhower's choice for secretary, threw as much cold water on farm programs as he was politically able to do. According to wags of those days, the principal function played by Benson, a devout Mormon, was to offer prayer at the beginning of Cabinet meetings.

If good and evil are the contesting forces in the world, as the ancients believed, Harold Breimyer rephrases them in terms of public versus private interest in the making of economic policy. The marketing research and extension program of the 1950s had as nearly immaculate a conception as can ever be hoped for in this grimy world. In the better-world dreaming at war's end, the idyllic image was that a growing and prosperous, fully-employed population would be provisioned bountifully by a productive agriculture. Consumers, healthier and happier than ever before, would claim the vast output of America's fields and flocks without any need for acreage controls. The dream was incorporated in the Hope-Flannagan Research and Marketing Act of 1946.

In the USDA, under the leadership of Harry Trelogan, Barton De-Loach, Kenneth Ogren, and others, scarcely a marketing pebble was left unturned. National marketing workshops delved into all that was known about marketing services such as information, grades and standards, and development. So much money was made available for marketing extension that, in many states, commodity specialists suddenly found themselves reclassified as marketers and sent to a workshop for training.

BARGAINING IN PRICE DISCOVERY

On entering the marketing field, Harold Breimyer took note of institutions for price discovery. He was convinced, for example, that the posting of non-negotiable prices, as in retailing, is significantly different from arriving at prices in market-clearing auction.

Livestock markets in the 1950s came close to meeting the criteria for perfect competition. As such, they were almost unique. Theories of oligopoly pricing were at least a century old, and those of monopolistic (or imperfect) competition dated from Chamberlin and Robinson in the early 1930s. Harold Breimyer concluded that most of the marketing system for farm products was oligopolistic or monopolistically competitive. He found himself rejecting the many marketing studies done on the premise that the perfectly competitive model is appropriate.

In later years he came to deplore the profusion of mathematical analyses with which younger economists filled scholarly journals, very nearly all of them contingent on a competitive model—perfect—that is to be found almost nowhere in farm-product marketing. He almost turned scornful. The reason so many economists assume competition to be perfect, he scolded, is that otherwise their models would be meaningless. They themselves would be technologically (or ideologically) unemployed.

Pursuing his new conviction about how the marketing system is constituted, Harold Breimyer became fascinated with the bargaining concept. During the 1930s labor unions had demonstrated the potential effectiveness of collective bargaining. In agriculture, West Coast producers of several specialty crops such as cling peaches had formed bargaining associations and shown them to be practicable. During those years Ralph Bunje, the cling peach farmers' bargaining agent, was a popular speaker at conclaves of agricultural economists.

Dairy cooperatives, sheltered by the marketing orders program, had learned to bargain for price premiums. But the most voluble advocate in the 1950s was the new National Farmers Organization. Arising in unchanneled frustration, the NFO searched for a mission until, under the evangelistic leadership of Oren Lee Staley, it turned to collective bargaining.

The NFO had dreams of enlisting enough of the national production of various farm products to be able to bargain effectively with processors. It used so-called holding actions, sometimes violent, both as a bargaining tactic and for publicity. In a holding action for hogs, for example, the NFO would choose a brief period when its members would withhold their animals from the market and would try to keep other farmers from trucking theirs. If the market surged noticeably, the NFO claimed credit. Harold Breimyer, who clocked livestock markets constantly, noted that the organization usually chose a time when a seasonal slowdown in marketings was a normal expectation. NFO leaders wanted the odds to be on their side.

In his article, "On Price Determination and Aggregate Price Theory," Breimyer applied Edgeworth's contract curve to theories of bargaining. He quoted Kenneth Boulding's dictum that imperfect oligopoly, which prevails so widely, "may not allow a position of stable equilibrium" (p.678).

Yet most business firms want "a position of stable equilibrium," with predictable if not predetermined prices. Breimyer had observed that they are more concerned for market-wide stability than for any narrow and temporary price advantage to themselves. Hence the appropriateness of collective bargaining to establish market-wide, fully revealed prices that give all processors a uniform starting pad for their non-price-competition games. Hence, too, the usefulness of the contract curve for interpreting the bargaining process.

DEBATES OVER FIXED VS. FLEXIBLE PRICE SUPPORTS

In farm affairs the 1950s were a tedium of interminable debate about fixed versus flexible price supports, relieved only by the foredoomed Brannan Plan proposal, the imaginative and effective Public Law 480, and the more prosaic Soil Bank.

Harold Breimyer was a close observer of what went on, although his personal contribution was to supply background data. He was part of a corps—essential in government—charged with keeping administrators statistically honest.

One observation he made is that policy issues often are kept alive and debated long after they have lost relevance. Farm leaders, congressmen, and USDA officials have a tendency to beat an issue to death—and then to continue the foray still longer. The postwar issue of fixed versus flexible price support rates was a case in point. During the first two years after World War II, prices of the major field crops were supported at 90 percent of parity (92.5 percent for cotton) under terms of the Steagall Amendment. Following the Steagall period the burning question was whether supports should be "fixed" at 90 percent, or allowed to flex between 60 and 90 percent according to supply conditions.

Caught on the horns of this dispute, Charles Brannan, who followed Clinton Anderson as secretary of agriculture, used a diversionary tactic. He proposed a scheme of direct income-supplement payments that became known as the Brannan Plan. Harold Breimyer made a small contribution to it. Brannan was not able to win congressional support. Not until thirty years afterward would a somewhat similar program be adopted in the 1985 farm law. Proposals for "decoupling" offered in the late 1980s would come even closer to Secretary Brannan's devisals of 1949.

SOIL BANK AND FOOD FOR PEACE

Early in the Eisenhower administration crop surpluses mounted, as Breimyer had predicted. The self-righteous Ezra Taft Benson wrung his hands about the high cost of holding stocks—a million dollars a day—and blamed Congress for farm programs that led to them. Otherwise he could do little. Congress had tied his hands. But there was one exception: He could use a ruse by which to sell Commodity Credit Corporation grain into the market.

Benson discovered that he was allowed to circumvent established release prices and dispose of any stock that was out of condition or in danger of becoming so. Thereafter, whenever the market strengthened even a little, the secretary's legmen found grain that the secretary could declare eligible for sale. After all, grain or other stock in storage is always "about to" lose condition. Except perhaps in an airless Egyptian tomb, any organic material will oxidate and lose quality eventually. Benson's flexible criteria for finding grain to qualify for sale were one of the conversation pieces that circulated through USDA's two buildings when he was secretary: "The corn market is poised to go up, except that Ezra will find some more damaged corn of the world's highest feeding quality." Such was the typical jocularity.

Soil Bank. Congressional drafting of a law is often alleged to be a mockery. Influential lobbyists are said to do most of the work and wield the crucial influence. The Soil Bank law of 1956 was a notable denial of the cynicism. So, in large measure, was the Food for Peace law—Public Law 480.

Harold Breimyer had no hand in either law. The two will be commented on because they were the most innovative steps in farm policy taken during the decade of the 1950s.

When Senator Ellender, chairman of the Committee on Agriculture and Forestry of the Senate, staged a series of field hearings, the call he heard was for a large program of general land retirement. The idea was not new or strange. Carroll Bottum and other economists at Purdue University had advocated retiring land by auctioning leases. Farmers would be invited to bid to leave cropland idle, and the lowest bids would be accepted.

The Soil Bank law called for an acreage reserve in which land previously planted to six major crops would be idled, and, separately, a conservation reserve that would hold land in conserving use for three to ten years. The conservation reserve of 1956 was prototype for the similarly named Conservation Reserve Program established in the Food Security Act of 1985.

The Soil Bank was only partially successful. It came at a time when production technology was advancing fast. As farmers intensified their cultural practices on land remaining in cultivation, aggregate national output showed little effect of the Bank.

Moreover, the bid system brought the largest offerings from marginal cropping areas, where so much land was put in the Soil Bank that local communities were injured seriously. Farm suppliers lost volume of business, and tenants could get no land to farm. Yet the payments were attractive enough that non-farm investors often would buy land for the exclusive objective of putting it in the Soil Bank and collecting the payments.

Public Law 480. P.L. 480, instituting the Food for Peace program, was truly one of the signal developments in farm policy following World War II. It was a case in which grubby selfishness combined with elevated objectives to arrive at a salutary outcome. P.L. 480 has put our commodity surpluses to use in the interest of international diplomacy and meeting human needs, even as it also has helped build up commercial markets.

Although the law had several titles, the principal programs were to sell surplus farm products for a country's own currency, and to make foodstuffs available free—the so-called grants. Two maxims or premises underlay the program. The first was expressed often: When we have so much embarrassing surplus on hand, yet people are starving elsewhere, why not make our food available to them? Second, why not use our stocks for export market development?

The first led to the grant portion of P.L. 480, and to government-to-government sales. In many cases, foodstuffs were delivered without cost to charitable organizations located in foreign areas of poverty and undernourishment. This has long been the least controversial feature of Food for Peace.

The market development idea took two different forms. The premise for the first was that poor countries would become good commercial markets for our products if they could develop their own economic activity. Yet they were strapped for funds for development. Our surplus farm products would be sold at low price, as a sort of capital-in-kind. Moreover, payment would be accepted in a nation's own currency, and much of it then would be reinvested in the country itself. Although the United States hoped long-term benefits would rebound to it, and the sales were attractive to U.S. producers and agribusiness suppliers alike, in other respects the program embodied about as much idealism as ever is to be found in a law.

But market development had a second interpretation. Sale of our products at cut-rate prices for local currency was seen as an entering wedge into the buyers' trade. We could force out competitive exporters or position ourselves to take advantage of the buyers' future economic growth. In either case we would generate a trade pattern that could prove persistent. Optimists promised that P.L. 480 buyers eventually would become commercial buyers.

Our market development by discount pricing generated intense resentment among other exporting countries. To be conciliatory, we purred assurances that we would not use the tactic to displace their traditional shares; we only wanted incremental increases for ourselves, we said. Not surprisingly, our stance was greeted skeptically.

A different criticism, offered by many of our own economists, was that our bargain-basement pricing would be damaging to indigenous producers. How could native farmers produce corn if we made our stocks available at discount price? An instance fitting the thesis, found in Colombia, has been cited repeatedly by P.L. 480's critics.

Another black mark often given P.L. 480 is that the government-to-government portion has led to local fraud. Where that happened persistently, the objective of financing economic development was not carried out.

Harold Breimyer has long defended the Food for Peace program against its harshest critics, even while admitting his regret that so many countries have refused to carry out honestly their end of the government-to-government portion. The program proved to be market-developing. Defenders who say it helped to open markets in countries such as Spain and Taiwan have solid data to back them up.

The humanitarianism of the grant portion is hardly subject to challenge. As to allegations that food grants impede indigenous farm production, the reply is that giving food to people who have no money docs not harm the commercial markets. The government-to-government operations are a different matter; and experiences vary so widely that sweeping denunciations and equally general defenses must be rejected. P.L. 480 experiences differ country by country, and any evaluation must be carried out on a specific-country basis.

The Food for Peace program was invariably plugged in terms of our abundance of food and how we could use it for humanity. By inference, nonfoods were to be excluded. But the question of whether food aid could somehow extend to tobacco and cotton had been resolved during the postwar food relief programs. At a hearing on the Hill (in Congress), USDA Secretary Clinton Anderson pointed out routinely and defensively that tobacco was, of course, excluded from food relief programming because it has no nutritive value. Thereupon Senator Vandenberg of Michigan puffed hard on a long Cuban cigar, blew the smoke, and said, "What do you mean, no nutrition?" Tobacco was quickly named a commodity eligible for exporting. Data for P.L. 480 shipments show entries for tobacco and cotton.

 *A Goulash of Experiences*

THE AMERICAN PENCHANT FOR FORMING ORGANIZATIONS, as reported by de Tocqueville a century and a half ago, finds almost universal expression in support groups for community schools. As a new young parent, Harold Breimyer found himself caught up in the fervor.

During the twentieth century Parent-Teacher Associations proliferated throughout the United States, becoming a potent local political force. In school districts where the board of education is elected, the occasion is presented for all the trappings and maneuvers of the political process. Advocacy and support groups abound.

All this has its *raison d'etre* in the decentralized structure of our public elementary and secondary schools. The Northwest Ordinance of 1787 set the pattern. In what may have been the most enlightened piece of legislation enacted by the Continental Congress, it provided for land grants in support of local schools, yet kept both financial and instructional control in state and local hands.

Also activating citizens' interest in schools is the importance Americans have attached to education. Harold Breimyer has observed many times during his career that, in both tradition and law, we permit freedom of religious belief and worship as a privilege but mandate that schools will be not only available but attended.

It has long been an article of faith that good schooling will yield both private and public benefits. It is the means of uplift for individuals and even whole ethnic groups that lack inherited property or distinguished ancestry. Separately, it is the key to enhanced national productivity — a contributor, in the Adam Smith precept, to the wealth of a nation.

PTAs AND THE SCHOOL BOARD

Harold and Rachel Breimyer's son, who at that time did not resent being called Freddie, first attended the Kensington elementary school. There, pupil and parents were lost among the established families of the town. The next year a new Oakland Terrace school was opened. Before the first pupil was enrolled, a PTA had been formed, with Harold Breimyer as one of the officers.

He found it easy to enter into school affairs. He had been immersed in "club" organizations ever since joining his first 4-H Club. In 4-H and other rural organizations all meetings were conducted according to formal parliamentary rules, and were an exercise in group structure and dynamics.

Remembering his own early instruction, Harold Breimyer has often wondered whether democracy and its processes are more thoroughly grounded in rural people than among the self-proclaimed elites of the cities. Rural leaders of the Jeffersonian tradition can readily believe so.

Two years later Breimyer was invited to be a candidate for PTA president. Having just gone through his "hiatus," he was not sure about his emotional stability and hesitated to accept. He rationalized the question in almost the same terms as had led him to join campus organizations as an undergraduate student at Ohio State. Persons who are shy and uncomfortable in informal social settings can respond well to structured activity. So it was with Harold Breimyer in 1952, and in fact has remained so ever since. He took the PTA office, and did so partly for his own emotional growth.

The year of PTA presidency worked out well. Thereupon Breimyer climbed the PTA ladder, becoming delegate to the Montgomery County Council of PTAs and then legislative chairman for that organization. In 1958 he decided to try for a higher post; he announced his candidacy for the county's Board of Education. He did so without any political base of support other than his prominence in the county PTA activities.

The school board election took place only a year following an event in distant, alien Russia that already was shaking up educational philosophies in our country: the successful launching of Sputnik I.

Americans were aghast. Those crude, atheistic Russians had put a satellite into space before we did. What a blow to our national pride!

Only the wisest of thinkers could sense that the experience would be the first of many to follow. Few Americans could suppose that our world primacy in science and invention, unchallenged in the first postwar years, was about to be abrogated.

Instead we asked how Russia could get ahead of us. What was at fault? Citizens stampeded to accuse our educational system, the schools. In their dereliction lay the cause for our nation's dropping behind in the international scientific derby. Such was the refrain.

In 1958 it could hardly be anticipated that almost thirty years later, following the Challenger disaster, the same accusation would be heard once more.

Harold Breimyer took the newly expressed public sentiment seriously—too seriously, as matters turned out. He regarded schools as encrusted with tradition. He questioned the invariable, inflexible curriculum and locked-in instructional techniques. "Standardized instruction for non-standard pupils," was the essence of his criticism. Montgomery's Superintendent of Schools C. Taylor Whittier was sympathetic. A one-time soccer star, Whittier introduced in a few venturesome schools the ungraded primary. And he moved toward more differentiation of course offerings.

Harold Breimyer's political career ended quickly; he was defeated in his bid for reelection. He should not have been surprised, as he is not endowed with the politician's peculiar talents. He is incapable of the hail-fellow-well-met pose and not skillful in remembering and recognizing individuals. He was and is an idea man, not a gregarious gladhander.

Nevertheless, he contributed to updating Montgomery County's school system. And apart from the experience of being "diselected," as his friend Tom Street put it, he made two discoveries. One was about himself, and it was reassuring. The other, naturally, was about others, and it was to prove negative, discouraging.

Harold Breimyer met the moral test of not giving way to political pressure. The most contentious issue in Maryland schools in the later 1950s was desegregation. The 1954 Brown decision of the U.S. Supreme Court had mandated an end to racially segregated schools. Maryland is south of the Mason-Dixon line, and its schools had long been segregated. Even though Montgomery County had only a few pockets of blacks (still called Negroes at the time) and the majority of its citizens were liberal and progressive, in many of the rural sections integration was resisted fiercely.

Following the *Brown* decision Harold Breimyer endorsed moving to desegregate step by step, to ease the transition. Within the county PTA Council he found himself locked in debate with flaming liberals including Paul Howard, with whom he would later serve on the Board of Education. The parlor liberals wanted to force desegregation down throats instantly. As events later worked out, owing in large measure to the good sense of Taylor Whittier, Breimyer's philosophy prevailed.

But Breimyer was on the losing side in one fight. A black junior high school in Rockville was scheduled for integration. A band of local white parents objected in strongest terms. They did not want to send their children to a school that had always been known as the blacks' (or niggers') school. So they mounted a vicious political campaign to force the school board to convert the old building into an administrative building, and to build a new junior high school.

Their scheme carried a cost of a half-million dollars. When the final Board vote was taken, Paul Howard and the other liberals gave way to the pressure; they lacked the moral courage to stand up to it. Only Rose Kramer, a stalwart lady, and Harold Breimyer voted "no." A half-million dollars was spent as a concession to prejudice.

A lesson learned was to be wary of the type of liberal intellectual as encountered in the school affairs of Montgomery County, Maryland. Persons of that temper can give drawing-room endorsement to all liberal causes but cannot be trusted to stay stalwart under fire.

A TRIP TO RUSSIA

World War II forced the United States to be international, in both outlook and conduct. One avenue of international activity that drew agricultural economists into participation was international economic development, with a specific focus on agriculture.

The highly successful Marshall Plan set the tone. President Truman declared international technical aid as Point Four. Later, the designated office in the Department of State carried various names until Agency for International Development (AID) was settled on.

Harold Breimyer's immersion into international waters had a different origin. In 1953 death mercifully removed Joseph Stalin from the Soviet Union's and the world's scene. After a series of maneuvers that would chill the spine of even a mystery-novel devotee, Nikita Khrushchev became First Secretary of the Communist Party and, as such, the Soviet Union's leader.

Khrushchev rapidly reversed many of Stalin's policies. He was oriented toward agriculture, and he gained wide publicity for opening up 70 million acres of virgin lands in semi-arid Asia. The U.S. press gave him a lot of lineage after he visited the Garst farm in Iowa and began to promote growing Iowa corn in the USSR. Unfortunately for him, most of the Soviet Union is a far cry climatologically from Iowa.

The thaw in the cold war was on. One form it took was an exchange of technical delegations between the USSR and the United States. In 1958 Harold Breimyer, as a livestock economist, was asked if he would like to be a member of an agricultural economics delegation.

The upshot was that at the end of June, he traveled as a member of a six-man team that was booked to fly to Moscow, join Soviet counterparts, and tour the more important agricultural areas of the Soviet Union. The team leader was Sherman Johnson, whom Harold Breimyer respected and even revered. Other members were John ("Wally") Kirkbride, a statistician; Carl Heisig, a production economist; Lazar Volin, Russian-born Soviet specialist in the Foreign Agricultural Service; and Harold Wingo, a professional photographer. They were met and hosted in Moscow by Alexander Tulupnikov, who had been stationed in Washington during the war to negotiate food procurement. He did not join the Americans in the tour, however. The two principal Soviet economists on the tour were G. G. Kotov, Deputy Director of the All-Union Research Institute of Agricultural Economics in Moscow, and Oleg Nichiparov. A journalist, I. Belousov, accompanied the economists, as did a superb interpreter named Yakovlev.

The four weeks' experience was barely endurable, but definitely unforgettable. Soviet agriculture had been forced into collectivization, at enormous human cost. It consisted in 1958, as it has since, of huge collective farms, even larger state farms, and millions of private plots on which the farm workers raised fresh produce and kept a few head of livestock.

The regions the delegation visited divided into the dry steppes of Asia suitable only for wheat; the cold north in which crop production was marginal at best (even potatoes had to be sprouted in greenhouses before planting, because of the short growing season); the Kuban of the south that alone resembled the U.S. Corn Belt; the attractive humid areas near the Black Sea, including the Crimea, that were suitable for fruits, vegetables, and tea; and the irrigated areas of central Asia, where the culture was Moslem with touches of the oriental. The United States delegation diplomatically abstained from preaching to the Russian hosts about the flaws visible in Soviet agriculture. But team members offered suggestions timidly that wheat in the new lands of Khazakstan requires alternate fallow years, and that only a few areas have growing seasons long enough for corn.

When the delegation left the USSR, its members remained unsure whether the nation's inability to provide a good diet for her people is attributable to natural or to man-made phenomena. Our home-grown Russia-bashers insist the Soviet system is at fault. Trying to model agriculture there (except for peasant plots) on the pattern of industry is a formula for failure, in the minds of that school of critics. But Sherman Johnson and his entourage were impressed by the limitations of soil and especially of climate, in a semi-arid nation located at the latitude of central and northern Canada.

Not long after his Russian tour Harold Breimyer became interested in the structural organization of U.S. agriculture. He found more than a little irony in conservative stances that the emerging large-scale industrialization of our agriculture is in the interest of efficiency but that the Soviets' insistence on their version of corporate farming is their undoing.

Farm Dinners. At each farm the delegation visited the sequence was the same. The tour group would be conducted to the farm's headquarters, an office unit that had the trappings of the head office of a U.S. corporation. In a conference room everyone would sit at a long, narrow table covered with the green cloth of a U.S. billiard table. Tea and chocolate bonbons would be served. The head man or his spokesman would explain in boring detail the organization of the farm and its accomplishments. The American guests would ask questions that mixed their genuine inquisitiveness with the requirements of protocol. When the conference concluded, the guests were invited, in the best rural tradition, to stay for dinner.

The dinner resembled not so much a U.S. farm-family dinner as a hospitality party of a corporation—of which, in fact, it was the Russian version. The table invariably was loaded with *hors d'oeuvres* that included, in addition to seasonal fruits, several cheeses and one or both caviars. Even more prominent were libations that ranged from bottled water and soft drinks to wine, cognac, and the omnipresent vodka. The dinner was garrulously ceremonial, lasted two or more hours, and was punctuated by joke telling and a series of toasts.

Abstemious and unpracticed at after-dinner repartee, Harold Breimyer nevertheless rose to the occasion and developed more than a little skill in composing his toasts. One theme he used drew on a U.S. observation that he had clipped and pasted in his scrapbook. "I can never travel from Omaha to Chicago," the author wrote, "without reflecting on what can be done with all this farm productivity." Then came the balancing phrase, "I can never travel from Chicago to New York without wondering how all the people can get enough to eat." It was easy to convert Chicago-to-New York to Leningrad-to-Moscow, and the midwestern leg to whatever rural area was being visited.

Reflections and Impressions. In 1958 the Soviet Union seemed to most Americans to be a primitive land of mystery and intrigue. The Johnson party was not prepared for the openness and the considerate hospitality experienced. Nonetheless, the Soviet political system was in evidence. At every farm visit an agent of the Communist party monitored what went on. Usually he was inconspicuous. Once in a while, though, the man assigned to watch the Americans thought himself versed well enough to join in the review of what the local farm was doing. He apparently wanted to show that he wasn't just a Party eye, but possessed of a brain.

On its arrival in Moscow, the Johnson group was lodged in the Moscow Hotel. That darkly repelling hostelry, of century-old brown decor and ponderous leather sofas, probably was chosen because it was suitably bugged. The innocent Americans gave no thought to the likelihood that everything they said was being listened to via modern electronics. Before they left Washington the five economists had been briefed by the CIA. They also were asked to solicit a bookful of statistical data that the CIA lacked. Sherman Johnson, a literal-minded Swede who was too honest to be devious or adroit, pursued the statistical quest to the predictable outcome — no success. The response at Gosplan, the Soviet's planning agency, is remembered: "If we can have more of these exchanges, it may become possible for us to give you the data."

Tiring of the futile begging for data, Harold Breimyer exploded to his companions one evening in a Moscow Hotel room: "Let's stop wasting time trying to get data. I'm not here as an agent of the CIA." Sherman Johnson accepted the suggestion. Thereafter the group was received more cordially than before, and Harold Breimyer noted that he seemed to be singled out for especially warm hospitality. Only much later did the likely reason occur to him. The interlopers in the hotel conversation knew how to identify the voices and recognized the one calling for an end to servicing the Central Intelligence Agency.

As one feature of the hospitality shown it, the U.S. exchange delegation was shielded against anti-American demonstrations. During the time of the tour, President Eisenhower sent Marines into Lebanon, whereupon the USSR burst into a blaze of indignation. Johnson, Breimyer, and company were kept under cover for a weekend. The tour then was resumed, without incident.

At two or three farms political demonstrations were staged. They were restrained, inoffensive. The message there, and indeed in all political conversation during the month in the USSR, was invariable. It was a plea for peace: "Miry-Mir" — Peace to the World. The pitch was political, yet the U.S. visitors were certain that the Russians and other Soviet peoples fervently hoped and even, perhaps, prayed that political rivalries will not once again immerse the Western world in armed conflict. The Soviet Union's dead in World War II, uncounted, are variously estimated at between ten and twenty million. Memories were poignant in 1958. One wonders if they have dimmed since. Probably not.

Another impression related to the character of the Soviet peoples. Most of the visits were with Russians, who proved to be the opposite of the stereotypes that had been publicized in the United States. Instead of the dour, stolid, stiffly formal mien that Breimyer called the "Molotov image," the Russians exhibited a garrulousness and an aptitude for banter that appealed to the American visitors.

The Russians also could be abrasive at times. The most cultured individuals who were met during the month-long odyssey were not they but, rather, the Uzbeks of Tashkent. The contrast should not have surprised the Americans. Russia ranks as a latecomer among modern nations; only the Bolsheviks settled and tamed the roaming tribes of Kazakhstan. The Uzbek civilization, located at the crossroads of the ancient world, is dated in millennia.

An impression received in the 1958 tour that was disturbing then and is disquieting even now is the deification of Lenin. Lenin's instrumental role in establishing the Soviet government is not disputed. But it appeared to Harold Breimyer that a not-so-subtle campaign was underway to convert him to a secular saint. And if Lenin were the equivalent of the deity of Christians or Moslems, Karl Marx was his apostle. The Lenin visage was seen everywhere the American group traveled. Often a portrait or bust of Marx was next to it. Stalin, though dead five years and discredited by Khrushchev, was still on view at some farms. At others, farm or Party officials were willing to bet on Khrushchev, putting his photograph alongside Lenin's on meeting-room walls.

The first-ranking "religious rite" in 1958 was to view the bodies of Lenin and Stalin in their crypt on Red Square in Moscow. Breimyer and his companions did so. They were fortunate in this unique experience, as the body of Stalin was removed soon afterward. Believers in the Communist orthodoxy now can pause to reflect at the glass-enclosed display only of Lenin. The Soviets have been converted to secular monotheism.

Religious practice has never been forbidden in the USSR, but it has been restricted tightly. The potential threat lies not in Christianity but instead in Islam. Muslim peoples, located in republics that were forced into union with the dominant Russians, have long been restive. Breimyer concluded in 1958 that they could pose the strongest threat to the liberalization that, in the later 1980s, Gorbachev was trying to bring about.

PRESTIGE WITHOUT PRODUCTIVITY: THE CEA YEARS

In the fall of 1959, Harold Breimyer made a major career change. He moved from the Department of Agriculture to the CEA (Council of Economic Advisers) in the Executive Office of the President. The Executive Office tag carried prestige. Those two years of residency were highly educational, years well spent. They also were without tangible product other than a few papers and journal articles.

The position as economist for agriculture on the Council staff was falsely prestigious and also misconstrued politically. It was a civil service position, nonpolitical. But it was regarded popularly as a patronage plum. During his years on the Eisenhower Council, Breimyer was labeled a Republican. Remaining for several months after John Kennedy became President, he was taken to be a Democrat. No political hermaphrodite, he was Democratic in allegiance throughout — and has remained so since.

Members of the Eisenhower Council were the chairman, Raymond ("Steve") Saulnier, Henry Wallich, and Karl Brandt. Saulnier was ultraconservative. His only instruction to Breimyer during eighteen months was that he as chairman be notified if the Food Stamp Program seemed to be moving forward. Saulnier wanted to set up a roadblock. The program did indeed move ahead, but not until Kennedy had replaced Eisenhower as President and Saulnier had departed.

Wallich and Brandt had in common their German lineage. Wallich was the more talented and less philosophically entrenched of the two. He wrote a thoughtful book, *The Cost of Freedom,* published in 1960, which allegedly was intended to facilitate the Nixon candidacy for president, not to mention enhancement of Wallich's position in the event of a Nixon success.

Harold Breimyer has always felt sorry for the Wallichs of this world, of whom there are more than a few. Keenly astute and affectively humanitarian, they are sentimentally conservative yet functionally liberal. For them the imbalance is stressful.

The best epigrammatic line in Wallich's book is, "The ultimate value of a free economy is not production, but freedom, and freedom comes not at a profit, but a cost" (pp.ix, x).

After Kennedy was elected, Wallich became a columnist for *Newsweek* magazine. Whenever he needed current data on the state of economic affairs in agriculture, he telephoned Breimyer. Later he served with distinction on the Federal Reserve Board until ill health overtook him.

Karl Brandt, a giant of a man physically, had been an up-and-coming agricultural economist in Germany in the 1920s and early 1930s. Appalled by the Nazi menace, he fled to the United States. After several years with the New School for Social Research, he joined the Food Research Institute at Stanford University. As Council member agriculture was his bailiwick. Possessed of all the attributes of a gentleman-scholar, he was a locked-in political conservative and essentially ineffective as a Council member. Harold Breimyer kept him informed on happenings in agriculture and cautioned him repeatedly, and usually successfully, against taking positions farther to the right than his president's. Otherwise, his assistant used the eighteen months of their association primarily for his own self-improvement.

When President Kennedy named Walter Heller as chairman of the Council, everything changed. Heller and James Tobin were pure blooded Keynesian macroeconomists, and Kermit Gordon was only a little less steeped in the doctrine. Heller and company set out to stimulate the economy via a reduction in income tax rates. They finally got first the ear and then the go-ahead of Kennedy, who was impatient with all economic thinking except that of his friend John Kenneth Galbraith. The tax cuts performed about as anticipated. Harold Breimyer, an agnostic about fine-tuning the economy, still thinks Heller and his crew were luckier than they were astute.

In 1981, when President Reagan's advisers proposed an even sharper tax reduction, they cited the Kennedy-Heller operation as supporting evidence. Heller and Tobin (Gordon had died) shouted their denials. One big difference was that the Economic Recovery Tax Act of 1981 created a host of huge tax shelters. It was redistributional. The Kennedy-Heller scheme primarily reduced rates.

Heller, Tobin, and Gordon knew little about agriculture and cared less. Willard Cochrane, top economist for new USDA Secretary Orville Freeman, sent Walter Wilcox as his emissary to Heller to negotiate with him a hands-off-agriculture agreement. Heller was all too happy to assent. Harold Breimyer continued to supply his chief with memoranda keeping him up to date on what was going on. These were filed unread. He was surprised that Heller did not suggest politely that he look for a congenial spot elsewhere. Breimyer took refuge in a two-months' assignment in Argentina. Not wanting to wither on a bureaucratic vine, he was receptive to an invitation from his old friend Robert Tetro to join him in the Foreign Agricultural Service. He went another route, and how it happened is worth relating as an example of how a bureaucracy often works.

Every agency in government has elaborately formal recruiting procedures. But when Harold's son Fred mentioned to his Sunday School teacher, Henry Herrell, that his father was considering going back to the Department of Agriculture, Henry forgot the story of Joshua or whatever was the topic for the day. "Oh, is that so?" he replied. Herrell was assistant administrator for management of the Agricultural Marketing Service. Within days the administrator, Sylvester ("Si") Smith, asked Harold Breimyer to interview with him for his staff economist position. Breimyer interviewed, was hired, and soon began a five-year stint with AMS that was in some respects the most interesting and rewarding half-decade of all his career. Recruitment came by way of a chance remark in a Sunday School class.

Within weeks after the emigre had left the Council of Economic Advisers, President Kennedy tripped his fiscal feet over the big budget that Secretary Freeman had submitted for agriculture. He turned to Walter Heller. "What do you people say about this?" he asked. Heller replied meekly that he had not given thought to agriculture and did not have an agricultural man on his staff. "Get one," the president ordered. Very quickly the capable Dale Hathaway was brought in from Michigan State University. Meanwhile Don Horton, Harold Breimyer's counterpart and friend in the next-door Budget Bureau, taunted, "You had the best policy economist in the country, and you let him get away." Never since has the agricultural spot on the Council staff been left vacant.

THE THREE ECONOMIES OF AGRICULTURE

The Argentine experience will be touched on in a later chapter. Not postponable, though, is a note on what may have been Harold Breimyer's crowning lifetime success in his economic writing. It is his article published in the *Journal of Farm Economics* in August 1962, "The Three Economies of Agriculture." It was judged the best article published in the Journal that year. The acclaim it brought its author is illustrated by a 1985 incident in Spain. While attending a conference in Malaga (of the International Association of Agricultural Economists), Harold Breimyer made the chance acquaintance of a Spanish professor whose English was minimally adequate. He said, when introduced, "Oh, Professor Breimyer, you wrote 'The Three Economies of Agriculture.'" Breimyer was pleased to be so identified.

The theme of the article was the difference in economic structure between the crop and livestock portions of agriculture and, further, between those and the marketing sector. Classical agricultural economics has related to the first of the three, the "enterprise of producing primary products from the unique resource, the soil" (p. 680). The marketing sector, by contrast, is industrial in character. The livestock sector is intermediate. All three economies have moved along a path toward industrialization, but the impact is "most telling upon the first, primary-product, economy of agriculture, converting it to a natural resource-industrial composite and removing it farther from the other two economies" (p. 685).

One lesson the author drew is that governmental acreage-reduction and price-support programs essentially conform to the industrial model. They are not agrarian.

"Three Economies" and the two other award-winning articles that preceded it established their author's reputation. Further, they identified him permanently as of the institutional school. Ever since, Harold Breimyer has been an economist of the structural make-up of the economy, and especially of its agriculture. He has let others engage in microscopic analysis of the economics of the firm, and, at the other extreme, in macro-modeling. Each to his own niche; while occupying his undemanding desk at the Council of Economic Advisers, Harold Breimyer found his.

CHAPTER 14

Brainstorming Marketing Services to Agriculture

IN THE FALL OF 1961, Harold Breimyer returned to the Department of Agriculture with a status enhanced by his two contemplative years with the Council of Economic Advisers. He was staff economist to the administrator of the Agricultural Marketing Service, S. R. Smith. He remained with the AMS five years, although during the school year 1963–64 he was absent on leave as visiting professor at the University of Illinois.

The years in AMS turned out to be gratifying. The agency, well-led, was vibrant with a sense of mission. Conventional marketing services were being performed capably. Food programs were newly in the limelight; commodity foods were being distributed, and the postwar Food Stamp Program was getting under way.

Breimyer found himself offering counsel on how the marketing system for farm products might be improved, and he also was a pamphleteer for the AMS's regulatory and service functions. Those activities, he said repeatedly, helped make the marketing system for farm products work more smoothly.

S. R. SMITH

The AMS administrator in the early 1960s, Sylvester R. ("Si") Smith, was a doughty veteran who had moved from California to the USDA at the beginning of the New Deal. For many years he directed programs for special crops; he became the resident expert on marketing agreements and orders, working especially with fruits and vegetables. He then moved up to be administrator of the agency.

His ·associate administrator, the affable Roy Lennartson, called Smith "Scrappy." The *nom de plume* fit. Resolute and incorruptible, Smith guided the marketing programs with a firm if considerate and talented hand. He was almost a chain smoker of cigarettes. He also had to fight alcoholism. His career ended, in fact, in the later 1960s when Secretary Orville Freeman came upon an intoxicated Smith at a field conference. Smith's indulgences doubtless contributed to his death at age 70.

MARKET STRUCTURE

It seemed incongruous at the time, and still does, that two contrasting personalities should professionally dovetail so smoothly. Key to the mystery is a term already referred to several times in these memoirs: "institutional economics." Both Smith and Breimyer were institutionalists. Smith had always been receptive to thinking about market structure; and of all marketing economists of the day, Breimyer was near the top among the structuralists. "How is the *system* constructed, put together?" both Smith and his economist would ask. "Form guides function," was the adage in the minds of both men.

Obviously, neither man was a *laisser faire* economist. It was not that either rejected the image of a self-regulating market system. On the contrary, both saw it as the ideal. But they also perceived how heroic it is, how vulnerable to any structural defects, and how dependent on a supporting institutional structure. An Agricultural Marketing Service was an essential part of that structure.

Likewise, neither Si Smith nor his chief economist subscribed to Adam Smith's "invisible hand" thesis — "theology," they would call it. They were sure the economy was run by highly visible human hands, which are not only greedy (as Adam Smith acknowledged — he referred to "vices") but ignorant and ofttimes devious as well. It would run well or badly depending on how it was structured.

Si Smith and Harold Breimyer truly believed the Agricultural Marketing Service had an obligation to monitor the structure — the system — of markets for farm products. Smith and Breimyer were dedicated to the already traditional marketing services such as market information (market news and other statistical services), grade standards and grading, sanitary inspection, and so on. Breimyer used his writing skills to assure the thousands of AMS staff members that their seemingly routine daily efforts were essential to operation of the magnificent system of markets in our country. Their place in the marketing system was equivalent to the jewels in a gold watch. The market news people, inspectors, and others were delighted with the notion, and even inspired by it. Breimyer helped build *esprit de corps;* and his doing that may alone have earned much of the support he got from his boss Si.

He never knew whether he had much direct influence on AMS administrative decisions. One instance, though, let him believe that his teaching, preaching, and advising had some tangible effect. During his year at the University of Illinois, he studied the broiler industry. When he returned to Washington, he found the poultry market news people still publishing a price of live broilers. It was a fiction. Virtually all broilers were delivered under contract, and any statistics on price were little more than bookkeeping entries. The market news chief, the capable Harry Rust, knew how flimsy were the price quotations. Only a little nudge from the agency's economist was necessary to bring about a policy change. Reporting of live broiler prices was discontinued.

NATIONAL COMMISSION ON FOOD MARKETING

Si Smith was convinced that the structure of markets for farm products was changing; that more power was being established past the farm; and that farmers would have to accept more joint action to protect their interests. He also regretted that marketing issues were not recognized and respected adequately. Year after year he plugged for a major attention-getting study by a blue-ribbon commission. The commission-study technique was in vogue at the time. Just as the food marketing commission idea was beginning to catch on, George Mehren, brilliant, irrepressible, and politically amoral, came to the USDA from the University of California as assistant secretary. He picked up the marketing commission idea and thereafter claimed almost exclusive credit when Congress acted favorably on it.

The commission that eventually was appointed had a balanced membership. One of the members, Elmer Kiehl, dean of agriculture at the University of Missouri, was instrumental in bringing the astute George Brandow from Pennsylvania State University as its executive director.

Harold Breimyer did not join the commission staff but worked with various of its economists. He was, and remains, strongly supportive of the studies that were published, and he was pleased with the commission's final report and recommendations. A majority of the members signed a report that could be termed activist, calling as it did for farmers and their organizations to develop more clout in marketing.

He was equally dismayed by the negative reception a great many agricultural economists gave it. At the 1966 annual meeting of the American Farm Economic Association, the commission's work was panned roundly. Aghast, Breimyer reflected that only a small contingent of agricultural economists understands institutional economics. Most are so indoctrinated in the neat principles of perfect competition, and so uncomfortable outside it, that they suppose it to prevail everywhere. In the language that Harold Breimyer learned as a farm boy, they wear blinders that keep them from seeing anything else.

FOOD PROGRAMS

Throughout the 1960s, food programs were on a crescendo. When John Kennedy as presidential candidate spent time and his father's money to wrest West Virginia's nominating vote from the more liberal Hubert Humphrey, he promised, if elected, to respond to the state's foremost wish. He would make food distribution programs more generous.

He was true to his word. His first executive order as president was to instruct that a better quality of food be made available to low-income families. At about the same time Congresswoman Leonor Sullivan of St. Louis, who was later to be a member of the Food Commission, introduced legislation to reestablish food stamps as pilot programs. Mrs. Sullivan intended the stamps not as poverty relief but, rather, as a way to enhance the diets of the working poor. A family would buy a basic quantity of stamps and would receive additional ones as bonus.

Meanwhile, the CBS broadcasting network was putting into living rooms, via the TV screen, pictures of families subsisting on spare, minimum diets. Those pictures helped create receptivity for the programs.

During the 1960s food stamps gradually replaced commodity food distribution. Later they were converted from a supplemental bonus to straight giveaway. Mrs. Sullivan, a devout Roman Catholic, was disappointed. She told Harold Breimyer that she didn't like what "*they* are doing to *my* program."

A YEAR AT ILLINOIS: INDIVIDUAL FREEDOM . . .

Early in 1963 George Brinegar, a professor of agricultural economics at the University of Illinois, asked Breimyer if he would consider
spending the next year on the Illinois campus, conducting a study funded
by the Eli Lilly Foundation. It would be the agricultural portion of a set
of studies relating to the principle of individual freedom in economic
affairs.

The invitation was attractive. The topic appealed to the institutional
economist, who had as much interest in political philosophy as in economics. Moreover, he had considered moving from government to a
university teaching post. Glenn ("Swede") Hedlund had tried to lure him
to Cornell. A couple of other department chairmen had inquired as to
his possible interest and availability. Breimyer's Ph.D. degree, acquired
in 1960, was paying off; those three letters added immensely to his
marketability. A year at the University of Illinois would make it easier to
decide whether to remain in government or to move into university
teaching.

THE INSTITUTIONAL STRUCTURE OF AGRICULTURE

As AMS economist Breimyer had written about market structure.
He was equally interested in the organizational (institutional) structure
of agriculture. Who will own the land? Who will farm it, and under
what terms? Ever since the days of colonization, yeoman farming had
been extolled; it was seen as a release from Europe's feudalism. The
family farm became a symbol, even an icon.

But trends under way, and threatened for the future, were trans-
forming the traditional system. What is at stake? What policy choices
are poised for the future? These were questions Harold Breimyer was to
address the next twenty-five years.

A Book on Freedom and Economic Organization. The year at Illinois
produced a book, *Individual Freedom and the Economic Organization of Agriculture,* published in 1965. Its opening chapters introduce
the book's subject and orient the reader; they review the origins of rural
institutions and include a note on the meaning of freedom. Later, three
case studies are reported: on vertical integration in broilers, on marketing agreements and orders, and on land rental and retirement. Of the

three, only the first will be commented on here.

The broiler study is the most original of the three topics. By the time of the early sixties, individual farmers no longer produced broilers for market sale, as Harold Breimyer had done in 1930 to earn money for college. Large integrating firms had crowded out all but a handful of independent poultrymen. They entered into contracts with farmers, who were called "growers"; or they produced the broilers in their own houses, employing hired workers.

Integration in broilers often was regarded as the first step in total industrialization of agriculture. As such, it was variously welcomed or feared. Harold Breimyer may have been the first economist to look into broiler integration from a vantage point other than corporate headquarters or a university library. He drove to two major broiler producing areas—the Delaware-Maryland-Virginia peninsula (Del-Mar-Va) and the Gainesville area of Georgia. In each place he guided his car along a back road until he spotted a broiler house. If he could find the farmer-grower, he visited with him. Later he interviewed officials of integrating firms, including D. W. Brooks, general manager of the Cotton Producers Association. The CPA, later renamed GoldKist, was a farmers' cooperative located in Atlanta.

The contractual system was similar in the two areas. The integrating firm, which often was a feed company, offered individual farmers a contract by which the farmer would provide housing and labor. The integrator would supply everything else including operating instructions. The farmer-grower would receive chicks on a specified date, feed them the firm's feed as specified, and make them available for trucking to the slaughter plant, again on the date the firm named. The farmer-grower would be paid a preset rate per pound of gain, corrected for feed efficiency.

Del-Mar-Va was the older and better established of the two broiler areas, and the farmer-growers interviewed were better educated and more politically alert. They welcomed the chance to earn income but resented the system that denied them managerial control and social status. One capable, alert Delaware farmer-grower blurted, "They say we are serfs, but I don't think we are." To Breimyer the significance of that remark lay not in the man's defiance of serfdom status but, instead, his awareness of the issue and even his knowing the word. "Serf" is not in the vocabulary of a typical U.S. farmer.

Aside from loss of control and their own status, the most general complaints heard from farmer-growers in Del-Mar-Va were the high cost of housing and a fear of becoming locked into producing for a single firm with no option of shifting to a different one. Most farmer-growers had to borrow money to build the costly facility; and matters were made worse, Breimyer was told, as each year the integrator demanded some new alteration to the house or new piece of equipment. So the person raising the birds was kept perpetually in debt — vassalized.

Initially, a number of feed-mills went into contracting and provided some degree of competitiveness. Farmer-growers believed they had a chance to negotiate. As the mills merged and became fewer, however, competition among them waned. Moreover, it was alleged that they refused to compete, or to sign a farmer-grower who had previously been a contractee for a different firm. Of course, the allegations were impossible to prove or disprove.

In Georgia, some of the farmer-growers had been cotton farmers. They were less vocal than the Del-Mar-Va people, although they joined in a regret that one man put in these words: "I'm just a nursemaid. All I have to do is stay home. The equipment does most of the work."

In principle, disaffected broiler growers were candidates for group defensive action. In the early 1960s several organizations including the United States Poultry and Egg Producers Association were trying to enlist broiler growers for collective bargaining. The American Farm Bureau Federation dallied with entering the fray. The bargaining threat came to naught. Integrators' ability to cancel contracts without advance notice gave them a whip hand.

The Farm Bureau might have been strong enough to defend its members against even the big integrators. But the Bureau president in one of the southern broiler-growing states proved to be himself not a grower but an integrator. He stopped the Bureau's timid venture into organizing broiler growers.

FARM POLICY IN THE 1960S; DIRECT-PAYMENT VOLUNTEERISM

Programs for acreage reduction and price support did not generate as much turbulence in the 1960s as they had done in the 1950s, yet they moved in a dramatic new direction. They were converted to voluntary sign-up for acreage reduction. Also, price-support rates were kept conservative as direct compensatory payments to producers, after a long hiatus, were re-legitimized. The option by which producers of a commodity could impose mandatory acreage allotments upon themselves eventually was abandoned for all crops except some types of tobacco.

As happens so often, abstract principle and happenstance events combined to set policy on a new path. Economists had contended for years that the high price supports that gave a temporary boost to farmers' incomes would shrink markets in the long run. The demand curve would be shifted to the left. They said that if a public component to farmers' incomes were necessary, it would be better, from a longer point of view, just to pay out Treasury money. Better to do that than to jeopardize markets via high commodity price supports.

Only when cotton people saw their markets disappear before the inroads of artificial fibers and watched cotton production expand abroad did anyone take the economists seriously. Yet, resistance to direct payments was deeply ingrained. Traditional groups such as the Farm Bureau said the only moral source of income is the price received for a commodity; to accept a Treasury income check is immoral. They added the more practical warning that compensatory payments always will be subject to undependable annual appropriations. In that respect, payments differ from commodity loans, which come from a trust fund. Payments would be vulnerable to whims of the Budget Bureau and Congress.

Arthur Ellender of Louisiana, chairman of the Senate Committee on Agriculture and Forestry (Nutrition had not yet been added to the title), declared his over-my-dead-body opposition. Some clever fellow then devised a scheme for paying participating farmers not in Treasury cash but instead in Commodity Credit Corporation commodities, and purred to the good senator, "We don't propose to give farmers any of the Treasury's money. We only want to turn back to them some of their grain and cotton." The senator relented. Payment-in-kind was reborn.

As might have been anticipated, shipping grain or the white fiber to the farmer proved clumsy, making it necessary for him to convert it to dollars. Before long, it was arranged that the CCC would sell the commodity and send the farmer the money received. The obvious next step was to contract to pay participating farmers in dollars in the first place.

But the subtle scheming against Senator Ellender is only half the story. Willard Cochrane, as Secretary Freeman's chief economist, came to Washington convinced that tight production controls were the only way to go. He especially favored them for a commodity such as wheat, for which the demand curve is inelastic. Also, most consumers of wheat, worldwide, do not shift readily to other cereal grains. Thus, the demand curve is not as shiftable as that for cotton. Cochrane and his Secretary-boss were spurred further by President Kennedy's opposition to big budgets for farm programs. They pressed for tight mandatory acreage reduction for wheat.

The campaign prior to the wheat farmers' vote was noisy and heated. The American Farm Bureau Federation led the fight against the

Cochrane-Freeman program. Charles Shuman promised wheat farmers, "Vote it down, and we'll get you something better." They voted it down. Shuman was as good as his word. He got farmers something better. He got direct payments in a voluntary program. For that to happen, two persons had to choke as they swallowed their previous stands. One was Shuman himself. He had warned of the sins of direct payments. Yet he actually became instrumental in converting programs to a payment form. President Kennedy, even as President Reagan more than twenty years later, also gagged as he found that he had to accept a rising cost of farm programs.

Even so, the direct payment feature of the programs of the 1960s was of small magnitude and carried a modest cost. Not until the payment-in-kind debacle of 1983 did the cost of price and income supports reach double-digit figures (in billions of dollars). And only with enactment of the Food Security Act of 1985 did direct payments, by that time called "deficiency" rather than "compensatory," become so firmly established as to erase cleanly from the blackboard the many aversions and apprehensions expressed in the first twenty postwar years.

FOREIGN ASSIGNMENTS

In the years after World War II, when the revitalized United States was sure of its economic, political, and military dominance and saw itself as the world's moral standard bearer, it felt charged with a mission to teach our ways to underprivileged peoples. Most of the teaching was technical. It began with President Truman's Point Four. During the 1950s, agricultural economists picked up the beat. They made agricultural development one of the profession's fields. In prestige and financing it crowded marketing from the limelight. A month or a year spent advising a Third World university or central government became an agricultural economist's badge of professional distinction.

Two private foundations, Ford and Rockefeller, made big waves with their national development projects. Ford's in India, directed by Harold Breimyer's friend Douglas Ensminger, was widely heralded. Rockefeller, which engaged outstanding economists such as Clifton Wharton, Jr. and Vernon Ruttan (also friends), worked in many countries and regions. The international development agency of the U.S. Department of State, which came to be known as USAID, dispatched its minions over the whole non-Communist, less-developed world. It drew on many U.S. university scientists, individually and under negotiated contracts.

Harold Breimyer was slow to get excited by the new obsession. His reluctance is not explained easily. Although holding the Ensmingers, Whartons, and Ruttans in highest respect, he was distrustful of others whom he suspected of being more interested in tasting foreign cultures than in helping anyone's agriculture. His sharper doubt, though, reflected professional modesty. "Who are we to believe that we can manage other countries' affairs for them?" The doubt was reinforced by an observation that quite a few of the economists who saw service abroad were not regarded highly by their peers here at home. What could they have to offer? Should second-raters be our emissaries?

Argentina. In spite of his reservations, when Albion W. Patterson, chief
    of an AID mission to Argentina, invited Breimyer to head a four-man team examining policies for the development of Argentina's cattle industry, the appeal could not be resisted. It was the time of President Kennedy's Alliance for Progress (Alianza para el Progreso) that put a missionary imprimatur on our country's resuscitating aid to Latin America.

In the company of James Rhodes, Jerry Goodall, and Roger Gray, during July-August 1961 Breimyer dug into all the analytical evidence available on the economics of Argentina's cattle production and beef distribution. The findings were so obvious that no elaborate research study was needed. Argentinians were gorging themselves on an immense consumption of beef that should not have been produced in the first place; the land tenure system, favoring big landowners, kept productive land in grass that should have been devoted to grain. The marketing system was tightly oligopolistic, dominated by one U.S. and one British firm, together with an Argentine government-sponsored cooperative that tried to provide active competition in defense of Argentine producers. And the shipping of fresh-chilled carcasses to Europe was doomed to decline in the longer future. The team found it inexpedient, however, to put all its misgivings in its report.

One exciting feature of the experience, for Breimyer, was his being received by Arturo Frondizi, president of Argentina. In the best diplomatic tradition the president conveyed his government's appreciation of the team's work, and indeed of President Kennedy's considerate attention shown to Argentina. He did not say that what was appreciated most was the sizable amount of loans that were received.

Via another avenue Harold Breimyer learned that the U.S. loans were appreciated by Argentinians in addition to their president. While walking through a cafeteria line, he was puzzled when a man behind the counter smiled and clasped his two raised hands in a gesture of tribute. Breimyer was puzzled until he remembered that the morning paper had carried an announcement of a large loan advanced to Argentina. The food vendor was saying "thank you."

In 1962 Harold Breimyer returned to Argentina on a new assignment. He, Howard Ottoson, and Louis Upchurch were charged with helping to redesign Argentina's program of agricultural economics research. The assignment was safe politically—a significant consideration in view of the change in government that had taken place. The Argentine army had staged a coup, putting President Frondizi under house arrest. As before, Breimyer reported to Roberto Risso Patron, and his new team worked with capable persons such as Alberto Amigo, Dario Bignoli, and Horacio Halliburton.

But the atmosphere was totally different. Breimyer's distrust of military people and philosophy was ingrained further as he listened to obnoxious ignoramuses sing a single refrain at every opportunity. It was a begging for U.S. loan funds to install "silos" (grain storage facilities). Harold Breimyer wondered if each dipping hand would come up with 5 percent, 10 percent, or even more. He hoped U.S. officials would not cave in.

Guatemala, Peru, Colombia, Spain. Later in the decade of the 1960s, Harold Breimyer would update his passport, put on his agricultural-development thinking cap, and travel to three other Latin American countries—Guatemala, Peru, and Colombia. In 1974 he took a different kind of assignment, working with the agricultural research station in Zaragoza, Spain. Always, he tried seriously, in spite of his reservations, to be helpful to his hosts. The best technique, he decided, was just to work directly with a local counterpart in each of those countries, introducing him to ideas and sources of information about which he had not known.

Ever since, Harold Breimyer has declared repeatedly that his principal contribution in his Latin American assignments was to "undo the harm other gringos (Americans) have done." He cited an example from little, beautiful Guatemala. Previous to his arrival a *norteamericano* from USDA's Agricultural Stabilization and Conservation Service had told Guatemalan officials that they should set up a price support and storage program for grains similar to ours. "Not so," Breimyer counseled. "It would be useful only to the big grain farmers located near the capital city. If you want to underpin prices to your farmers, send trucks into the foothills, offering to buy grain at a decent market price, and so

protect them against the below-market prices the sharks have been offering."

No matter. It's doubtful that the Guatemalan government paid any
attention to the ASCS man, or to Breimyer. It is probably just as well.

But Harold Breimyer bought some beautiful fabrics from Guatemalan Indians. At least he put some money into the money-starved Guatemalan economy.

THE AMS YEARS: WASHINGTON'S CAMELOT

The five years Breimyer served with the Agricultural Marketing
Service were the most gratifying of his career to that date. How is the
good feeling explained? What causes any individual to experience episodes of euphoria and others of discouragement? Are the influences
introversive, arising from within? Or are they explained by external
events? Both the internal and external were favorable during those years.

In 1961, when John F. Kennedy was inaugurated as President,
Harold Breimyer was already a twenty-five-year veteran of the New
Deal's ministering to a once-distraught agriculture. The verve, the vitality, that had carried forward to the first postwar years had been muted
during the administration of Dwight Eisenhower and his foot-dragging,
pontificating secretary of agriculture. The later 1950s were unexciting.

Thus it was that the election of a vibrant Kennedy was a breath of
fresh air. Federal civil servants such as Harold Breimyer heard with
relish his call for "vigor," pronounced in a Hyannisport accent. They
were inspired to respond.

President Kennedy's appointee as secretary of agriculture was of the
same temper. Orville Freeman was trained in the law, but his career to
that point had been meteoric in the politics of his native Minnesota. He
also had been an officer in the U.S. Marines. Although Breimyer's opportunities for conversation with him were few, the two had in common
their service in the World War II campaign for Bougainville, an island in
the Solomons. Breimyer remembered how he, as his LST's executive
officer, spent an anxious afternoon trying to keep his ship from broach-
ing in heavy winds. It was beached as it provisioned troops on the island
that likely included Freeman. On Bougainville, Freeman narrowly escaped decapitation as a Japanese sword cut a groove in his cheek. In all
his public appearances Freeman kept the gashed cheek turned away from
cameras.

Freeman drew on his Marine-officer qualities more than his legal training as he sought to guide programs in agriculture, about which he knew little. He was courageous and, to continue the military analogy, a straight-shooter. His eight years were marred, however, by the relentless bickering and hooting between his economist, Willard Cochrane, and the American Farm Bureau Federation. Most of the Farm Bureau's diatribe was launched by Roger Fleming and other henchmen. It was an ugly demonstration that conferred credit on no one. Harold Breimyer could have been more defensive of Cochrane had Cochrane not been guilty of firing Oris Wells.

The *esprit,* the sense of purpose, that marked the Kennedy Camelot years did not fade immediately on Lyndon Johnson's accession to the presidency but did so later as Johnson dragged the nation into the quagmire of Vietnam. In Breimyer's observation it has not been reestablished since.

THE AMS YEARS: APOGEE TO PERSONAL GROWTH

Human beings are individually unique but collectively fall into recognizable categories. One classification relates to rate of growth and maturation. In everyday language, people divide between early and late bloomers. We may suppose a block of average-speed bloomers lies between the two, but it gets little attention.

Harold Breimyer was a late bloomer. As a child he was slow to learn to talk. Emma Schlamb, his beloved teacher in Sunday School, worried whether he would ever pronounce consonants correctly. As a teenager, puberty and the outgrowing of clothes came late. He added the last half-foot of his eventual 74½-inch height during his college years. Each Christmas break when he returned to his home church, older members took note of his increasing height by remarking in an invariable phrase, "You need to put a brick on your head."

His professional growth was not rapid. He gained professional confidence and stature only as he approached forty.

Receiving Awards. Chronicled in preceding pages have been experiences in entering community life and in professional productivity. Not mentioned are the occasions of formal professional recognition. In 1954, a month after his fortieth birthday, Breimyer sat on an improvised platform located on the grounds of the Washington Monument, and listened to Vice-President Richard Nixon eulogize the employees of the Department of Agriculture who qualified for the awards that were about to be conferred. It was the USDA's annual awards ceremony.

In the alphabetical priority that his name gave him, he was called forward early to receive a Superior Service Award. It was the first such formal tribute he had received. More were to come, during his USDA tenure and his years at the University of Missouri.

Studying Great Books. Also not touched on in the account thus far is an enterprise that, in the jargon of educators, could be called a "learning experience." Almost all Harold Breimyer's formal education had been technical. At Ohio State's College of Agriculture in the 1930s, few courses taken in remote disciplines such as history and the arts could be credited toward graduation, although he enrolled in some, the rules notwithstanding.

During the 1950s, sensitive to his deficiency in liberal education, he joined a Great Books group. Not long before, Stringfellow Barr had made a name for himself and for St. John's College by advocating study of the classics as the magic key to superior education. Winter after winter, one or two evenings a month, Breimyer and his companions mulled over the writings of Plato, Goethe, and other giants.

They pondered St. Augustine on education. Augustine had called his boyhood dislike of rote learning (arithmetic, for example) a sin. Nonetheless, as an adult he decided that "a free curiosity has more force in our learning . . . than a frightful enforcement" (p.15). So wrote Augustine in the fifth century on an issue that excites and divides in the last years of the twentieth.

Or consider Aristotle and his *Politics:* "In all sciences and arts the end is . . . justice" (p.24). Also, is "the virtue of a good man and a good citizen . . . the same?" Before answering, Aristotle reminded that "the virtue of the citizen must . . . be relative to the constitution [i.e., community] of which he is a member" (p.6). The question is still germane.

Among all his Great Books readings, though, Kant's *Prolegomena* was Harold Breimyer's favorite. Empirical observation does not self-categorize. What, then, are "the sources of metaphysical cognition?" They must be metaphysical knowledge, "*a priori* knowledge, coming from pure Understanding and pure Reason" (p.11).

How can literate Americans waste their time reading or listening to insipid chatter when the words of the world's great minds are available in the Great Books' inexpensive paperbacks? Harold Breimyer had that question during his concluding years of employment in the U.S. government, and he has it as this account is written.

Final Reflections. In December of 1966 Harold Breimyer turned from government to academia. His thirty years in Washington had been years of ascent, by any test. By the end of that period, had he reached a plateau? He did not know the answer then, and he has not learned it since. Life on campus was so sharply different from that in government that moving from one to the other was not transitional, but a disjuncture.

It suffices to be said that the thirty-year veteran was well-prepared for the second stage of his lifetime career that followed as he moved to the University of Missouri. And it is glorious to affirm the satisfaction he felt as he concluded his government service. It was not just that he felt a glow of personal accomplishment. More important was his sense of having contributed, in his own small way, to significant missions of the federal government relative to agriculture and the rural community. During all the thirty years, he believed in the worth of what he was doing. He held in high regard the agency in which he worked, as well as its officials, his bosses. Only later did he come to realize how rare is such an experience.

His positive reflections proved indelible. In 1984, when he addressed the 250 persons who attended his retirement dinner, he quoted the words of Sherman Johnson. Johnson, whom he respected so much, had been chief of the six-man party that toured the Soviet Union in 1958. In Johnson's autobiography, Breimyer recounted, Johnson declared himself proud to have been a bureaucrat. "So was I," Breimyer added, "and I still am."

As of the date of writing these memoirs, he still is.

CHAPTER 15

The Cresting Years: the University of Missouri

As a farm boy Harold Breimyer remarked one day as he watched Earl Whitesell at the Fort Recovery cooperative elevator wearily heave the day's seventy-fifth bag of grain into the grinding chute, "Earl, you're getting old."

"No, I'm not," came the retort. "I'm fifty, in my prime."

The youth thought it inconceivable that a man of fifty years could regard himself as in his prime.

Breimyer was fifty-two when he left the U.S. Department of Agriculture and became a professor of agricultural economics at the University of Missouri–Columbia. At that time the change in his career was too dramatic, and his anticipations were too upbeat, for him even to think about whether he was at the prime stage of his life. A reflective judgment, made as these memoirs are written, is that he was indeed at his lifetime peak. It was due to last a while. At the university Harold Breimyer's career crested.

PARALLEL BETWEEN PERSONAL EXPERIENCES AND NATIONAL TRENDS

Do people commonly see a parallel between their lifetime experiences and those of the community of which they are a part, even of their nation's? Harold Breimyer has long sensed such a relationship in his case. The crucial experiences and turning points in his life almost synchronized with major national developments during the twentieth century—his century.

What a century it has been! First it brought World War I, which began at Sarajevo in 1914, the year of his birth. The United States came out of that conflict almost unscathed. It was newly appreciative of its rising status in world affairs but tempted to stay out of them. Isolationism was rampant.

The Great Depression gave the nation a new jolt. Weathering it, the country took alarming note of the storm clouds of a fascist threat in Europe. It dallied and equivocated until the Japanese forced its hand at Pearl Harbor.

The 1920s proved to be the last decade of *laissez faire* philosophy. Upon the election of Franklin Roosevelt in November 1932, as Dean Acheson put it, the American people turned "from the hope of salvation by faith to the doctrine of salvation by works" (p.101). They endorsed action by government to relieve the Depression. Next it became necessary to muster all hands to win a war. Both efforts were by their nature social, all-hands-joined; even, it could be said, statist. In both enterprises the country's resources were mobilized in collective enterprise.

Shared fear always makes for collaboration, a putting of everyone's shoulders to the wheel. The paradigm fits the events of the 1930s and 1940s.

The national confidence, restored by victories over both the economic and military threats, preserved, for a time, the sense of common purpose and subordination of private aggressions to common goals. It was in this moral climate that a postwar Congress enacted a law (Employment Act of 1946) designed to protect against a new depression even as a rainbow, in the Biblical account, promises no new inundating flood. In that climate, too, the United States led in establishing a United Nations. It extended developmental aid worldwide, even to former enemies.

The enlightened benevolence brought its rewards. The nation entered its Golden Age. During the 1950s and 1960s the Gross National Product increased steadily. Material prosperity facilitated the endowing of blessings, material and nonmaterial, upon deprived social classes. When the television screen revealed hungry people in our land, food programs were expanded. When it pictured starvation abroad, food aid was dispatched. When brutal police in the South tried to limit the civil rights of blacks, national resentment forced enactment of civil rights legislation. And southern governors were not allowed to forestall the desegregation of public schools mandated by the Supreme Court's decision of 1954.

Martyrdom helped advance the cause of civil rights. Not only that of Martin Luther King, Jr., did so. The assassination of President Kennedy on a fateful day in November 1963 gave a major impetus to the civil rights movement. In its shadow Lyndon Johnson as President won congressional acceptance of a series of laws that were as significant as the Emancipation Proclamation of 1863. They might not have been enacted had Kennedy lived.

The Golden Age lasted scarcely longer than twenty years. It lost its brilliance as the nation found itself caught in the maelstrom of Vietnam. It's likely, though, that the Vietnam conflict and the divisiveness it engendered only speeded a trend that would have been under way in any event. National dedication to a common purpose is invariably transient, short-lived. Pericles's Athenians tired of his good government. Americans of the later 1960s and 1970s were sated, "fed-up" they would say, with calls for economic and political justice. In 1980 Ronald Reagan exploited the new national temper, radicalizing and redirecting (but not reversing) a concept of government that had lasted almost fifty years.

In any nation defeat is soft-pedaled, and Americans of the 1970s were loath to acknowledge their retrogression. But a decade later either perceptions sharpened or courage strengthened, for scholars began to call attention to a dimming of the nation's previously bright lights. Mancur Olson speculated on where the United States fit in *The Rise and Decline of Nations*. Paul Kennedy's *The Rise and Fall of the Great Powers* was an instant best seller. Arthur Schlesinger, Jr., wrote about *The Cycles in American History*. The most recent cycle, it might be supposed, was an eclipsing phase. The portents were discouraging.

Synchronized timing between national history and Harold Breimyer's life experiences is easily sketched. The 1920s, when the country was newly feeling its oats, were the boy's years of 4-H Club and school achievements that qualified him for college. The early 1930s, a time of economic recession, were for the Ohio State student troubled years of emotional insecurity. World War II was revealing of potential to the nation and confidence-building for Lieutenant Breimyer. The 1950s and 1960s were golden for the United States of America and for many of its citizens who reached their personal pinnacle at that time, as did Harold Breimyer.

The coincidence in chronology between a nation and one of its 200 million citizens would be unworthy of remarking were it not that as civil servant Breimyer became Professor Breimyer, he enveloped national events into his study and teaching. He joined the small crowd of general scholars.

TRANSITION FROM CIVIL SERVICE TO CAMPUS

A question poses itself. If Harold Breimyer was so happy working for Si Smith and the Agricultural Marketing Service, why would he uproot himself and wife Rachel from comfortable Kensington, Maryland, at age fifty-two, and take his chances in a new career at a small college city in a state of inauspicious social standing, Missouri?

The circumstances of making the move are explained easily. The invitation came from V. James Rhodes, a member of the Argentine study team of 1961. As collaborators, Rhodes and Breimyer had gained a mutual respect. In 1966 Rhodes was chairman of the Department of Agricultural Economics at the University of Missouri–Columbia. Fred Heinkel, president of the Missouri Farmers Association, had just funded a professorship in agricultural marketing. An inquiry went to Breimyer: Would he be interested in the new position? "No, thank you," came the reply. But within weeks he changed his mind and called Rhodes: "Is the position still open?" Rhodes replied that it had been filled, but added, "If you're willing to come, we'll make a place for you." Breimyer was, and Rhodes did.

Why the change of heart? Did Harold Breimyer sense, in the spring of 1966, that the Golden Age of the nation was tarnishing, and particularly that the surge for liberal legislation was losing its momentum? Did he suppose that enlightened public purpose was about to disappear from government service? Or did he find himself retracing familiar ground in his marketing work, a clear signal that the time had come for a change?

The clinching consideration in his decision to accept the Rhodes offer was his chagrin at the growing politicizing of the Department of Agriculture. Two of the guilty parties were agricultural economists of Breimyer's acquaintance, George Mehren and John Schnittker. Mehren violated procedural rules brazenly in his handling of dairy programs. A big dairy cooperative later rewarded him with an executive position, but Mehren mishandled that and lapsed into an obscurity that for him must have been distasteful.

As under-secretary of agriculture, John Schnittker had ambitions for an even higher office. Schnittker, a friend then and since, surely could have had no idea that a decision that he thought to be of no import was the deciding factor in Harold Breimyer's fleeing from government to academia. Breimyer was a member of a transportation-rate review committee headed by the splendidly capable James Lauth. Southern Railway Company wanted to give concessionary freight rates on poultry feed shipped from the Midwest to Gainesville, Georgia. The proposal was flagrantly anticompetitive. The committee recommended strongly that the USDA oppose it. Schnittker saw a political advantage in taking the opposite stand. He rebuffed the committee. "If that's the way things are going to be, I'll leave," Breimyer reflected. Leave he did.

Among all the capable agricultural economists who have tried to serve in high political office, only two are regarded as having performed ably. They are Don Paarlberg and Dale Hathaway. Otherwise a general judgment is that agricultural economists make poor politicians.

SURPRISES IN STORE

Harold Breimyer was no novice in the classroom and no stranger to a university campus. As early as 1956, he had taught an evening class in the graduate school in the U.S. Department of Agriculture. For three semesters he was instructor at Montgomery Junior College, in Takoma Park, just north of Washington. At that college he taught the first course in economics (principles) to clerks and secretaries who were ambitious to move into a professional career. Some were superb students. During his year (1963–64) at the University of Illinois, he taught one class. Speaking dates and seminars had taken him to perhaps half the land-grant universities in the United States.

He was respectful of higher education and pleased for the chance he saw for his own scholarly growth. But he was not prepared for the surprises, some positive but some not, that lay ahead for him. The first surprise was that he found himself engaging in activities that did not conform to stereotype. He had supposed that he would spend his time preparing and delivering classroom lectures and conducting research projects that would be reported in the form of dry, barely readable (and rarely read) station bulletins.

He did in fact begin teaching a class within weeks after arriving on the Columbia campus. But almost immediately there came invitations to talk to some farm or agribusiness group in the state. He undertook a couple of research projects, including one on food programs that was carried out well by two other Harolds, graduate students Harold Love and Harold Loyd. But it became clear soon that monastic mulling over masses of research data was not Harold Breimyer's best employment. Within a year James Rhodes and Clarence Klingner announced that inasmuch as he was taking lots of Extension dates, he would be put half-time on Extension. Research would be downplayed.

He remembers the first off-campus speaking experience clearly. Elmer Kiehl, Breimyer's longtime friend and Dean of Agriculture, was

unable to fill a speaking date for a luncheon of the agribusiness committee of the St. Louis Chamber of Commerce. Would Breimyer substitute?
Of course he would. The warmest response he got from the audience was
to his reporting that Midwest politicians' sense of honor betrayed them.
"They think they must act faithfully to their political stances," he explained. "I have watched politicians from all regions operate in Washington. The southerners are the most effective, and midwesterners least so.
Midwestern senators and congressmen think that if they talk conservatively, they must act accordingly. The southerners feel no such obligation and are free of inhibitions. In economic matters they routinely
announce how free-enterprise they are. But when a federal handout is
available, they disregard the rhetoric and are first in the receiving line on
behalf of their constituents."

A Shortage of Scholars. The surprise that was most disappointing was
the discovery that scholars were fewer and high scholarship rarer on
the University of Missouri–Columbia campus, and by inference on most
university campuses, than Harold Breimyer had supposed and expected.

Lest this remark be misinterpreted, Harold Breimyer's end-of-career
reminiscences on his eighteen years as professor of marketing and policy,
and Extension economist in public affairs, are entirely felicitous. Nonetheless, as he took his place in the activities of the Department of Agricultural Economics and College of Agriculture, he was shocked to observe how wide was the range of competence and productivity among
individual faculty members. In the U.S. Department of Agriculture, that
citadel of government bureaucracy, he had known a few incompetent
time-wasters. But somehow the huge USDA was better able to command
acceptable performance than was the University of Missouri–Columbia.

Breimyer came to the judgment, still held, that a modern university
relies on an elite corps of scholars to give it standing and, ideally, acclaim. Their crucial role reminds him of Winston Churchill's tribute to
the air defenders of Britain—that so many owed so much to so few.
Midway in Breimyer's university tenure Rose DeWever, an older graduate student, remarked laconically, "Not more than one in ten of the
faculty members of this campus qualifies as a scholar." She added, with
no trace of obsequiousness, that Harold Breimyer and James Rhodes
were the only two in agricultural economics. Breimyer thought her too
selective in the nominees but not far in error in her statistical estimate.

Around the middle of the 1970s, the University of Missouri and
most state universities began to suffer a slow attrition in both status and
funding. Among land-grant schools particularly, burdened or blessed

(however viewed) as they are by their public service obligation, hand wringing became epidemic. Harold Breimyer the institutionalist wondered if the uniquely American land-grant school, advertised and advocated worldwide as an engine of development, was indeed in an atrophying decline. Institutions do have life cycles.

In 1983 his friend Robert Finley invited Breimyer to address the University Club on the institutional outlook for the modern university. Breimyer chided his fellow faculty members that "university scholars must be the most innocently and delightfully naive contingent of human beings." They go about their daily business "in quiet confidence that their role is not only revered but guarded by impregnable defenses." It's just as well, he told his listeners. Professors could turn neurotic if they brooded about how subject the scholarly role is "to the winds of cultural and political acceptability" (p.1).

If institutions fade and eventually die, do they do so because of external hostility or of internal dry rot? The question has been debated for centuries. Applied to the U.S. university in the ending decades of the twentieth century, it asks whether the American public has turned anti-intellectual and therefore less supportive. Or have the institution's (university's) own people become so inward-looking, so preoccupied with in-house jealousies, that they not only tolerate but even contribute to institutional decay?

Private Consulting and Research Funding. Harold Breimyer served one three-year term on the campus-wide Faculty Council. He found it a depressing experience. Most of the members were devoid of institutional vision. They were concerned only for professors' salaries and perquisites, and for the rivalries among the Columbia and other three campuses of the university. His salty judgment, rarely expressed, was that insofar as the University of Missouri was in trouble, it had largely brought it on itself.

No gladiator, Harold Breimyer did not run around wildly, lance extended, battling all institutional opponents. He directed his attack primarily to the threat he regarded as most insidious of all—the compromising of scholarly precepts by acceptance of private dollars. Specifically, he objected to two practices that were growing rapidly: the private funding of university research and the individual professor's acceptance of consulting pay. It was not surprising, to be sure, that as public research funding diminished (in real terms), administrators would turn to soliciting private contractual research. Breimyer warned his University Club audience of the danger of thereby compromising "that most precious of all the distinguishing qualities of university education, namely, freedom of inquiry."

Private consulting, Breimyer believed, was equally noxious or maybe even more so. He had seen professors at other schools, Iowa State and Stanford universities, for example, become indentured to firms for whom they performed consulting services. ("Intellectual prostitutes" was the term Si Smith had used for the type.) As most of his speaking and writing would relate to public policy, Breimyer thought any financial liaison on his part to be particularly sordid. Upon arriving at the Columbia campus, he pledged to himself that he would accept no payment for outside speaking or writing. If a payment were made, the check would be endorsed to the university's development fund. Not until after he retired did Harold Breimyer accept a consulting dollar.

The monies received went first to a student loan fund set up in his name, and then to the Breimyer seminar fund. Harold Breimyer always allowed himself some pride for having abstained from any financially induced temptation toward bias in his teaching about public affairs.

Harold Breimyer was never lured into any appeasement regarding his stand on professors' consulting and a university's accepting private research funding. "Private financing of a public educational institution," he said at his retirement dinner, "is a contradiction in terms" (p.6). But university officials, at Missouri and elsewhere, cannot resist the temptation. They are begging for private monies. Breimyer has believed, and continues to believe, that the institutions—and land-grant universities especially—are inviting their own doom.

CHAPTER 16

 *Extension Education in Public Affairs*

AMONG ALL NATIONS ON EARTH, the United States surely distinguishes itself by the trust it places in education. "Education," says David Boroff, "is our secular church—the one faith that unites us all." (p.33).

In spite of claims that may be made by Harvard or the California Institute of Technology, the exceptional quality of our educational institutions is not found in classical schooling or even in Nobel-prize performance in physical sciences and engineering. Nor is it lodged at the other end of the spectrum—instruction in the "3Rs" provided to the children of wage workers. The most unusual, "American," feature of our educational system is the extracurricular, off-campus, teaching of youth and adults.

The land-grant university system that was established in 1862 was charged particularly with serving the entire citizenry. By and large, land-grant schools have carried out the mandate faithfully. They have done the best in agriculture and home economics, and especially so following enactment of the Smith-Lever Act of 1914, which set the nationwide Cooperative Extension Service in motion.

Harold Breimyer learned about Extension at about the age he got to long division in elementary school. In 1923 George Henning, the county extension agent, enlisted Fred Breimyer in leading a pig club that his son Harold joined.

As a student at Ohio State University, Harold continued an association with Extension as he summarized farm accounts in the "mill." He maintained a close Extension tie during his thirty years in Washington, working frequently with Extension economists in the respective states who held outlook responsibilities. So when Clarence Klingner and James Rhodes invited him to shift to half-time Extension, he was not looking at a strange new field of activity.

218

EXTENSION'S METHODS AND MEDIA

Agricultural Extension is a unique educational institution. It has had its own personnel, formal teaching methods, informal improvisations that often substitute for formal instruction, a special tradition and folklore, and an intense internal rapport and group loyalty.

If education is America's secular religion, county extension agents were agriculture's high priests. The early agents were indeed a caste, an order. They were dedicated. Until country roads were improved so that a Model T Ford could get through, the agent rode horseback to reach a farmer in trouble, or to hold a local meeting on the magic (nitrogen-carrying!) property of legume forages. When Mercer County's third agent, O. H. Anderson, brought a group of 4-H Club members back from Columbus and one of them, Harold Breimyer, found that his Ford would not start, no garage was called. Anderson got out a rope and towed the youth's recalcitrant tin-Lizzie the twenty miles to the Fred Breimyer farm. His doing so fit with the Extension *esprit* of the time.

Three Media. In its educational activities Extension has long employed three media. One is the printed bulletin/report/ newsletter. From the state university and local county offices, those publications have gone out in a steady flow.

A second is the public meeting. In Missouri the state specialists located on the campus in Columbia have been — and probably still are — on call to meet with groups scattered over the big state. They run up high numbers each year on the odometer of their own or the university's automobiles. They know where to find motels with the most comfortable beds, and they are even better informed as to which restaurants serve the tastiest meals at reasonable prices and have the prettiest waitresses.

The third medium consists of radio and television. Because most Missourians prefer to see their Extension teacher in the flesh instead of on a TV screen, the electronic medium did not catch on fast. But in the 1970s, when OPEC boosted the price of motor fuel and cost of travel, radio and television were turned to more and more.

Clarence Klingner's first instruction to Harold Breimyer was that he take over the monthly Extension "letter," *Economic and Marketing Information for Missouri Agriculture.* His recruit was delighted to do that. Breimyer always felt more confident of his ability in writing than in speaking. He would have the opportunity to report and comment on a wide variety of issues of the day. He set two terms: (1) that a review board go over each month's draft, and (2) that he be granted the privilege of adding editorial comments. The terms were met.

The titles for the first letters Breimyer wrote give a clue what was to follow: "Food Programs for Low Income Families — Welfare, or Market Building?"; "Economics and Politics of Extending the 1965 Farm Law"; "Corporate Farming — a Bird's Eye View"; "A New Protectionism in Foreign Trade Policy." During the sixteen years he edited the E&MI, writing more than three-fourths of the articles, Harold Breimyer affected the thinking of Missouri farmers and farm leaders.

Public Meetings — Reading the Audience. Harold Breimyer had taken part in meetings held at various places in Missouri before Klingner and Rhodes put him on the Extension payroll. He already knew that his first problem was the same as the one every Extension specialist wrestles with: how to present technical information in language that unschooled audiences can comprehend. To make matters worse, it often is impossible to know the composition of the audience that will attend his next meeting.

Breimyer sensed the soundness of the advice given by the syndicated columnist Raymond Clapper. "Never overestimate the people's knowledge," Clapper wrote, "nor underestimate their intelligence." Also germane was an epigram of the poet William Butler Yeats: "Think like a wise man but communicate in the language of the people."

A few Extension economists in other states were prone, Breimyer noted, to "talk down" or "write down" their message, reducing it to mush. He would have none of that. Yet, in teaching about public affairs, the greater hazard lies not in the prior knowledge or vocabulary of the audience but, rather, in the baggage of opinion already held. The adults who come to a session devoted to a public issue rarely lack opinions, which often are held dearly and given up grudgingly.

Sixteen years after beginning his Extension teaching at Missouri, on the occasion of his retirement dinner, Breimyer reflected on the challenges that go with teaching about public policy. "Not for a moment," he said, "have I forgotten that education in public affairs is highly sensitive. One cannot make even the blandest statement on a public or political issue without touching on the interests of some person or group" (pp. 4–5). Breimyer believed then, and still does, that he was moderately successful in staying within the boundaries that are implicit in Extension education in public affairs, without diluting the factual, or compromising the moral, content of what he wrote or said.

He assessed each of his audiences as accurately as he could and pressed upon each as much sophisticated understanding, and as much challenge to cherished beliefs, as he could get by with. Don Paarlberg, his good friend from Purdue University who had been chief economist to four secretaries of agriculture and to President Eisenhower, wrote Harold Breimyer on the occasion of his retirement that he had been "the conscience of the economists." Perhaps so; but Breimyer also understood that every person in his audiences had a boundary line beyond which he could not be persuaded, and he was careful not to breach that line.

Once in a while he either misjudged his listening audience or became unwary. At an Extension meeting in eastern Missouri in the mid-1970s, at a time when both crop and livestock prices were up and just about everything in agriculture was going well, the extension economist from the University of Missouri dared to ask rhetorically why farmers kept complaining even in good times. "We could wonder if they are paranoid," Breimyer suggested. The word was a mistake. A nice-looking lady in the back of the room jumped to her feet and blurted her question: "How can you object to farmers' being paranoid when they have so much to be paranoid about?" Harold Breimyer never again used the word or even the idea.

In spite of his efforts, Breimyer ran afoul of one big audience—the Missouri Farm Bureau. For several years after coming to Missouri, he had been invited to make a presentation at various Farm Bureau meetings. One such meeting that related to soybean marketing proved to be his nemesis. It was a time when the soybean people were ecstatic about the blessings of soybean promotion. Without really intending to prick their bubble, Breimyer commented *sotto voce* that promotion was not the most important issue in soybean marketing. The promoters of promotion were indignant. His statement was correct, of course; integrity of markets always outranks promotional devices in significance. Jim Ragsdale, the university's good-common-sense grain marketing specialist, tried to calm down the outraged farmers. He was not successful. Breimyer was excommunicated.

Losing touch with a farm organization was naturally disappointing, but it did not vitiate Harold Breimyer's end-of-career reflection about the Extension part of his role at the University of Missouri–Columbia. On the contrary, he felt good about it. His further remarks at his retirement dinner are worth noting.

> I am eternally grateful to the people of Missouri who have let me present data and offer ideas that don't always fit with the way they want to see the world.

Missouri is a wonderful state in which to teach about public affairs. It is the Show Me state. Missourians almost brag about the term but also sense that it is not entirely complimentary. It's very positive for education, because show-me means a willingness to be shown. It does not extend to a promise to accept what is said. But in my extension teaching I never try for a kill. I only ask to be listened to.

Missourians have let me pour out a lot of ideas they would prefer not to hear. I have told farmers that the tax deductions they like individually are hurting them collectively. I have said getting price supports too high will shrink markets; and that import quotas on beef become export limits on soybeans. Missourians have listened, and I thank them. (p.5)

EXTENSION EDUCATION: VERSATILITY FOR A VARIETY OF ISSUES

Extension teaching has little in common with formal research or instruction in the classroom. Unlike the latter two it does not extol intricate investigation or rest on highly specialized knowledge. It puts a premium on the opposite—a catholic capacity to address a variety of issues that phase in and out of view in lunar fashion, if not quite lunar speed.

By its nature all Extension is contemporary-applied. Justice Oliver Wendell Holmes once had occasion to say that "we need education in the obvious more than investigation of the obscure." He did not have Extension in mind, but he could have. Extension addresses what is currently of interest or concern.

Somnolence in Farm Program Debate. In the later 1960s, when Harold Breimyer began his career at Missouri, farm programs had phased out of political prominence. Following several years of jockeying, direct Treasury payments had become accepted as an alternative to mandatory acreage allotments. India had suffered two monsoon failures in a row, giving the United States the opportunity to shovel its surplus wheat her way as fast as that hapless nation could take it. For a brief moment we were spared our chronic worries about surpluses.

The law in effect at the time had been enacted in 1965. What the 1965 law did, as Harold Breimyer wrote in *Economic and Marketing Information* for September 1968, was "to avoid tight restrictions on farmers, and to steer clear of high support prices as well. The U.S. Treasury finances those policies, at a cost that is large by any standards.

Thus, Treasury checks protect farmers from compulsion, and consumers from paying higher prices for food" (p.1).

Twenty years later, the line about a "cost . . . large by any standards" seems bizarre, even ridiculous. Yet in 1968 that amount of government spending (perhaps one or two billion dollars a year) seemed attractive enough to farm interest groups that they were eager to keep it.

In November 1968 the Republicans and Richard Nixon unseated the Democrats in the White House. Clifford Hardin was named secretary of agriculture. Hardin came from a land-grant university career, having moved from Michigan State to be chancellor of the University of Nebraska. He epitomized the Peter principle of being elevated to successive spots just above his level of competence. Basically anti-program, he offered a plan by which the old diverted acres would be renamed "set-aside," and would be a hybrid between land retirement commodity by commodity, and general land retirement. Hardin specified an upper limit for loan rates, but no floor. The secretary would be able to pitch the loans as low as he wished. It was a foregone conclusion that Congress would not assent.

A corn blight in 1970 eased lingering fears of a new surplus production. Late in the year the Agricultural Act of 1970 was passed and signed. Secretary Hardin got his language ("set-aside") and some administrative latitude but not the bottomless loan rates. Congress was careful to set a loan minimum close to the rates then in existence.

The 1970 law had two landmark features. First, it put more of the compensatory principle into direct payments. Thereafter, payment rates were to be more of a compensation for shortfall in market prices. Second, the law imposed a ceiling on the amount of compensatory payment a farmer could receive in any one program. The farm law had long carried the heavy baggage of public resentment over the giant size of some individual payments. Following previous unsuccessful attempts, the 1970 law put a lid of $55,000 on the amount a farmer could collect from a program.

Collective Bargaining in Agriculture. Not farm programs, but collective bargaining, was the *piece de resistance* in agricultural circles in the mid- and late-1960s. At least two farm organizations put little faith in traditional acreage-reduction programs, and bided their time until group action by farmers could take over. The two were the old American Farm Bureau Federation and the new National Farmers Organization.

In *Economic and Marketing Information* for September 1968,

Harold Breimyer wrote: "The American Farm Bureau Federation is the principal farm opponent of present policies. It wants to rely almost entirely on land retirement. And eventually it hopes to replace government programs with bargaining arrangements sponsored by its American Agricultural Marketing Associations" (pp.1–2).

The National Farmers Organization had sprung into existence in the early 1950s as a spontaneous protest movement. With the charismatic Oren Lee Staley at the helm, it soon adopted collective bargaining as its banner. As was stated previously, the NFO announced goals of enrolling enough of the national production of a crop or livestock to be able to exert a bargaining lever over the price paid to farmers. It engaged in periodic holding actions that occasionally became violent.

The holding-action episodes drew enough media attention to indict the NFO in the minds of many citizens and of most economists. Harold Breimyer was not so negative. As was made clear many pages back, he did not subscribe to the neoclassical doctrine that impersonal forces akin to gravity predetermine economic values. He liked to quote Richard Kohls, a professor at Purdue University. Writing about livestock markets, Kohls declared, "Prices are not made by a special heavenly angel bringing supply and demand together. They are made by people working with the information and in the institutions they have at hand" (p.4).

In his classroom teaching Breimyer liked to draw the usual supply-and-demand curves on the board, note the point of intersection, and then tell the class that it represents the price that no one except some silly economist wants. Every seller tries for a higher price and every buyer a lower one. Only as a last resort do they accept that price, and when they must do so, both are unhappy.

Kohls legitimized human participation in price making. He stated, "Joint agreement between two parties may definitely improve some factors and therefore aid in the discovery of a more satisfactory and more accurate price for both sides" (p. 4).

Various leaders in farmer bargaining sought legislation to codify bargaining practices—and so protect farmer bargainers. While still in the U.S. Department of Agriculture, Breimyer supported legislative proposals to establish fair practices in bargaining and especially to outlaw blacklisting. But he took a firm stand that any law must apply equally to private and cooperative integrators. In doing so he stirred up the proverbial hornets' nest. He was favorably inclined toward farmers' cooperatives but was unwilling to regard them as holy and sinless or free of obligation to conform to established rules of fair play.

A fair-bargaining-practice law was enacted—S. 109, the Agricultural Fair Practices Act of 1967. In its original draft it called for strong, effective protection of collective bargaining. During the legislative process the food trade showed its political power. The version as enacted was almost the opposite of the first draft, and essentially innocuous. Randall Torgerson, who studied S. 109 while working under Harold Breimyer's tutelage at the UMC, concluded, "At best, S. 109 offers a foundation statute for the bargaining activities carried out by general farm interest organizations. At worst, . . . [it] may provide handlers and dissident members with an excuse to harass bargaining associations" (p. 211).

In an Extension bulletin that he edited with the help of Wallace Barr of Ohio State University, Breimyer defined collective bargaining as "successful negotiation between two or more opposing parties to arrive at prices and other terms of trade including the terms of contracts" (p.5).

Price making via bargaining is indeed an exceptional means for what economists call "price discovery" in the marketing of farm products. Collective bargaining, Breimyer told everyone who would listen, is appropriate only where the conditions for effective, if not perfect, competition are clearly absent. It makes sense only where organized entities are found, or can be established, on both the buying and selling side. As viewed from the selling (farmers') side, bargaining is more likely to be feasible for a specialty crop that is produced in a small geographic area or one sold under a marketing order; or, more generally, in any situation where market buyers are few.

The critical element in bargaining is the *threat*. George Ladd's coinage of "opponent-gain power" and "opponent-pain power" helped soften the sting of the term. Each party to a bargained agreement must find something positive in it, even as each must have the ability—to be used rarely—to do something undesired or even harmful. The positive often was assurance of tight quality control. Farmers agreed to deliver the kind of product the processor wanted. The usual negative was (threat of) withholding.

The evolving tactics of the National Farmers Organization provided an example. The NFO was not able to sign up enough volume of any major farm product to make itself a national bargaining agent. It drifted into block marketing, wherein the sale of a sizable "block" of a farm product was negotiated.

The NFO was still block marketing in 1990, but Staley had lost the presidency mainly because of flubs in administration. He was a spellbinding evangelist but an erratic administrator. Before succumbing to a fall that fractured his skull, he wandered about, trying to recapture past glories. He never succeeded. It's hard to climb down from Olympus, even as modest a version of that pinnacle as the presidency of the NFO.

CHAPTER 17

Policy Making in the 1970s

GOVERNMENT PROGRAMS to control acreage of major crops and put a floor under commodity prices and farmers' incomes have always received less than stouthearted endorsement. They are the most politically sensitive of all government activities relative to agriculture. Moreover, support for them has been almost apologetic. They were first advanced during the Depression on grounds that they were emergency, therefore temporary. Later, when the programs failed to fade into oblivion, any advertised new hope for agriculture's economic salvation, or any diversionary focus, was welcomed.

Just after World War II, marketing claimed the diversionary attention. A few years later, when post-Korea market prices dropped low, and farmers' spirits with them, the Soil Bank was seen as the answer to production-control prayers. The newly enacted Public Law 480 was anointed as Food for Peace and trusted as a solution on the demand side.

In the 1960s a flurry of excitement about collective bargaining claimed the spotlight. During that decade commodity programs were redesigned to draw more on direct payments from the federal Treasury. The change was taken in stride, and at decade's end the farm policy front was as nearly quiet as at any time since 1933.

In the 1970s a series of events again pushed acreage programs and price supports to the sideline. The first was the Russian buy-out of our grain stocks, which initiated an export boom. Soon after, the Organization of Petroleum Exporting Countries sent oil prices skyrocketing. Steps taken to relieve the ensuing business recession set a rapid inflation in motion. It extended to farm products, and especially farmland.

Significantly, these were happenings outside our agriculture. The pattern was to persist in the 1980s, when economists such as Luther Tweeten and Harold Breimyer would declare that no longer was the agricultural sector in command of its own destiny. During the two decades, it had become subservient to forces arising from outside it.

EARL BUTZ AS NEW SECRETARY OF AGRICULTURE

Acreage and price-support programs were not absent from the policy agenda of the 1970s. And the two new laws of the decade, those of 1973 and 1977, introduced several changes in policy that remain significant as this memoir is written.

U.S. farm policy in the mid-1970s was dominated by one person and two events. The events have already been named: sudden increases in our grain exports, and OPEC's oil prices. The person was Earl Butz, primarily a raconteur and secondarily an agricultural economist, whom President Nixon named secretary of agriculture just before the 1972 election.

Butz's move into the secretary's office is a story of its own. It illustrates the occasional crudity of personnel management in government. When Clinton Anderson was secretary of agriculture, Louis Bean was in his office as economic adviser. Bean learned he had been displaced when, on returning from a trip, he found his furniture in the hall.

President Nixon did not fire Clifford Hardin quite as brusquely. But prior to the 1972 election campaign Nixon decided that Hardin was not colorful enough to give him the support he feared he would need. Butz, who had been an assistant secretary when Nixon was vice president, was anything but colorless. While Hardin was abroad, Butz was named to replace him.

Butz was basically anti-program. It galled him to have to enforce acreage controls. He rejoiced when exports relieved the gluts and he could call not for acreage reductions but instead for increased output. In hundreds of news stories, he has since been credited with urging farmers to "plant fence row to fence row." Did he really say it? Wayne Rasmussen, the USDA's superb historian, searched for the phrase in Butz speeches. He could not find it. Queried as to whether he had called for fence-row to fence-row planting, Butz told Rasmussen, "I don't remember ever using those words. But I could have; I said the same thing in other words."

Harold Breimyer was not anti-program. But he regarded the secretary's judgments as correct and endorsed the laxity of those years. Actually, the law provided for phasing acreage reduction in and out as needed. Breimyer upbraided Butz only one time. The testy secretary had hit the airwaves early one summer, a couple of days before a crop report was due to be released, with a forecast of the year's crop production that was politically appealing but factually wrong. Breimyer editorialized that when his own Crop Reporting Board is about to announce the official data, the secretary of agriculture should button his lip. The comment was picked up by the press. The secretary may have read it.

Butz's verbal insensitivities — to put it nicely — finally got him into trouble. On an air flight he made an ethnically crude remark. By that time Gerald Ford had succeeded Richard Nixon as President. When he heard of the incident, he excused Butz from further service.

THE 1973 LAW

Earl Butz was not the only one who rejoiced in the placid atmosphere of the early years of his secretaryship. Many farmers did, too. At a Perry Seminar on the University of Missouri campus in the mid-1970s, Harold Breimyer suggested that a quiet interval was a good time to plan programs for the future. A farmer in the audience jumped to his feet. "Don't you understand, Professor Breimyer," he said scornfully, "that there won't be any need for farm programs in the future?"

Undaunted, the professor inscribed the same suggestion in a letter to his friend Butz. A functionary's coldly negative reply was couched in almost the same language as the Missouri farmer's. Years later, Breimyer told Butz about how rudely he had been treated. Both laughed about the callous working of bureaucracy. Earl Butz would have responded cordially if the letter had reached him.

Even though the setting was low-pressure, or perhaps because that was so, both the 1973 farm law and the 1977 one that followed it were noteworthy pieces of legislation. The "Agriculture and Consumer Protection Act of 1973" was distinguished for introducing the term "target price" as the governor of the amount of deficiency payment to be paid a farmer.

As Harold Breimyer wrote in his Extension letter *Economic and Marketing Information* for November 1973, "Direct Treasury payments [had previously] wiggled their way into farm programs as a substitute for relying on high price supports. . . ." Also, "in the 1970 law direct payments, land retirement ('set aside'), and price supports were all wrapped up together" (p.2). The 1973 law codified the whole matter. It established a relationship between target prices and loan rates that became a fixture. Data of the time illustrate. The target price for wheat was set at $2.05 for both 1974 and 1975. The loan rate was $1.37. If the market price were to average below $2.05, eligible farmers would receive a payment equivalent to the shortfall. The maximum amount, however, was $0.68, the difference between the target price and loan rate.

Breimyer sensed, perceptively, a self-limiting feature of the program. If markets were to weaken and set-asides were announced, he wrote in his November Extension letter, "any deficiency payment is then not just a supplement to income, . . . but also payment for setting land aside. . . . " The farmer who signs for the program would be gambling—gambling that markets would be weak. He would retire some of his productive resource on the expectation of weak markets. But he would be left "without any assurance that he will get a payment" (p.3), for if markets turned out to be strong, he would receive no benefit from his participation. Worse, he would be helping to give nonparticipating farmers a free ride.

The whole scheme is partially self-defeating. Insofar as farmers anticipate stronger markets, they will abstain from participating. If enough do so, the program proves ineffective in limiting production and strengthening markets. These implicit features were explained in an editorial comment in the November Extension letter:

> It would have been better to separate the deficiency payment principle entirely from rental payments for set aside.

And further,

> If [set-asides] become necessary, the self-defeating contradiction will come painfully into view. Required set asides cannot be used successfully to keep prices near or above target levels, because insofar as they do that the farmer gets little or no return and will not participate. (p.4)

Fourteen years later, in 1987 testimony before the Committee on Agriculture, Nutrition, and Forestry of the U.S. Senate, "Targeting as a Principle in Farm Policy," Breimyer begged for farm-law changes that would separate from the deficiency-payment formula the portion that is "reward for a farmer's . . . idling land . . . The sensible course is just to make those payments as straight per-acre rent—paid diversion. Pay the same rate to everyone. . . . " "An acre idled," Breimyer explained, "should draw the same reimbursement irrespective of size of farm" (p.2).

THE 1977 LAW

The Food and Agriculture Act of 1977 continued the terms of the 1973 law. The two laws were similar in that neither promised or demanded much. The two fit the temper of the times. In his November 1973 Extension letter Harold Breimyer had written, "The new farm law will work well if it is not expected to do too much" (p.3). In January 1978 he used identical language in appraising the 1977 law (p.4).

As was to be expected, the 1977 law increased the target prices and minimum loan rates. For wheat, the data for the 1978 crop were $3.00 and $2.35 respectively. One wrinkle was to provide for some annual modification of the statutory prices. Price history bore on the loan rate: If the market price weakened, the rate could be reduced 10 percent. Crop size entered into the target price formula: The 1978 wheat target would be increased slightly if the crop proved to be short.

The most innovative contribution of the 1977 law was to offer participating farmers two choices in storage loans. The first was the familiar non-recourse loan. The second was a farmer-held reserve, in which farmers could elect to put their grain in storage for as long as three to five years. They would receive a storage payment for doing so. Only if the market price were to rise to a trigger point would the storage payment be discontinued. At a second, higher, trigger level the loan would be called.

Crop Insurance and Disaster Payments. Ever since the 1930s it had been a credo of successive secretaries of agriculture that although the government provided subsidized protection from the vagaries of unsteady demand, it felt less responsibility to offset the effects of variable weather. Any shielding against crop losses should be funded by insurance premiums, in their view.

A federal crop insurance program was framed and offered as early as 1938. Harold Breimyer had a small hand in designing it. The program was narrow in both coverage and access, and not a howling success.

Temptation had never died to put crop-loss protection of some kind into price-support programs. The 1973 law provided for disaster payments. They were not insurance but, rather, a handout. Breimyer wrote in his Extension letter of November 1973:

> If drought, flood, or other natural disaster prevents producers of feed grains, wheat, or cotton from planting their crops, they will be eligible for payments at the rate of one-third the target price on the normal

yield for allotted acres. If a farmer is similarly prevented from harvesting two-thirds of his normal crop, he shall be paid an amount based on the nonharvested portion. (p.2)

The 1977 law essentially continued the same program.

A new enterprise found its way to U.S. farms. It was to farm the disaster program. Many farmers found the attraction of taking high risks in seeding crops to be irresistible. Disaster claims and payments shot upward as a meteor. The story was told, and vouched for as true, about a farmer in a low-rainfall Colorado county who was visited as he pulled his grain drill over his field, lap after lap. "But there's no seed in the drill," the visitor ejaculated. "Why waste it?" the farmer asked. The question was sensible; he was only farming the disaster program.

Secretary Bergland called the disaster program "a disaster" and pressed for revitalized crop insurance to replace it. Just before he and President Carter left office, a major new crop insurance program became law — the most significant agricultural law of the Carter years. It broadened the coverage and, for the first time, provided specifically for government subsidy toward its operating cost. Federal funds were to pay 30 percent of the premium charge for the two lower levels of coverage. A farmer who elected the highest protection (the third level) had to pay the incremental cost. Private insurance companies lobbied so hard against a federal program that they were granted authority to write insurance contracts — for a fee, of course.

Although he did not care for private agents, Harold Breimyer generally defended the new program. He regretted that only a minority of farmers enrolled in it. "Farmers are splendid corn-growers but lousy actuaries," he told one and all. They simply could not appreciate how high is the risk of crop loss, and therefore mistakenly regarded premium rates as too high. A bargain was available to them, but most passed it up.

Breimyer as a Populist Puritan nonetheless was bothered by the opportunity for farmers to be paid as much when low yields are caused by bad farming practices as when they result from bad weather. For years he had praised the proposal of his friend Harold Halcrow of the University of Illinois. In a year of drought, advocated Halcrow, let drought areas be delineated where the shortfall of precipitation is nearly uniform. Then pay off all farmers in each area by the same percentage of their normal yield. In that way the careless farmers are denied a program bonanza. Other kinds of damage, as from hail, would be assessed farm by farm. To date no one in authority has acknowledged the Halcrow-Breimyer wisdom.

Although the disaster provisions of the 1973 and 1977 laws were discontinued, in 1988 a severe drought brought a generous $4 billion aid package. It seemed likely to discourage participation in crop insurance. "Why pay a premium," farmers were wont to ask, "if the government is going to come through with drought aid?"

Perhaps the day will never arrive when farmers will have to depend on a solid, actuarially sound insurance program as their guard against crop losses. Too bad.

CHAPTER 18

Oil, Energy, and the Supply and Price of Land

THE FARM POLICY BULLRING may have been comparatively quiet during the 1970s, but in other respects the decade was turbulent. The turbulence not only reached to farm affairs, but it actually enveloped them.

CLUB OF ROME, OPEC, AND A RAID ON U.S. GRAIN STOCKS

In the early years of the 1970s, an unlikely team of thinkers and an even stranger gang of activists, each scarcely aware of the other's presence, reinforced each other in reminding the Western world of an incontestable fact: Planet Earth, on which we all depend as we whirl through space, is an isolated ball possessed of limited resources.

The Club of Rome, a study team, shocked all literate populations as it portrayed not only the progressive, and geometrically speeding, rate at which Earth's stock of depletable resources was being used up. It also showed, on graphs that suggested the imminence of Armageddon, the rapid increase of pollution.

Also from the scholarly crowd came Barbara Ward and Rene Dubos, writing *Only One Earth*. The book admonished, as its subtitle indicated, "The Care and Maintenance of a Small Planet." Harold Breimyer assigned it to his bright students in honors courses, and it doubtless was drawn on similarly on many campuses. It, too, told how profligate are our practices in using up and failing to protect the planet's physical resources.

As though the thinkers lacked convincing power, early in the 1970s

233

the world's major petroleum-exporting countries activated their long-quiet cartel, the Organization of Petroleum Exporting Countries (OPEC). It was alleged later that the instigation came not from Sheik Zaki Yamani of Saudi Arabia and other bright U.S.-educated Arabs, but instead from Armand Hammer of U.S. Occidental Oil and other Western oil men. Those practical Americans could foresee that if Arabian or Libyan oil were to go up in price, so would the dollar yield of their U.S. wells. Khadaffi of Libya probably had a hand in it.

The price of oil at Middle Eastern ports, which had been in the range of $2.00 to $3.00 a barrel, was pushed up in 1973–74 to $8.00 to $9.00. That increase was only the first thrust. Later, in 1978–79, the price was doubled. In the early 1980s it escalated further, to a peak that held briefly at about $34.00.

Virtually all the physical components of Western civilization have long been based on cheap energy. OPEC's action was a jolt of atomic intensity.

The high prices created serious problems for oil-importing economies. They also told the world, with more convincing power than any professor's eloquence, that petroleum is a depletable resource and its reserve stock is being depleted fast.

In a strange sequence, yet another group of actors helped get across the message that the planet's productive resources — land, in this case — are basically limited. They were the world's grain traders. In the early 1970s they began to move grain around the globe in increasing volume. Country after country entered the market to fill its bins. Episodes of dry weather limited production, even as economic prosperity added to demand. The export boom of the decade got under way. It enriched exporting countries but revived ancient fears that food could run short.

The flamboyant actor in the episode was the Soviet Union. As early as the spring of 1972, that nation had begun to buy wheat. Its objective was to compensate for short crops and to improve diets. In 1973, following a poor crop, the Soviet government quietly contracted for all the wheat it could find. It bought out U.S. wheat from under the thumbs of the Commodity Credit Corporation, at bargain prices made even lower by an export subsidy. When the public-exposure lid blew off, the ebullient Secretary Butz was embarrassed. He not only had been asleep at the switch but also had been outfoxed by the Russians.

In reality, as Butz's economist Don Paarlberg was quick to point out, more than the Soviets were buying our stocks. A great many other countries were doing so, too. And although Japan spent money earned in her burgeoning export trade, Third World countries soon entered the fray by recycling petrodollars. Earlier, as the oil exporters began to rake in dollars, pounds, and other Western currencies, they socked them away in developed countries' banks. The banks, in turn, lent the funds everywhere. They sent a lot to the Third World. The Third World then used part of its borrowings to enter the grain market and, in doing so, contributed to the turbulence of the 1970s.

Events in the grain trade during the decade carried the message of a limit to resources. In turn, they also set the stage for the bust that was to follow in the 1980s.

The surge in world demand for grain was made to order for the United States, which was quick to capitalize on it. Unlike most other exporting countries, the United States had stocks on hand. Also, the 50 to 60 million acres of idled farmland (idled as set-aside) were available to be put back into production, at the beck-and-call of the secretary of agriculture. Furthermore, devaluation of the U.S. dollar made it easy for U.S. grain traders to outbid others. Our nation rejoiced in its good fortune. Consumers, though, began to worry. It seemed to them that the numbers on their check-out tabs at supermarkets climbed higher each week. They did not take the higher food prices lightly; and their protests converted readily into apprehensions about food-producing resources.

EXTENSION EDUCATION ABOUT LIMITED LAND AND SCARCE ENERGY

The events of the surprising 1970s set the tone for Extension education in public affairs. Economists always are more at home with notions of scarcity than of plenty. After all, what is economics about, other than the allocation of scarce resources?

The Puritan-tilted Harold Breimyer began quickly to shift his Extension teaching to preservation of cropland and the economics of energy. He gave less attention to the former, although he joined in seminars on the subject. He supported the legislation introduced in Missouri and many states to authorize preferential assessment of cropland. He knew that allowing cropland to be assessed at farming rather than developmental value would not keep it in farming indefinitely. But the law could slow the trend toward erecting office buildings and condominiums on the black alluvial soil of the Missouri River bottom near St. Louis. Besides, the law had educational value.

Energy. In Harold Breimyer's car pool in Washington just after World War II was an attractive brunette lady named Abbadee. Light, frivolous talk is resorted to in car pools for relief of tedium. Breimyer chanced upon the theme that the automobiles that crowded the streets of Washington were drinking petroleum by the barrel. How, he asked his comely companion, would she get about when the wells run dry? Would she walk, or buy a horse?

Twenty-five years later, in his Extension teaching at Missouri, he addressed the subject again. This time he found no reason for banter. A paperback book the National Academy of Sciences published in 1969, *Resources and Man,* jarred him with its data on how finite indeed are world stocks of fossil fuel and many metallic minerals. He also took note of the projections of fossil fuel supply made by the respected geologist M. King Hubbert. Hubbert showed annual petroleum production as climbing to the peak of a hill and then descending in a smooth arc, completing a silhouette as symmetrical as that of the Japanese mountain Fujiyama (remembered from Lt. Breimyer's war's-end weeks in Japan). Hubbert's critics scoffed, but his estimates of the rate of depleting the world's petroleum stock have since proved remarkably accurate.

Modern agriculture in the United States and elsewhere, Breimyer declared to one and all, is steeped in the economics of energy. Today's technology in farming is highly energy-intensive; agriculture is a big user of fossil fuel. But, by its nature, agriculture is a producer of energy. Growing plants capture the energy of the sun's rays and incorporate it in foodstuffs as well as fibers and tobacco leaf.

Convinced that a scarcity of fossil fuels would make itself known and felt about the turn of the century, Harold Breimyer schooled himself in energy economics. He studied two classic articles, long forgotten, written by Lewis C. Gray and Harold Hotelling. The bountifully rich United States had treated all buried minerals as though they were infinite, and put no reservation price on them. They were made available at the cost of extraction. As the stock becomes smaller and drifts into fewer and stronger hands, the monopoly-exploitation power will become enormous. So Breimyer concluded.

Breimyer joined the biomass crowd. He was persuaded that as supplies of industrial raw materials become tighter, materials of organic origin will be turned to. But he did not endorse farmers' own production of ethanol. In his Extension publications, Breimyer and his colleague Coy McNabb presented data showing that on-farm distillation is difficult and costly, as is utilization of the wet mash by-product. Moreover, the entire process is energy-inefficient; more energy is used in getting the ethanol from the grain than is contained in the product.

Breimyer joined Extension engineers, agronomists, and animal scientists in holding meetings around the state. He has long remembered the session at Warrensburg. Farmers packed the room, hoping to be told they could profitably set up stills on their farms. As they left, Breimyer searched their visages. He seemed to read, "I had hoped for a brighter message, but I'm glad I came and found out how things really are." Thus does Extension perform its grandest role, Breimyer reflected.

To the day of writing this memoir, Harold Breimyer remains convinced that biomass is a wave of the future. But that future is not close at hand.

As he writes these words, Harold Breimyer cannot know what length of life will be vouchsafed him. His genes and healthful regimen may keep him alive yet a number of years—long enough that he might witness and even experience the accuracy of the Club of Rome study and his own predictions. When the Western world approaches a terminal point for its living luxuriously on buried treasures, its cherished institutions for security and civility will come under intense strain. The consequences in terms of government, art, and even religion can scarcely be envisioned—with one exception. One outcome is inescapable. Tilling of the soil and cultivating of plants to capture the sun's energy as means to mankind's wherewithal—that is, biomass—will come into its own.

Warning of the Speculative Bubble in Farmland. Breimyer's second success story of the decade was his sending up gale warnings about the dangerous speculative buying of farmland that was going on.

In Missouri the average price of farmland in 1970 was $224 an acre. By 1975 it was up to $396. It more than doubled the next five years, reaching $878 in 1980.

Bare statistics are less graphic than an account of a South Dakota scene of about the year 1979. A grizzled old rancher and his wife of careworn face were watching an auctioneer run up the sale price of a neighbor's ranch. Eager bidders pushed the price higher and higher. The rancher turned to his wife and, applying the numbers to their holding, exclaimed, "We are millionaires!" Thousands of farmers and ranchers who had started with a small stake found the book value of their property at the end of the 1970s to reach into seven digits, often to their astonishment.

The idea that money could be made just by buying and holding property was so attractive that it caught thousands of investors in its grip. The psychology had its root, though, in the general price inflation of the 1970s. That, in turn, is easily accounted for. Deficit financing of the Vietnam conflict set it off, and it soon got a huge push from OPEC's sharp increase in oil prices, mentioned earlier. A cost-push price escalation followed. Some monetarists called for tight money in order to arrest it, but neither the Nixon and Carter administrations nor the Federal Reserve Board was willing to force the economy into a 1930s-style industrial depression. Instead, monetary policy accommodated the expanding demand for enough money to do business (at the progressively higher prices). The policy served, it must be admitted, to finance the inflation even though the money managers were innocent of an intent to do so.

It was sometimes said that the growing export demand for farm products was the prime mover behind higher land prices. It was not; it only gave an added fillip. Likewise, although the inflationary psychology did not set inflation going, it both speeded and sustained the pace. An inflationary spiral, once under way, tends to perpetuate itself.

Reckless investors had no Odysseus to put cotton in their ears. Harold Breimyer tried to perform that ear-plugging service, without much success.

Harold Breimyer knew the basic economics of land price. Over time, that price is the discounted value of income flow. By the late 1970s the price of land was at least twice as high as its income-producing capacity justified. The numbers told him that.

Moreover, he had read about the Credite Mobilier in France, Holland's tulip mania of 1634–1637, and the South Sea Bubble of 1720. He remembered the Florida land boom and bust of 1926. His bachelor uncles were tempted but, good Württembergian Germans that they were, they didn't buy Florida land that sometimes proved to be in a lake, or the ocean.

In his Extension talking and writing, Breimyer explained, and he warned — accurately, as events proved later. His Extension letter of September 1975 carried this message:

> Appreciation of capital values in agriculture has yielded a windfall income to many thousands of farm families who have been in position to cash in on it. We can rejoice in their good fortune.
>
> It promises a paper profit, not yet realized and perhaps not realizable, to two million more. A great many will not get it.
>
> This is the sort of moral situation that poet and priest have deplored since at least Old Testament times. Its benefits are brief and false and confined to a few. Its harm can be excruciating for many, when the bubble bursts. . . .
>
> No real wealth is created by a chain letter game, a lottery, or speculation in land. Any nation that tries to build upon such manipulation is headed for trouble. (p.4)

Did anyone listen? Two farmers did. Regrettably, their names have escaped memory. Early in the 1980s a letter was received from a farmer, newly retired, in northeast Missouri. "You are the greatest," he wrote (approximate paraphrase), "and the University of Missouri is outstanding. You put on a seminar about the future of family farming. When I learned it had no future, I went home and sold every one of my 680 acres. I put the money in CDs, and I will be comfortable the rest of my life."

In the spring of 1985, when filling a speaking date in eastern Illinois, Breimyer was accosted by a young farmer carrying a letter that he, Breimyer, had written to the farmer in 1980. The farmer had asked whether he should buy more land. The two-page response carried the advice: It was no time to buy land. The young man did not buy, and he was solvent in 1985 solely for that reason.

So two persons listened and acted. Perhaps a few more did so but remained silent. Insofar as some farmers took heed, Harold Breimyer's waving of red flags was a success story, a hit, on not one but two counts. It proved accurate, and a few farmers were helped.

ONE BIG MISS

It is conceivably excusable for even a memoir-writer to abbreviate his confession of error. Harold Breimyer misinterpreted what underlay the export boom of the 1970s and guessed wrong on what could be expected in the 1980s. He was too optimistic as he predicted that the uptrend of the 1970s would continue. He expected the rate of increase to slow but did not even guess that export movement would turn down sharply after its peak of 1980–81.

Data are that the value of agricultural exports, which had been only $7 to $8 billion at the beginning of the 1970s, climbed to almost $44 billion in 1980–81. That increase in value is attributable in part to price inflation, but the volume expanded substantially.

To Breimyer, the United States was in the enviable position of being almost alone among exporting nations in its ability to expand output, and therefore exports, in response to demand from an ever-growing world population. He drew on charts showing that the United States had contributed the largest part of the increase in world grain trade during the 1970s.

Events were to convince him of his error. The export value turned down in 1981–82 and descended to a low of $26 billion in 1985–86.

How could he have been so mistaken? One reason is excusable, the other not. The inexcusable reason was national pride, even chauvinism. Breimyer did not believe other countries could match ours in productivity. In particular, he regarded it incredible that crowded, industrial Europe (including the United Kingdom) could coax bountiful harvests from its northern-latitude lands. Only when he learned of England's 100-bushel wheat yields did he acknowledge his blunder. More defensible was his over-faith in a continued uptrend in world demand. He did not know that much of that demand had originated in recycled petrodollars. When he learned the data, he knew he was in trouble. His earlier optimistic export forecasts were wrong.

CHAPTER 19

Who Will Control
U.S. Agriculture?

IN THE WINTER OF 1977–78, the new and aggressive farm organization that called itself the American Agriculture Movement chose to demonstrate its members' unhappiness and its corporate political power by sending an entourage of tractors to Washington. The cavalcade ("tractorcade") camped on the grounds between the Washington monument and Capitol building. A detail of the farmers barricaded the office of the secretary of agriculture, Bob Bergland.

Bergland promptly took off for the Old Executive Office Building, where he began to catch up on his reading. What did he read? Among other papers he read several written by Philip Raup and Harold Breimyer relating to what academics call the organizational structure of agriculture. Extension economists put it in the form of the question that is the title for this chapter: Who will control U.S. agriculture?

Bergland was a dairy farmer from the cold north woods of Minnesota who became active in Minnesota farm organizations. He was elected to the U.S. House of Representatives, where he was assigned to the Committee on Agriculture. President Jimmy Carter named him secretary of agriculture.

As a Minnesota farm leader he had been in touch with Raup, a professor of agricultural economics at the state's university. Bergland became acquainted with Harold Breimyer when Breimyer appeared on the program of several Minnesota farm meetings. So, during a snowy Washington winter, the lean, astute countryman secretary, holed up in the marble halls of a building that, according to folklore, had been made ornate so as to forestall moving the seat of government out of Washington. There he read the opinions of two old friends. He took seriously what they said about contemporary threats to traditional proprietary ("family farm") agriculture.

When the AAM cleared out (or relented) and Bergland returned to his USDA office, he told the Economic Research Service to get busy studying the topic of the structure of agriculture. He assigned the bright and beauteous Susan Sechler to ride herd on the show. Capable economists such as David Harrington were drawn into the project.

Harold Breimyer was delighted. He and others reflected, "So USDA has finally caught on that structure of agriculture is a policy issue! Where have they been? What took them so long?"

Breimyer was called to Washington to review the first papers the ERS wrote. He told Susan Sechler they were terrible. She scolded and counseled the ERS people, and the next batch was better. The final report from the project, *A Time to Choose,* is excellent.

As a part of the project, Secretary Bergland held ten regional hearings. Breimyer spoke at the Sedalia, Missouri, one. He had lunch with Secretary Bergland. Two memories remain from that day. He learned that Bergland liked to sneak a chew of tobacco. The other memory was the loudly-voiced statement of Dale Lyon, president of the Kansas Farmers Union. He told the audience that the University of Missouri had in Harold Breimyer the country's best-informed person on the structure of agriculture. He should be listened to, Lyon said.

EARLY BREIMYER WRITING AND TEACHING

For the first time, this memoir is using a device novelists like so much — the flashback. But before Harold Breimyer's first work is annotated, the sequel to Secretary Bergland's highlighting of structural issues can be stated quickly. In short, there was none — no follow-up.

In November 1980 Ronald Reagan's election victory held Jimmy Carter to a single term as president and pushed Bob Bergland out of office. Soon afterward a congressional committee addressed the structural question. Richard Lyng, newly appointed deputy secretary of agriculture, testified. "What about the structural issue?" he was asked. "There isn't any," was the substance of his long reply. As far as he and new Secretary John Block were concerned, structure was a non-issue. So it remained, officially, during the Reagan years.

Even at the time of this writing, Harold Breimyer finds it hard to explain why he was preoccupied for so many years with who will own and control agriculture and what the role of the farmer will be. The explanation may begin with his sensitivity to the human side of all economic matters. In agriculture he was concerned for the status and welfare of the man and woman who do the actual farming. He did not want to see them disfranchised, reduced from freeholding to a subservient role. As a 4-H Club member in his native Ohio, he had joined lustily, if off-key, in singing the 4-H song with its words, as recited earlier in this memoir: "Sons of the soil are we, men of the coming years. Turning our sod, asking no odds, lords of our land we'll be." He may not have expected, or desired, to be a lord of land, but he wanted his fellows to have a chance.

During his USDA years Harold Breimyer had learned about the meaning of status from the well-known economist-philosopher John Brewster. Next after meeting the minimum necessities for survival such as food and shelter, Brewster pointed out, human beings need a sense of their worth, their status. He called the impulse the "striving for significance." "Men the world over," he wrote, "strive for an ever finer image of themselves in their own eyes and the eyes of others." (pp. 8–9).

Farmers on their land have treasured their status, their self-image. During the 1980s thousands of farmers went into despondency when they were forced to leave their land. A commonplace explanation was that they feared loss of income. It missed the Brewster point a country mile. They had been lords of their land. Thereafter they were not sure even of being serfs.

In his 1965 book, *Individual Freedom and the Economic Organization of Agriculture,* Harold Breimyer set forth several reasons why it matters as to what kind of agriculture our country is to have in the future—what its organizational structure is to be. Aware of the exploitive power of landholders under Europe's onetime feudalism, he saw merit in not converting agriculture into what he called a layer-cake class (caste) system, with its inequity and smoldering social unrest. "Until men learn to live in more amity," he wrote, "a plus value must be marked up for those forms of economic organization that keep the social pot from boiling too hard or too often" (p.77).

As another facet, he saw family farm agriculture as "virtually the last outpost of small entrepreneurship" in the economy (p. 16). He wondered if there might be social merit in keeping one economic sector in comparatively modest entrepreneurial hands.

From his first writing he disappointed many defenders of a family farm agriculture by not building his case on moral values, even though not necessarily denying them. "[The question] is not whether agriculture can claim an implicit superiority or even whether it contains or instills personal qualities that are unique. It is rather whether agriculture, and rural life generally, as an integral part of total society any longer has anything to offer it" (p.15).

Harold Breimyer had presented his first paper on the structure of agriculture at Moorhead, Minnesota, in January 1962. He included the subject in a series of seminars he gave at Texas A & M University in 1963. Thereafter he wrote and talked on the subject on many occasions.

As Extension economist at Missouri he developed a presentation that he used at county meetings. He had his "gingerbread man" that he would put on a flannel board. The family farmer is a composite man, he explained. He is at once owner, manager, laborer, technical expert. In a different kind of agriculture, the gingerbread man would be pulled apart and each portion would become a separate man. One would be owner, another manager, a third hired worker, and a fourth technician. They would not be of equal status. Which kind of agriculture do we want?

He hooked the structural question into his teaching about farm programs. He told both his Extension audiences and students in the classroom that structure is a part of policy for two reasons. One is that our price and income policy always has been designed for a decentralized, pluralistic agriculture. If agriculture were an oligopoly, there would be no farm programs as they have been known since 1933. Second, any preference for a particular structure is itself a policy matter.

The structure of agriculture is determined by credit policy, he explained; by how the benefits in farm commodity programs are distributed; by income and estate tax policy (this above all others); and by research-and-education policy. Also bearing on structure are a number of state laws that limit the largest corporate farming entities.

NORTH CENTRAL EXTENSION

During the 1970s the Extension Services of a number of states developed an interest in the structure of agriculture. In the North Central Region a regional committee wrote a series of bulletins, all under the title, *Who Will Control U.S. Agriculture?* Breimyer was one of a dozen contributors to the lead publication, which came out in August 1972. He, along with James Tucker, Hoy Carman, Richard Fenwick, and Fred Woods, published, in 1974, *How Federal Income Tax Rules Affect Ownership and Control of Farming.* A year later he and Michael Boehlje wrote the third part of *Death and Taxes: Policy Issues Affecting Farm Property Transfers.*

It was not hard to teach about structure in Missouri. Almost all Missouri's farmers are family farmers or think of themselves in those terms. Very few megafarms or giant corporate farms are to be found in the state.

Harold Breimyer almost got his comeuppance, though, when he accepted an invitation to talk about structure of agriculture before a group of California farmers. He flew to the airport in San Francisco, where a room had been reserved for the day's session. A few dozen California farmers and ranchers came in from the valleys or mountains, often flying their own planes. They were not of the genre of Missouri's family farmers. Also present was a sprinkling of small-farm activists, long a thorn in the flesh of big California farmers who use minimum-wage migratory Hispanic workers to work land that is made fabulously productive by subsidized irrigation water.

By that time Breimyer was so inured in Extension teaching that he could smell a risky situation. At San Francisco he could sniff potential hostility. To this day he does not know how he chanced on a visual-graphics device. On the blackboard he drew the outlines of fish of successively larger sizes. The smallest fish on the left was about to be devoured by a somewhat larger fish behind it, that fish was followed by a still larger one, and the last on the right was at least a dolphin, if not a whale. The farmers and ranchers got the point before their instructor explained it. No matter how large a farmer may be, and how intent on swallowing smaller farmers in the neighborhood, an even larger predator lurks silently behind. The dolphin/whale was probably Tenneco or whatever investment giant was regarded as the greatest threat of the time. The Californians got the point, and their instructor escaped unscathed.

Some years later Breimyer came across other demonstrations of the identical instructional device. These, however, were complete with neatly drawn fish silhouettes instead of the crude sketches he had improvised in a San Francisco airport room.

"FARMING'S NON-INSTINCT FOR SELF-PRESERVATION"

During the years of his Extension work in public affairs, Harold Breimyer drifted into political science, philosophy, and other related disciplines. He made his students learn about "values," for instance. He insisted that the basic issues relating to a desirable structure of agriculture have little to do with material considerations including operating efficiency. They are a matter of preferred values. What do we envision as a desired role for people in agriculture? What kind of fabric of rural society? These are the value questions, he said.

He became impressed with the political-science aspects of a decentralized family-farm agriculture. He perceived a tenuousness to it and in fact to all forms of social organization to which the term "decomposed" can be applied. The unit that is at once the essential constituent and exalted object of the system is itself powerless either to put the system in place or to assure its continuity. Worse, emphasis on the heroically individualistic aspects discourages the jointness of action that alone can preserve the system.

At the April 1972 convention of the Farmers Cooperative Grain Dealers Association of Oklahoma, Breimyer gave a talk carrying the title, "Farming's Non-instinct for Self-preservation." He was to use the phrase and the message countless times thereafter. He made his classroom students wrestle with it, as an illustration of the textbook principle of fallacy of composition.

Farmers, he pointed out, are so individualistic and so preoccupied with what appears good on their own income-and-expense and balance sheets that they cannot even perceive that what may look attractive to them individually may be harmful to farmers as a whole.

The several examples he offered need not be cited here, except for the one he highlighted most often: Income tax concessions. Farmers take delight in any expensing they can write off in calculating their tax liability. They can be deaf to whether the concession helps or hurts them relative to other investors in farming. Breimyer tried hard to get across the maxim that any deduction from income subject to tax is of advantage in proportion to the taxpayer's tax bracket. As most family farmers are in the lower brackets, they gain less from deductions than do high-bracket competitors. The neat line he ended with was, "The family farmer fails to see that what looks good to him individually can doom him collectively"; or, in another version, "What looks good to the family farm*er* can kill family farm*ing*."

Harold Breimyer nudged and poked and inveigled Missouri farmers to understand his pedagogy about income taxes and non-self-preservation, and maybe even accept it. He quoted others. He liked his friend Phil Raup's line, "It is ironic that family farmers have provided much of the voting strength for the continuation of . . . policies that discriminate against them."

During the profitable 1970s, when some Missouri farmers climbed to higher tax brackets, the response was ambiguous. Tax-paying farmers would beg their organizations to press for more sheltering write-offs. But in responding to the opinion polls that Harold Breimyer took at three- to five-year intervals, the majority would acknowledge that shelters were harmful to family farming. (They of course, almost to a man, declared their preference for family farming.) When the awful 1980s came and few farmers owed income tax, it was easy to support tax reform. Farmers generally supported the Tax Reform Act of 1986.

A couple of years later they reverted to form. Cattlemen begged for restoring a tax deduction for the cost of raising heifer calves. In 1988 Breimyer editorialized about "The Irresistible Appeal of Tax Concessions" in *On the Economy,* shrugged his shoulders, and philosophized for the ninetieth time, "They won't learn until it's too late."

For the journal *Challenge* Harold Breimyer extrapolated in 1985 from his theses about the vulnerability of a pluralistic, decentralized ("decomposed") agriculture to a matching generalization about any social or political system in which the unit that is the intended beneficiary is neither oriented toward nor capable of saving the system. In "Agriculture and the Political Economy" he subtitled the concluding section, "The hazard of pluralism, even democracy."

> The final message of this review of the political economy of agriculture is a cosmic extrapolation. It suggests that the incapacity of an atomistic agriculture to mobilize for its survival may illustrate a flaw in any political system that enfranchises its constituent parts, even democracy itself. It also calls to mind scholarly introspections, ancient and modern.
>
> If traditional institutions of agriculture disappear, as they likely will do, the root cause will be the failure of individual farmers, glorying in their independence, to delegate centralization of power for collective defense. The paradox finds a parallel in all pluralistic economic and political systems, including political democracy. Therein may lie the most penetrating lesson an agriculture under stress has to teach in our day.
>
> For therein does agriculture today illustrate timeless issues in social structure and political organization. If the first concern in agriculture is for the welfare of farmers and not of the sector, an analogy is struck, Adam Smith aside, with all inquiries into the wealth not of a nation but of its people. Propositions, ponderable but scarcely resolvable, are those of ancient Plato and his *Republic* and *Laws;* of the more modern Edmund Burke, preoccupied with *Natural Society* and *Discontents;* of the Germans' dichotomy of *Gemeinschaft* and *Gesellschaft;* and of what the sociologists of our day, less intellectual, simply call the search for community.
>
> Whatever else can be drawn from the agricultural economy in its present peril, the deepest meaning lies in demonstration value for the political economy. (p.21)

Harold Breimyer may have been hallucinating, but he dared believe that the political economy of agriculture into which he had delved for so long contained a lesson applicable even to the democracy of the nation.

CHAPTER 20

The 1980s: The 1920s Deja Vu

UPON THE ARRIVAL OF THE 1980s, winds of change blew across the United States of America with the force of a hurricane. The incarceration of Americans in Iran during the Carter tenure, unprecedented in our national history, helped Ronald Reagan unseat the Georgian from the presidency. Reagan represented the "wild and woolly West" wing of the Republican party, which had displaced the liberal Eastern establishment at the party's control center. Although he and his team were not able to deliberalize national affairs totally—they only clipped the wings of labor unions, for example, rather than abolish them—they instituted profound changes in our national life.

Pundits and scholars invariably vie to interpret any new era. They did so valiantly as the Reagan years began to take shape. Old debates came to life once again about the relative importance of the people and the times—of the person(s) in leadership, and of the era. Was Ronald Reagan a product of his time or a shaper of it? The puzzler is identical with that asked about Franklin Roosevelt. Did Roosevelt make the New Deal, or did the crisis of the 1930s make him a New Dealer? The question was asked often.

The personality of Reagan as president was so transparently visible and his policies so graphically revealed that it was easy to write about him. He was known to be lax in his work habits (just plain lazy, it could be said, and was). His aides kept his press conferences to a minimum because he invariably was guilty of gaffes. It became a favorite game of journalists to ask whom Reagan resembled more closely, the incompetent Warren Harding or Silent Cal (Calvin) Coolidge.

Harold Breimyer thought the question to be apt, and as his memory began with the years of the two presidencies, just to ask it reminded him of the *deja vu*. He was back to where he had already been—was seeing what he had previously seen.

Lacking knowledge about the government they headed, Harding and Coolidge relied heavily on members of their cabinet and staff. Reagan did the same. Harding was guilty of cronyism, a mark of Reagan. Reagan's attorney general, Edwin Meese, bore a resemblance to Harding's Harry Daugherty, whom Harding took from Washington Court House, Ohio, to Washington, D.C. Mishandling of money in the Iran-Contra affair, a major blemish of the second Reagan term, brought to mind the Fall-Sinclair scandal of the Harding years.

Breimyer was more attentive to public sentiment and the political process than to the personal qualities of a sportscaster and western-movie actor whose microphone poise and political pliability had induced wealthy Californians to promote him first into the state's governorship and then into the presidency. His indignation soared, nevertheless, when at the 1985 Gridiron Club dinner Reagan told the white-tie crowd that he had found a solution to the farm problem. "I think we should keep the grain and export the farmers." When the line fell flat, the President was asked if he regretted saying it. "Yeah, he replied, cause I didn't get a laugh." Crude, thought Breimyer.

Midway in his second term several of Reagan's former staff members wrote of their White House experiences. Their disclosures often were defamatory. David Stockman, for example, revealed that he never could get Reagan to understand the significance of a budget deficit.

Quotations from two well-known journalists illustrate the kind of commentary that was commonplace during the Reagan years. Kevin Phillips, a Republican spokesman, summed the Reagan philosophy and policies in this way: "First and foremost it's a politics of easy, feel-good victories . . . and the economics of free lunches. In Reaganology, budget deficits don't get in the way of tax cuts, trade deficits do not call for cutting back on imported automobiles and cappuccino machines."[1]

Hodding Carter, III, had served in the Jimmy Carter administration. A sharp-penned correspondent, he expressed in a 1986 column a viewpoint that had high currency among both Democrats and at least Eastern Republicans: "The fundamental fiscal reality of our time . . . is that a conservative government in a conservative time has managed to borrow and spend the nation into the status of debtor abroad and bankrupt at home. The name of the public-policy game for six years has [been] the encouragement of private selfishness and public irresponsibility."[2]

[1]*Kansas City Times,* April 28, 1987.
[2]*Wall Street Journal,* November 6, 1986.

HOW TO ACCOUNT FOR THE 1980s

For Harold Breimyer the 1980s were *deja vu* in many respects. In taking him back to the 1920s, the new decade closed a circle.

To regard Ronald Reagan in his role as president as a reincarnation of Warren Harding was eerie. It seemed especially so when voters, after four years of observation, chose him for a second term. But the 1980s resembled the 1920s in so many ways. The notion of cyclicality of human affairs, noted earlier in these pages, came again to mind. The Russian Kondratieff had suggested a cycle with a pulse-beat of about half a century. The periodicity fit the 1920s–1980s.

Why should Homo sapiens trace a cyclical pattern in his affairs? Do people weary of innovation and revert periodically to *status quo ante?* Harold Breimyer found the thesis credible, inasmuch as the liberalizing, progressive, innovative spirit of the 1930s faded during the years after the war, was revitalized briefly during the Kennedy euphoria, then virtually disappeared. It was followed by the 1980 reversion to the 1920s. Or so he saw things.

But chance events enter in, too. The Vietnam debacle left America dispirited. OPEC, with its redistribution of world wealth, jolted all Western oil-importing nations. The Toyota automobile that crowded city streets reminded one and all that the center of industrial enterprise and finance capital was moving from the United States to the Rim of Asia.

In national affairs the white-hot branding iron for the 1980s was, of course, fiscal irresponsibility. Persistent deficits in the federal budget added rapidly to the internal government debt. Because they contributed to a negative imbalance in foreign trade, they had the further and more alarming effect of literally selling out the great United States to foreign lenders and investors. By the end of the Reagan years, Japan had not only lent untold billions of dollars but was rapidly buying our country's productive assets.

The president of the United States and a majority of his constituents stood silently and idly by.

The 1920s Revisited in Agriculture. In agricultural affairs the collapse in land values in the early 1980s was almost an exact duplication of the dreadful similar experience beginning in 1921. Even the antecedents were almost alike. In the 1920s an end to strong wartime demand turned land markets downward. In the 1980s it was the speculative boom of the 1970s, partly export-fueled, that came to a crushing end.

The similarity between the two times did not end with their origins.

In the Harding years the only action taken was to hold high-level conferences as farmers were dispossessed. Under Reagan, as farm liquidation devastated families and claimed farmers' lives (by suicide), David Stockman opined that there were too many farmers anyway.

The commodity support programs of the 1980s retained the general pattern they had held for a long time, but they fell more and more under the dominion of large cash-crop producers. They did so to the extent that Willard Cochrane announced in 1987 that he wanted to terminate them. Cochrane, as economist to USDA Secretary Orville Freeman, had been their staunch defender. But he could tell a Missouri audience in 1987 that the programs have contributed "to a growing concentration of landholding in U.S. agriculture." "By virtue of this process," to which he applied the term "cannibalism," "productive resources in farming have been concentrated into the hands of fewer and fewer, and larger and larger, farmers" (p. 29).

The Farmers Home Administration continued to be charged with supplying finance capital to farmers with limited resources, but it squirmed to avoid fulfilling that mandate. It showed more interest in making emergency credit available to big borrowers.

Less Hands-On Government. During the 1980s the progressive ("graduation") feature of the federal income tax was compromised severely. In 1981 President Reagan pushed through a reluctant Congress, with the help of a nest of conservative Southern Democrats called Boll Weevils, the Economic Recovery Tax Act of that year. Neil Harl, economist-lawyer at Iowa State University, called it "the most irresponsible congressional act of this century." It threw the federal budget into a huge deficit, offered enormous tax write-offs via countless shelters, and paved the way for the 1986 law that scaled down the progressivity in rate structure. Thereafter, everyone paid less tax than before, and the rich a lot less. The government increased its borrowings, primarily from other countries.

The two dramatic revisions in income tax law during the 1980s illustrate an internal inconsistency in federal policies of the time, one not understood by citizens whose thinking processes were cauterized by the persistent pitch of the Reagan administration that it was getting government off their backs (the precise language that was used).

During the decade the direct, hands-on role of government—to aid or to restrain individuals and businesses—was indeed circumscribed. The federal government curtailed legal aid to the poor and antitrust action against big business. But in sharp and stark contrast, the 1980s continued a trend toward an ever more powerful indirect government influence over the economy. Macroeconomic control was enhanced greatly. The big three among policies were monetary, fiscal, and income tax. Monetary policy was the province of the Federal Reserve Board. That august body took actions, especially under Paul Volcker's chairmanship, that could make or break whole sectors of the economy.

Thousands of new businesses were creatures of the 1981 tax law, and then became victims of the partially-corrective 1986 law. What a vicious sequence!

Persistent fiscal deficits had so many evil consequences that it's pointless to enumerate them. Not to be overlooked is the building up, as the conservative columnist George Will pointed out, of a rentier class of recipients of interest payments on the debt that the deficits gave rise to.

On every occasion when he could discreetly do so, Harold Breimyer gave the lie to the line that the role of government was reduced during the 1980s. The role was not reduced, he said; it was just converted from overt to covert. And the latter is harder to deal with. It is insidious.

Yet another ingredient in the strange mix of government and politics in the 1980s came to mind: the near-reversal of party roles. The Republicans had always been, or at least had portrayed themselves, as the party of a discretely limited government and fiscal responsibility. They enforced the antitrust laws so as to allay the need for a regulatory function by government. All these identifying precepts were violated blatantly during the 1980s.

In the same vein, it occurred to the 1930s' veteran Breimyer to ask: Where were to be heard the noisy catcalls that had daily denounced Franklin Roosevelt? Who was the new Westbrook Pegler to excoriate any official who raised his head?

Breimyer decided that what had happened was that the political rightists, unable to junk the New Deal machinery, took over its control. They metered out Social Security and food stamps as tranquilizers and hired the most talented journalists to mold, or at least sway, public opinion. Does every social revolution end in capitulation to the forces that initially had been revolted against?

A sequel to engaging both major political parties in a contest for the macroeconomic policy helm was to open the door wide to the newest among nihilists, the Libertarians. They were quick to organize and profess the pure anti-government doctrine. They became the True Believers of the kind the literate longshoreman Eric Hoffer had denounced a generation before.

Glorified Materialism. Harold Breimyer observed that the 1980s reverted to the 1920s in various public mores. The 1920s had opened with a carryover of the austerity of the war years, which had culminated in adopting the Eighteenth Amendment to prohibit the manufacture, sale, or transportation of intoxicating liquors. The moral ambience shifted rapidly during the rollicking 1920s. America discovered how quickly it could industrialize and promise, if not provide, everyone the means for self-indulgent living. Even the so-called prohibition amendment became a facade for its raucous and widely publicized evasions. Puritan tradition gave way to materialism at breakneck speed. By the time of the stock market crash, a car in every garage and a chicken in every pot were said to be everyone's lot, and buying stock shares was the assured means thereto.

In a paper given at the annual meeting of the American Home Economics Association in June 1980, Breimyer struck the similarities between the mores at the onset of the 1980s and those sixty years earlier. He said the 1920s' materialism had reappeared in full glory. He reported that during the years of his youth, "the three most advertised symbols of material comfort were home refrigerators with cooling unit on top [i.e., General Electric], sleek automobiles, and cigarettes." "Alcohol was later re-legalized" he added.

Even in 1980, he explained in "Our Common Future," Americans liked to say they continued to hold to a nonmaterialistic ethic: "Still today my rural audiences proclaim their allegiance to that ethic." He went further:

> The ethic is essentially ascetic. By contrast, no single trend during my lifetime stands forth so graphically as the steady, insistent, relentless glorifying of sensual pleasure. We are a nation of professed Puritans and practicing hedonists.

Then he introduced the futuristic kind of query that engaged his interest more and more during the 1980s:

> Our present drug culture is a logical extension of past trends and should have come as no surprise. It will be interesting to see whether the excesses of narcotic and hallucinating drugs will force us to reconsider our hedonistic value system. The question takes on poignancy because our high material productivity made it easy to indulge our hedonistic urges. That productivity is now in some jeopardy. Will we be forced to change our value system? (p.3)

EXTERNAL DESTABILIZATION OF AGRICULTURE

In 1945 Theodore W. Schultz, who was later to receive the Nobel Prize for economics, wrote a small book titled *Agriculture in an Unstable Economy*. Twenty years later Harold Breimyer found occasion to remark that the tables had been turned; it was then a case of unstable agriculture in an (almost) stable economy.

In the 1970s and 1980s the original Schultz phrasing became germane once again. The indefatigable Luther Tweeten at Oklahoma State University was one of a number of economists who proclaimed that most of agriculture's troubles were not generated internally but arose from outside. They were explained by an unstable general economy and erratic general policies.

Tight Money. The saga of the 1980s, following the upheavals of the 1970s that were recounted above, was reported voluminously in the press of those years. It will be a rich lode for historians for years to come.

The first landmark (or decade-mark) event anticipated the 1980s by three months. In October 1979 the Federal Reserve Board let loose a blockbuster. It turned to a severely tight monetary policy, designed and intended to lift interest rates high enough to choke off the inflation of the 1970s.

The action arrested inflation, but it also threw the economy into a tailspin. The 1982 recession that followed was the deepest since the Big One of the 1930s.

Meanwhile, an obscure professor of economics named Laffer convinced Ronald Reagan, who was eager for any rationalization for tax reduction, that if tax rates were cut sharply and tax shelters erected, the economy would burst into a blaze of prosperity. It would generate enough tax revenue to offset the initial temporary reduction — and more. Thus was born supply-side economics, also known as Reaganomics. It was incorporated in the 1981 tax reduction.

The economy recovered after 1982, but tax revenues did not. Federal on-budget receipts in fiscal 1983, in constant (deflated) dollars, were 18½ percent less than those of fiscal 1981. On a per-capita basis the reduction was more than 20 percent. The deficit in the federal budget, which had been $28 billion in 1979 and $79 billion in 1981, shot up to $208 billion in 1983.

In his public talks Breimyer read the scene in terms of an independent monetary authority doing battle with the Executive Office. The Federal Reserve Board thought it had to keep money tight to offset the inflationary effect of deficit financing. Breimyer surmised that Paul Volcker saw himself as Horatius standing at the Executive Office-Federal Reserve bridge. He fought valiantly. The Executive, on the other hand, justified its fiscal policy in terms of keeping industrial activity from being suffocated by high interest rates. Each gladiator counteracted the other. It was a standoff.

Another entry in the diary of the 1980s recorded the ups and downs in exchange rate for the U.S. dollar. Monetary exchange had been freed, early in the 1970s, from control by the International Monetary Fund. Rates were allowed, according to the propaganda, to "float." In reality only a few nations really allowed their exchange to float; the image of a trading world of floating exchange rates was illusory.

When U.S. budget deficits combined with large-scale private borrowing to bid for foreign loan funds, the dollar's exchange value went up — as did, quickly, imports of foreign goods. Our exports, especially the exports of our farm products, went down. A scenario unfolded wherein private and public borrowings from abroad increased so fast that the United States converted within a few years from being the world's biggest creditor to the world's biggest debtor.

At mid-decade six other nations cooperated to bring down the exchange value of the dollar. Thereupon huge borrowings from abroad were replaced, in substantial part, by a rush to sell assets. Japan and other countries of the Rim of Asia were the big buyers. Several European nations also entered the melee. The proud United States of America was selling itself out.

This record of the 1980s, more fantastic than any work of fiction, provides the background for issues and actions in agricultural policy during those years.

Decapitalization of Agriculture. The usual label for agriculture in the 1980s is its shrinking export markets together with the major effort of writing a 1985 farm law. Neither was the truly outstanding event of the decade. First ranking was, instead, the devastating decapitalization of assets and matching distress of farm families. It was the principal subject of Harold Breimyer's Extension teaching and writing.

Breimyer was alerted to what might be in store for the 1980s when, in November 1979, he heard Sheldon Stahl exclaim over the Federal Reserve's blockbuster action of the previous month. Breimyer concluded that $300 billion would be stripped from the asset value of U.S. agriculture. He found few believers then; they came along later.

The gross value of farm assets peaked at $1 trillion in January 1981. Breimyer's direful prediction amounted to reducing it to a figure somewhere around $700 billion.

This is not written as a drama. Let the climax be announced: In January 1987, the low point, the estimated value was $692 billion.

The forecast of capital loss was translated into the count of farmers who would be in serious trouble. Of the nation's 650,000 full-time commercial farmers, a fourth to a third would find themselves hard-pressed to stay solvent. On the other hand, a small fringe of farmers would benefit from the Fed's monetary policy. Older ones who had paid for their land by the time the 1970s' prosperity ended and who held CDs in their bank vaults would be enriched by the high interest rates. The farmers hurt badly were not the poorer farmers but, on the average, the better ones. Younger farmers who had borrowed to modernize their operations were the preponderant victims. Studies in Missouri, Iowa, and elsewhere provided confirming evidence.

In interpreting what had happened, Breimyer acknowledged, as did everyone, that farm investors had gone overboard in the 1970s. They had paid prices for land far in excess of its earning power. But he put more emphasis on the Federal Reserve Board actions, first to reduce interest rates and thereby encourage an investment boom, then to reverse its policy and choke off, brutally, the boom it had helped bring about.

He also called attention to a major change in lending practices. He wondered why other economists were blind to it. A growing number of lenders had swung from lending at fixed rates to plugging-in variable rates. The ostensible reason was valid. It was to shield lenders from the effect of future inflation. But the Federal Reserve Board crossed up lenders and borrowers alike. After late 1979, interest rates were manipulated not to match inflation but, instead, to exceed it and thereby halt it. Harold Breimyer wailed, in company with farmer borrowers, that inflation was being broken on the backs of those farmer borrowers who were paying interest at variable rates.

Before the press picked up the sensible idea and long before Washington bigwigs even admitted anything was happening, Breimyer observed laconically that it was silly to force good farmers off their land to get the capitalized value down. Foreclosure did not preserve land values. Foolish people, those lenders! Countless instances were reported in which foreclosed land was sold at a price, and a new loan extended at a level, that the ousted farmer could have borne. What sense does that make? Why not just write down the principal of the loan in the first place? Breimyer asked the questions, but neither politicians nor farm credit officials deigned to answer them.

In different words Breimyer queried, in a paper delivered in 1986 at Augustana College ("Causes Consequences, Correctives, and Christian Responses to the Farm Crisis") whether "it is socially necessary . . . to force so much dispossession in order to accommodate the decapitalization process. . . . Ought it be possible to reestablish (reduce) land values and the principal of debts without forcing so many good farmers off their land?" (p.6).

Many private banks rewrote the terms of farm mortgages. Some went broke doing so until, finally, the Federal Deposit Insurance Corporation turned sensibly accommodating. Some insurance company lenders acted considerately; some others were Simon Legrees. The Farmers Home Administration, under legal mandate, restructured some loans. The Farm Credit System, which is farmers' own cooperative, may have been the hardest-nosed of all creditors until Congress, in the Agricultural Credit Act of 1987, told it to do better.

The shoddy public record of first heavy-handedly initiating a decapitalization of agriculture, and then blindly disregarding its consequences, revealed to Harold Breimyer how far the public conscience had sunk below that of the Golden Years before and after mid-century. And how closely it resembled the barbaric 1920s. *Deja vu.*

FARM POLICIES OF THE 1980s

Ronald Reagan was confirmed into the presidency in January 1981. The nation acquired a new president and a new secretary of agriculture, but it still had an old farm law. The 1977 law carried a four-year term. The new secretary and his newly appointed crew were faced with drafting a legislative program before they could school themselves for the task.

As though to make matters worse, neither the new president nor his secretary was favorably inclined toward farm programs. Reagan as candidate had essentially promised farmers that they would thereafter be free of such annoyances.

President Reagan wanted to name as secretary of agriculture the man who had been his director of agriculture when he was governor of California. Richard Lyng, although perhaps more agribusiness- than farm-oriented, was capable. Reagan's advisers, of whom he had a trainload, put a lid on how many Californians he could appoint. Stymied, Reagan named the Illinois Director of Agriculture, John Block.

Block was a West Point graduate, large-scale hog farmer, and even larger-scale land speculator (and borrower from the Farmers Home Administration, if press accounts are correct). He was innocent of knowledge of farm programs or of economics. He was less deficient in confidence. He announced that he could spark enough revival in exports to keep a generous farm program out of trouble.

The 1981 Farm Law. Secretary Block was one of the few persons who could not see by late 1981 that the export boom was waning and surpluses were mounting. And the ill-fated secretary ran into yet another problem: The irrepressible David Stockman, director of the Office of Management and Budget, decreed that target prices must be held down close to the loan level, to economize on government costs. For some grains the target price named in the 1981 law was actually less (for the 1982 crop) than the Farmers' Reserve loan rate. What a formula for trouble!

The 1981 law was unsuited to the surplus situation that was coming to light fast in the 1980s. Harold Breimyer and his colleague Abner Womack commented editorially in *Economic and Marketing Information* for March 1982:

> Following enactment of the 1973 and 1977 farm laws, this column's comment was that each would work well if it was not expected to do too much. Now the identical judgment can be offered about the 1981 law. The law will work well if not many demands are made on it.
>
> Already the 1982 wheat and feed grains programs seem headed for trouble, unless crops in 1982 are small. The problem begins with design of the 1981 law. In order to minimize Treasury cost of deficiency payments in the short run, the Farmers' Reserve program was turned to as a way to induce participation in acreage reduction. But that laid the base for major problems in the long run. . . . We question the workability of present programs.

The 1983 PIK. By the winter of 1982–83, the surplus overload about which Breimyer and Womack warned had come into being. Rarely are forecasters proven correct so soon. Secretary Block and his undistinguished economist William Lesher tore their hair and scratched their heads until they came up with a 1983 version of the payment-in-kind (PIK) program of 1962–63. Farmers who signed for the regular acreage reduction program could elect to idle additional land, up to half their base. For this second stage they would be paid not in dollars but in commodities from CCC storage ("in kind").

But that was not all. In addition, farmers could offer to leave the rest of their base acreage unplanted. They would make a bid as to how much reimbursement (in commodity) they would want. It was a bid-and-acceptance device.

In his February 1983 Extension letter Harold Breimyer wrote that the program was "at once a move of desperation and a reasonable, logical step to take under 1983 conditions." Much of the logic carried the name of David Stockman. Paying a farmer in commodities involved no current budget appropriation. Breimyer drew the obvious inference: There would be a "day of fiscal reckoning." "Commodities under loan," he pointed out, "can fund PIK now, but eventually it will be necessary to restore CCC capital, at high budget cost" (p.4).

It was easy to acquiesce in the 1983 PIK as announced. But when Secretary Block decided to accept 22 million of the bid-and-acceptance acres in addition to the 60 million contractual acres, Harold Breimyer hit the ceiling. "A total of 82 million acres idled is too much!" he protested.

In testimony before a U.S. House of Representatives subcommittee July 11, 1983, he gave air to his feelings:

> No farm program could have kept farmers' prices and incomes on an even keel the last couple of years . . . [of] the worst business recession experienced since the 1930s. . . . But mistakes have been made. The first mistake is that administration of farm programs was in unsympathetic hands. . . . no program should be turned over to non-believers. . . . Perhaps, in view of the situation that had developed by the winter of 1982–83, a PIK program was justified. It seems ironic, though, that once the Secretary of Agriculture decided to turn aggressive he went to the other extreme, accepting 22 million of the whole-base acres. (pp.2, 4, 5)

Forty-five years earlier, Harold Breimyer had calculated supply and disposition balance sheets for major U.S. farm crops, under alternative program options. Armed with memory of that experience, in 1983 he needed only a pencil and the back of a used envelope to reconstruct the same kind of data. Secretary Block and his economist were allowing almost no safety margin, on either the supply (low yield) or disposition (strong demand) side. Harold Breimyer and Oris Wells would never have made that mistake.

A drought did come. Prices shot upward, and farmers became over-confident about the future. Export markets shrank. Whenever export buyers are deprived of their normal purchases because of unavailability, they turn elsewhere. Their trade is not recaptured easily. The pattern fit the short-supply year of 1983–84.

At a seminar held in Kansas City in 1986, Harold Breimyer did verbal battle with Richard Lyng, who was soon to become secretary of agriculture. Lyng trotted out the exhausted demagoguery about how the 1980 Soviet embargo had damaged our exports. Breimyer replied sharply that all the embargoes of the last twenty years had done less harm than the unavailability of supply caused by the excessive idling of acreage in the 1983 PIK. Lyng did not respond.

THE 1985 FARM LAW

In the long history of acreage reduction and price support, never had so many organizations given so much attention to writing the basic law as was done prior to enacting the 1985 law. For two years, meetings and seminars and symposia were held from the Atlantic to the Pacific.

It's hard to account for the exceptional interest. To be sure, the Reagan administration's announced opposition to programs in general gave courage to all opponents. Harold Breimyer found himself addressing agribusiness groups, telling them, "No, we aren't going to abolish all programs and 'let the market do it.' " He convinced few of them. A sizable contingent of university professors, True Believers in the wonders of a totally free market economy, also rejoiced at the prospects of ending all the foolish New Deal farm programs.

A second reason for giving so much attention to a new farm law was the obsession with export trade. A dozen or more explanations were offered as to why the United States had lost ground — followed by an equal number of recipes for recovering it.

Soil and water protection was on a roll in the 1980s. And advocacy groups made their presence noisily known.

Yet another part of the melange was a desire to make life easier for the 200,000 or so heavily indebted commercial farmers who were trying hard to stay financially alive under the burden of their debts and the high interest rates. Breimyer remonstrated that debt problems should be dealt with as such. Acreage reduction and price support are instruments to influence current income flow and should be confined to that purpose, he declared. They are not debt-aid measures.

Subsequent events gave a strange twist to the debt-aid issue. The 1985 law, as written, had a few clauses relating to debt, but it was not primarily an aid statute. But the debt bind that prevailed so widely lent political urgency to getting some kind of farm law on the books. Republican congressmen and senators such as North Dakota's Mark Andrews told President Reagan, following congressional enactment of the

1985 farm law, that it was essential that he sign it. Otherwise there would be a big exodus of Republicans in farming country, they warned. The president found it necessary to abandon his earlier opposition. His signature on the bill did not help much, though. Breimyer regretted the loss of Senator Andrews, a capable legislator.

International Trade The Food Security Act of 1985 was enacted late in 1985, following expert leadership in writing it, given principally by Tom Foley in the House and Robert Dole in the Senate. It was signed by President Reagan about Christmastime. The law had two principal features as its banner, its nameplate. First, it reduced support prices sharply in the interest of expanding exports, relying on increased deficiency payments to protect farmers' incomes. And, second, it included significant measures for soil conservation including a Conservation Compliance rule that would attach an ineligibility penalty to farmers who failed to protect highly erodible cropland.

Ever since the 1920s the discipline of agricultural economics, and its practitioners, have been dedicated to empirical observation and objective research. "Get answers to problems by studying them!" That has been the dictum.

In spite of the rule, economists apparently failed to study foreign trade. When U.S. exports diminished beginning in 1981, they rushed to their computers to calculate elasticities of world demand for U.S. export products. The numbers they got ranged from very inelastic to highly elastic.

Perplexed, one school—the influential school, as matters turned out—simply announced that we had priced ourselves out of the market. Accordingly, the new law reduced support prices sharply, gave cotton and rice a virtually bottomless support level, and provided for a PIK certificate system by which CCC-held commodities could be used to reduce prices further. Funds were made available for direct subsidy (export enhancement) and for guarantee of private loans made to finance export sales.

As farmers' incomes were protected by means of target prices, the stage was set to run the Treasury cost of deficiency payments higher than anything known before. Harold Breimyer pointed out at once that the deficiency payments were an implicit subsidy to both domestic use and exports. He disliked to see domestic livestock and poultry operations expand in response to feed prices held low by Treasury disbursements. For surely those disbursements could be cut off at any time the Congress chose.

He deplored the international effect of our policies. Well-heeled competitive exporters such as the European Community, he said, could match our export subsidies dollar for dollar (or franc for dollar). Others such as Argentina, Brazil, Thailand, and even Australia would find themselves in a painful bind. They could not afford to compete with us in subsidization. They could only accept a loss of their export markets.

Breimyer asked in purple prose if it really were our objective to undermine the fragile democracy of Argentina, or the new Aquino government of the Philippines. Our export policy threatened the political stability of both countries, and several others, too.

He also alleged that what we really were doing was to subsidize the consumers in buying countries. In a paper given at the 1987 policy seminar that had been renamed the Breimyer Seminar, he noted "the anomaly that Japan, for example, uses the currency she saves by buying our grain so cheap to fund, by loans, the deficit in our budget caused by our subsidizing of sales to her." He added, "It's an interesting, if distressing, kind of recycling" (p.27). He wondered if the audience would understand his sally. It did.

After dropping to a low point in 1985–86, export values began to rise. Partisan supporters of the 1985 law rejoiced. They claimed full credit on behalf of the wisdom (theirs) built into the law. Meanwhile another school of thought took issue. Led by Edward Schuh, it attributed the export rebound to the newly depreciated dollar. Within a couple of years the U.S. dollar had fallen by half against the Japanese yen, and almost as much against some European currencies.

Harold Breimyer, a spoilsport wherever he thought economists were playing doctrinal games, observed that the international purchasing power of the new agricultural export values, in terms of the newly depreciated dollar, was actually less than before. So had there really been an improvement?

Near the end of the 1980s, a third school found yet another cause for our export problems: the trade-restrictive policies of other countries. If the European Community would just let us export unmolested, and if Japan would only buy grain from us in the way we buy automobiles from her, our problems would disappear in the morning mist. It was another version of the devil paradigm. Unfortunately, it had considerable validity. It gave rise to an effort to get all countries to reduce their agricultural trade barriers.

Soil Conservation. In the farm law of a half-century earlier, 1936, acreage reduction and soil conservation had been linked, although not very effectively. During the years that followed, an incessant clamor was heard to make price and income benefits contingent on farmers' protecting their soil. It came to naught. It was fruitless, that is, until 1985.

By the time of writing that law, soil and water issues had moved front and center in public attention. The political maneuvering that led to incorporating four conservation clauses need not be recounted. Conservation organizations, and the sparkling lobbyist Maureen Hinkle of the National Audubon Society, had an exceptional influence.

The Conservation Reserve provided for converting highly erodible cropland to grass or trees under a ten-year contract. Among the three other provisions, anti-swampbusting and anti-sodbusting limited the opening of new plowland. Conservation Compliance called for retiring highly erodible land already under the plow. The three provisions had the common feature that the incentive was denial of eligibility for price support, crop insurance, Farmers Home Administration loans, and several other kinds of benefits.

Decoupling and Targeting. In the year or two after enactment of the 1985 law, peace and quiet reigned. The law was working, in its costly and world-trade-disruptive fashion. Harold Breimyer was astonished that a $25 billion annual cost was accepted so supinely. A little stir was made around the catchwords "decoupling" and "targeting." Breimyer got his argumentative oar in, partly because he deplored the maneuvers taking place as big farmers sought to avoid the limitation on size of individual payments. Landholdings were broken up into minifundia — nominally, for program-participation purposes. One new owner, it was alleged, bore the name of the family cat.

Decoupling meant paying out deficiency payments without requiring that a farmer idle an acreage of land to qualify. Targeting referred to directing at least part of the deficiency payment to preferre ! recipients, presumably full-time family farmers.

In congressional testimony and on other occasions, Breimyer warned sternly against decoupling: "Don't give farmers money without requiring them to do something." The fact that decoupling was even considered indicated how much the ideology of programs had changed since the moralistic first years.

He asked that deficiency payments be broken up into three parts. One would be a straight per-acre payment for idling land. It would be paid irrespective of the size of farm. A second would be compensation for unrealistically low loan rates. This portion of payments would be disbursed about as was done under the 1985 law. The third part would constitute an income supplement. That part could be targeted, Breimyer said, to the most worthy category of recipients.

OTHER EXPERIENCES IN THE 1980S, AND REFLECTIONS

The 1980s were dotted with many crises, *ad hoc* events, and emerging trends. Harold Breimyer was sensitive to the human cost of writing off $300 billion in agriculture's asset value. He was pained by the statistic that 140 Missouri farmers were suicides during 1986 and 1987. He was indignant at the callousness shown in many communities, even by ministers in local churches. He was equally respectful of supportive efforts, including the manning of hot lines. He applauded the sympathetic work in Missouri of his friends William and Judith Heffernan, rural sociologists. He made the acquaintance of two Ohioans, Brien McGarvey, a Methodist minister, and Dean Kite, a farmer, who extended counseling to troubled farmers of his home state. He wrote their story in his *On the Economy* of July 25, 1987.

Also noteworthy was the MoFarms program the Extension Service of the University of Missouri set up. Staffed by retired Extension farm management specialists and bank loan officers, it was both humanitarian and professional. All power and glory to it!

Farm credit was a hot topic in the 1980s, and the machinations that led to writing the Agricultural Credit Act of 1987 gave cause for rebuking the cooperative credit community. At the same time, some members of Congress, especially Congressman Ed Jones of Tennessee, were applauded.

At the end of the second Reagan term, international trade stood almost alone in the farm policy limelight. In 1969 Breimyer had become acquainted with Clayton Yeutter, as Breimyer responded to a call to review the joint U.S. AID-universities technical aid project in Colombia. He gained high respect for Yeutter, whom Reagan appointed as his special trade representative. In that position Yeutter tried to carry out the assignment of inducing all trading nations to drop their farm programs and accept universal free trade. It was the most insurmountable assignment of his career, to that point. Whether his duties as secretary of agriculture under President Bush would prove to be even more arduous could not be known.

Harold Breimyer editorialized that universal free trade was Mission Impossible. He also insisted that what was needed above all else was to get the European Community and the United States to call off their costly subsidy war.

The Breimyer discomfiture with the 1980s—his unhappiness with both public attitudes and political policies—has been made clear. During that decade as never before, the fortunes of agriculture were determined less by what happened within its own borders than by the course of events in the general economy. Not the secretary of agriculture but, rather, the secretary of the treasury, the chairman of the Federal Reserve Board, and the director of the Office of Management and Budget, not to mention the president of the United States, held the fortunes of agricul- ture within their grasp. Harold Breimyer did not like the situation, but for a whole career he had tried to conform to the ungrammatical admonition to "tell it like it is." That's the way it was, in his judgment, and that's the way he told it.

CHAPTER 21

Nominal Retirement

EARLY IN THE YEAR OF OUR LORD 1984, the designated subalterns of the University of Missouri–Columbia notified Professor and Extension Economist Harold F. Breimyer that he was about to overstay his tenure. In conformity with the institution's rules, he would conclude his affiliation August 31 of that year.

The professor was, of course, not surprised. He knew the rules. The calendar governs much of human destiny. He had reached mandatory retirement age.

The notification was sweetened by conferring of emeritus status. Appreciated more was the invitation of Bruce Bullock, his department chairman, for the unseated Breimyer to come back into the classroom in the fall and teach the undergraduate course in farm policy.

A civil service office added an unexpected emolument. Harold F. Breimyer would complete, on August 31, forty-seven years, one month, and nineteen days of creditable federal service for retirement benefits. He would soon receive a check for $18,528.69 as refund of excessive retirement deductions. Deductions had continued to be taken past the time when annuity benefits reach their maximum.

THE BEAUTIFUL DINNER PARTY

A university customarily ritualizes the departure of one of its members into retirement. Harold Breimyer knew what kind of retirement party he preferred. Early in 1984 the prospective honoree told the newly appointed Breimyer-retirement committee that he wanted a lighthearted dinner affair in which the usual "this is his life" would be presented in the form of skits and songs. Omit eulogies, he said. The committee replied that Breimyer did not understand; the practice was for the university establishment to do what it thought proper to honor the retiree. After some persuasion the dinner party was staged as Breimyer wished it. It was a grand success.

Heroes were three. Charles Cramer, Harold Breimyer's longtime colleague, was chairman of the retirement committee and emcee of the skits. Breimyer will be forever grateful to him. By great good fortune Naomi Jensen, a thespian friend living in Florida, holidayed locally a few weeks before the date of the dinner. She pointed out how the script could be improved. "Lift the grandchildren episode out of the middle and begin with it," was an example of her advice. The third hero was Breimyer's onetime secretary, the musically gifted Judy Hamilton. She performed magic in reconciling the Breimyer-written ditties with scores borrowed from Rodgers, Sullivan, and Irving Berlin.

The 250 persons who attended included former graduate students William Bailey from Minneapolis, James Ahrenholz from Mt. Vernon, Illinois, and Tahira and Labh Hira from Ames, Iowa. A number of persons came from Kansas City and St. Louis. Herbert Koch, a farmer, arrived from Tarkio, Missouri. Some kinds of appreciation can only be testified to. Language is inadequate for verbalizing them. So it was with Harold Breimyer's deeply felt gratitude toward every person who conferred honor by being present at the celebration dinner June 29, 1984.

The evening turned out as the retiree had dreamed. Grandchildren Elizabeth, Lauren, and Paul played their parts in the skits beautifully. Graduate students and colleagues having roles got into the spirit of the evening. As vocalists, Vicky Willows and Randy Wilson provided a musical comedy touch.

In the more formal part of the program, the testimonials were few. The one surprise was presentation of a scroll conveying a resolution of appreciation from the General Assembly of Missouri. Harold Breimyer's friend, father of his former student Lori, D. R. ("Ozzie") Osbourn, had arranged for the resolution. Osbourn would succumb to leukemia within a year.

Harlan Lynn, Extension's expert, made a tape recording of the evening's program. It is one of Harold Breimyer's most treasured possessions.

UNINTERRUPTED PROFESSIONAL ACTIVITY

Harold Breimyer did not miss a day in continuing his professional activity. Bruce Bullock, chairman of agricultural economics, generously allowed him to keep his office, his private telephone, and the superb stenographic service of Jody Pestle, who subsequently word-processed this memoir. Services solicited in exchange were to teach farm policy, write occasional Extension papers, and edit the proceedings of the annual Breimyer seminar.

In the spring of 1985, the new retiree responded to an invitation from Joseph Havlicek to teach farm policy at his alma mater, Ohio State University. The experience was redolent with nostalgia. The highlight was presenting, in team with Neil Harl of Iowa State University, an Extension-type review of farm policy in a meeting held on the university's campus. The date was almost exactly fifty years after Harold Breimyer had left Ohio State, master's diploma in hand.

Among two negative experiences at Ohio State was the absence of a single individual who had been on campus during the student years, 1930–1935. But Breimyer did have dinner with Lucille Sitterley, widow of his friend John. A visit with Wilbur Bruner dated not from Ohio State but back to Fort Recovery, where Bruner was student Harold's vocational agriculture instructor. It was poignant with memory.

To his deep regret Breimyer learned that his friend Walter Stout, an M.D., who had been best man at his and Rachel's wedding, was ill with amyotrophic lateral sclerosis (Lou Gehrig's disease). Then and later, the two old friends visited as Walter punched out his responses on a computer screen.

Returning to Missouri, Breimyer accommodated the wishes of Ralph Havener, university archivist, for a copy of all the Breimyer papers and correspondence. The pack rat was able to fill several cartons.

For several years Breimyer had written a weekly newspaper column, *On the Economy,* distributed by agricultural Extension. Following retirement he made it available by subscription. Takers were few but enough to finance writing it. Breimyer found that having to stay informed and alert enough to compose for each Friday's mail a column on economic issues in agriculture was a mental stimulus as acute as having to prepare for the probing questions of a classroom of students or a farmers' meeting.

Obviously, the writing of this memoir was a major post-retirement activity.

CHAPTER 22

A Life, a Career, and
Farm Policy: A Resumé

By luck of the demographic draw, Harold Breimyer was born during the early years of the dramatic twentieth century and was able to write this memoir as the century neared its close. Most autobiographies, and biographies too, relating to lives dating within the 1900s give prominent place to the century's material and technological wonders. Breimyer's birth did not antedate invention of the automobile or airplane. But in his earliest years the plane was still rare, and only a few of his parents' neighbors possessed the exciting motor car. Likewise, the radio had been invented but was just beginning to become available to common folk. He remembers one uncle's searching a small crystal with a hair-thin wire, headphones clamped to his ears. Another uncle twisted three (or five?) dials of an Atwater-Kent (or Philco?) radio and shouted when music or a gospel message came through.

Breimyer would see television come into being—and antibiotics in medicine, jet planes, the transistor ("small gadget with a great future," Eric Larrabee had written in *Harper's* magazine not long after World War II). Later followed the world of computerization and microchips.

Being about one-quarter philosopher, he wondered about the dictum of Karl Marx and other thinkers about mankind's becoming hostage to his machines. He posed the *Deus ex machina* thesis before more than a few audiences. Are we at the mercy of our material inventions?

But that was not what Harold Breimyer's life or his intellectual adventures were about. Nor, therefore, is that the focus of this memoir. Only casual mention has been given to the infrastructure of U.S. agriculture or the accoutrement of rural people.

This memoir falls, instead, in the category known in academic circles as economic and cultural development. The chronology is of Harold

Breimyer's personal development and experiences. But Harold Breimyer is also surrogate for a generation of farm youth whose lives were reshaped by a paroxysm of emancipation throughout the rural America of their time. He and his fellows saw and felt the rural community—theirs and all others'—emerge from circumscribed opportunity and outlook into vistas of worldwide dimension.

A FEW HEROES

In this account are a few heroes. Grandma Pauline was one, and the beloved English teacher Lucile DeSelm Seedorf another. Among Harold Breimyer's mentors highest respect is accorded Murray Benedict, his California professor; Fred Waugh, Bushrod Allin, John Brewster, Mordecai Ezekiel, and other super-bright minds who made the Bureau of Agricultural Economics an intellectual mecca; James Cavin, with whom Harold enjoyed a long association; and the brilliant Oris Wells and crusty Si Smith, who taught without meaning to.

This is least of all a chronicle of the heroics of the author. Any subtle suggestion of self-adulation is denied, here and now, as unintentional.

To be sure, in the game playing of forecasting economic events, Harold Breimyer claims several successes and admits only one egregious error. He foresaw accurately the inflationary surge following World War II. He predicted that farm programs would be converted from mandatory allotments to a voluntary design featuring direct ("compensatory" or "deficiency") payments. In the 1970s he warned of an explosive end to the farmland-price bubble of that decade. He called the 1981 farm law unsuited to its time and accused USDA Secretary Block of playing a dangerous game in accepting so much cropland in the 1983 PIK program.

Breimyer's big mistake was to expect farm product exports to retain in the 1980s their large volume of the later 1970s. His lame excuse for the blunder is tucked away somewhere in this memoir and need not be extracted here.

At some risk a contemporary forecast is now offered. The presidential election campaign of 1988 was marked by implicit promises that the farm program then in effect would be continued with only little change. Harold Breimyer believes, and warns, that any program costing $15 to $25 billion annually will get its comeuppance. That scale of expenditure is not sustainable. Either the need for programs will diminish or their terms will be changed.

SATISFACTION VALUE

Scarcely mentioned as such in foregoing pages is the sense of gratification, of satisfaction, that has come to Harold Breimyer throughout his career. The absence of heroics including attainment of a position of high distinction and luminosity does not detract from the many positive rewards that have been his. Harold Breimyer thought his first talent to lie in writing, the one learned from Lucile DeSelm. Whether it constitutes vanity or not, he takes pride whenever he writes something that meets his own standards.

Isn't it permissible for an artist in oils to enjoy his or her own canvas? Cannot an automobile mechanic get a morale boost when a reassembled motor runs? If those self-appreciations are legitimate, so should be those of a writer.

Classroom teaching is redolent with rewards. When a final examination paper reveals that a student really has advanced his or her knowledge, the professor has cause to glow. Professor Breimyer had the opportunity to read the students' ideas because, as he said at his recognition dinner, he always gave examinations that included one or more essay questions.

Breimyer remarked often that a university regime is so easy and comfortable, and the satisfactions so palpable, that half his salary was producer's surplus. He was saying, in economists' language, that 50 percent of the salary he received would have been enough to keep him in the classroom. He has had short patience with a contingent of professors who regularly protest that they are underpaid.

Teaching adults in his role as Extension economist carried equal rewards. In fact, at times Breimyer regarded Extension as more exciting than classroom teaching and research.

Several appreciated honors came his way. The two of deepest meaning to him are his election as a Fellow of the American Agricultural Economics Association, and his receiving the Thomas Jefferson Award of the University of Missouri. The latter, an award of the university's four campuses, may have been the only one on the appendix list of which Harold Breimyer thought himself deserving. He rarely gave time or emotional energy to self-evaluation. He sensed, though, that his philosophy and his career record were in keeping with the ideals of Thomas Jefferson. A four-campus committee came to the same conclusion.

A NATIONAL OPERATION UPLIFT

A few of his faults and failings also have been cited in this memoir of the life and career of Harold Breimyer. But the intended focus is less personal than sociological.

During the years of his youth, he and a host of his fellows in rural America were blessed by the esprit and the active effort toward elevation of status that pervaded all levels from the local community to the nation. The year of his birth was the year when the Smith-Lever Act was enacted. The act established a nationwide Agricultural Extension Service. As an early beneficiary of that Service, a later participant, and a lifelong observer, Harold Breimyer can readily call it the most important law affecting U.S. agriculture in the twentieth century. He would even let it outrank the path-breaking Agricultural Adjustment Act of 1933.

Two years after Smith-Lever came the Federal Farm Loan Act, which provided for Federal Land Banks. Not to be overlooked in the legislatively fertile 1916 are the beginning of federal cooperation with states in constructing rural roads, and several pieces of marketing legislation, including the Grain Standards Act.

Is it necessary to persuade further that Harold Breimyer began his life at a time when the nation, without quite realizing it was doing so, or calling it that, was initiating Operation Uplift? The spirit of the time reached Washington but did not begin there. It had a grass-roots origin. To this day Breimyer does not understand how the hamlet of Fort Recovery, which was not only sleepy but also Rip-Van-Winkle-inert, somehow roused itself to instill its brighter young people with a sense of opportunity. The best judgment he can make is that faith in education was the key.

THE EFFERVESCENT NEW DEAL

The Depression years of the 1930s retarded or halted both the awakening of and the progress in rural America. The interruption proved brief. The nation responded to the entreaties of Franklin Roosevelt to have faith and press ahead. Henry Wallace and Milburn Wilson led a coterie of reformers in the Department of Agriculture who crusaded for a democratically self-developed rural America. They were checkmated first by an entrenched political establishment and then by World War II. Yet the notion that the race is not solely to the quick was never entirely dislodged.

A sweeping conclusion that Harold Breimyer has reached is that nations are truly generous and forward-looking only during and immediately after a crisis. A second is that they almost invariably martyrize their prophets — whose good work nevertheless, in partial and sometimes scarcely recognizable form, survives them.

THE GOLDEN AGE

The war came so soon after the Depression that it overlapped and in fact ended it. The two cataclysms forced the United States to take a look at itself and address its future. Breimyer regards the years from war's end to about 1970 as the nation's Golden Age. Those years were marked by a promise, akin to that of the rainbow's pledge about floods, that deep unemployment would never be allowed to recur; it was contained in the Employment Act of 1946. The Marshall Plan may rank as the most altruistic aid one nation has ever given another. Farm policy bogged down in pointless debate about fixed versus flexible price supports, but Public Law 480 was fully as internationally humanitarian and developmental as it was internally self-serving.

The study of rural poverty commissioned by Lyndon Johnson as President, and its report *The People Left Behind,* may have been waylaid by Vietnam, but meanwhile farmers' families had become eligible for social security, rural electric lines were extended to very nearly all of them, rural telephones came in fast, and before long most farm homes other than the most remote had a blacktop road in front of the lawn.

Rural America was not excluded from social ills of the time, but it shared in the positive efforts made to correct them. Televised pictorialization of undernourished Americans brought a speeding of food-stamp aid to both urban and rural families alike. The civil rights movement was brutal and even bloody, but it led to reforms.

The years may have stayed Golden because of the lingering conscience bestirred by a depression and a war. But also contributory was the almost uninterrupted economic growth. The nation's production record in those years was indeed sterling. Oris Wells repeatedly had expressed conventional wisdom in equally conventional language: People don't worry too much about the size of their and others' slice of the pie when the pie itself keeps getting larger. In the 1950s and 1960s the nation's economic pie steadily enlarged. Infighting was suppressed.

Economic growth and the confidence that it would continue entered into the federal government's fiscal policy. Harold Breimyer was a half-convinced Keynesian who regarded deficit financing as necessary during depression, but he was also a veteran of Great Depression years when private debts were an anchor around the neck. Except for assuming small mortgages when they bought their first two homes, he and wife Rachel abstained from all borrowing. He fretted each time the Congress chose to spend more money than was coming in. The spenders took refuge in prospects for larger revenues from a growing economy. During the Golden Age they were proved right. But later, Reagan-era spenders tried the same gambit, to the outcome of a costly futility.

Growing prosperity in the nation and on its farms during the Golden Age contributed to releasing farm acreage programs from their mandatory-allotment shackles. It had more bearing than economists and farm leaders were prepared to acknowledge. Thereafter, farmers could enter a program or not, as they wished, and would rely on minimum pricing via commodity loans, and direct payments, as benefits when they did so.

AFTER 1970, TARNISHED GOLD

The events of the 1970s and 1980s have been logged and remarked on in this memoir. They nevertheless are a puzzle. In a true sense the account of Harold Breimyer's life and career, and of the evolutionary changes in rural America to which he was so sensitive, followed a progressive course until about 1970. His career peaked about that time, leveling out into an asymptote. More significant is that the national temper entered a new phase. Shakespeare would have written, as he did in The Tempest, that it suffered a sea-change.

Breimyer formed a few hypotheses to account for the altered national mood beginning in the 1970s but remains uncertain how valid they are. It appeared to him that the decade of the 1980s was in a major way a repetition of the 1920s. *Deja vu.*

As one example, the reluctance during the 1980s to soften the human cost of decapitalization of agriculture fit with the cold indifference of the 1920s. On the other hand, during the 1980s commercial agriculture was bolstered by programs of a scope and cost of which neither Henry C. Wallace of the 1920s nor his son Henry A. of the 1930s would have dreamed. Programs for protecting ("conserving") the nation's soil had become a fixture. Hence, facile generalizations are suspect.

OPPORTUNITIES LIMITED, DEVELOPMENT ARRESTED

This memoir is only incidentally a political commentary. Least of all is it an exegesis of the 1970s and 1980s. It relates instead to the experiences of Harold Breimyer as proxy for a generation of rural youth for whom the doors of opportunity had been opened wide. They had been opened by others—by those close at hand, and by the nation in its (onetime) supportive national policies.

Breimyer's most trenchant judgment on the 1980s became a theme of his remarks at his retirement dinner in 1984. He wondered if Americans of that day were giving a quality of support to their rural youth equal to that provided him and his fellows. He implied his doubts. He admitted his sensing a "sardonic quality in the air . . . a superciliousness," that he never knew in the 1920s and 1930s. Maybe, he added, the folk of his native Ohio were naive as they put so much faith in education, but if so, he was glad they were. They "believed in what they were trying to do," His father and his father's neighbors taxed themselves for schools "much more heavily relative to their income than Boone County, Missouri, does today" (pp. 3, 4).

He cited his own financial history. He had attended Ohio State University on a scholarship. He received a fellowship to the University of California. His graduate work at American University was financed by the GI bill. The GI benefits fell short only of paying the fee for the dissertation. Altogether, Breimyer told his listeners, "I received 20 years of education at a total cost to me of . . . $100." In recent years even public (state) universities have increased their tuition charge annually. Breimyer would pass no fiscal judgment, he said, but "only declare that something of a heritage that was mine is not that of the youth of today." He added, "I think America is losing something" (pp. 2–3).

A FINAL WORD

This memoir ends on a note that will be regarded as somber. It is that, but is not intended to be negative and, least of all, despondent. Let it not be forgotten that Harold Breimyer grew up in the tumultuous 1920s and struggled through the dangerously discouraging 1930s. A cloudy denouement in national affairs following the glorious quarter-century just after World War II does not abrogate the message of this memoir.

The memoir is a testimonial to how a community's support within a national Operation Uplift enabled a farm youth to over-fulfill his early expectations. It is told as the story of Harold Breimyer's life, but it enlarges, as though under a giant lens, to the account of an entire generation of rural youth who found cultural emancipation during the years when it was a national purpose to help them do so.

What was accomplished in the past can be repeated in the future. Sensitivity to the dispirit of the time—any time—does not invalidate the moral derived from the experience of over-fulfilled expectation recorded here.

National Policy for Agriculture. Also a part of this account is the record of national policy for agriculture during almost six decades. Harold Breimyer has always declared the overarching objective of that policy to be to enable a proprietary agriculture to survive in an increasingly industrial, commercial, and technological farm-and-food system. As of the late 1980s and early 1990s, traditional proprietary units were giving way before super-farms and agribusiness integration on the one hand, and a host of smaller part-time units on the other. Insofar as giant units take over, the farm policies known since 1933 will fade into history. To the extent that individual proprietorships are retained, the Breimyer prognosis is that the intense individual-commodity orientation will be replaced by farm-unit contracts that allow more planting freedom and will protect, jointly, the soil, groundwater, farmers' income, and the consumer's food supply.

Community Democracy. The dreams of the late 1930s for democratically developed rural communities will never be realized. Nor, for that matter, is there a chance that farmers' interests and farmer leadership will dominate. On the contrary, as farm families continue to be a diminishing part of rural America, they will find their welfare, and their own citizen role, to be woven into the community fabric as a whole.

Rural communities ought always to be responsive to the aspirations of their youth and aggressively supportive, even as Harold Breimyer's Fort Recovery and Mercer County were supportive of him. They should be more attentive than they were during the frustrating years when this memoir was written.

As communities help their young people to fulfill their expectations or even, perhaps, as in Harold Breimyer's case, to over-fulfill them, one caveat is added. The supportive aid will be granted to all young people, farm and non-farm alike, rich and poor alike, and prominent-family and other-side-of-the-tracks alike. It will be truly democratic.

This memoir is written of its author as a onetime farm youth, because he was that. But the moral to be drawn is generalizable to all Americans born or brought to the countryside, there to form expectations for their future and there also to be responsive to the educational, cultural, and developmental environment provided for them.

A Futuristic Epilogue

ON TWO SUCCESSIVE SUNDAY NIGHTS in the late 1920s, the villagers and nearby farm families of Fort Recovery, Ohio, filled the Trinity Lutheran Church to capacity to view a tableau, *The Striking of America's Hour.* On an improvised stage the lines were recited from a text written by Laura Scherer Copenhaver, Katharine Scherer Cronk, and Mathilde Vossler. The hour of history has struck, the thespians announced in sepulchral voice, for Egypt, Babylonia, Greece, and Rome. It will strike next for America.

For each of the ancient cultures, the failings and missed opportunities were recounted. Thereupon the Spirit of Justice intoned, "Thou art weighed, O Egypt [Babylonia, Greece, Rome] in the balances and found wanting."

When America's turn came, it was "summoned to judgment" in the name of "Liberty, Justice, and Brotherhood." An Indian, a pioneer, a Negro, and an immigrant came successively on stage, each to tell of his trials. Following the procession the Spirit of Brotherhood announced, "America, the hour of thine opportunity is striking, not only in thine own land, but in all the nations of the earth."

The American destiny was yet to be determined, the chroniclers said. The Spirit of Justice began the warning, "Thou shall be weighed in the balances and found wanting, O America," as Liberty set the condition: "If thou does not set thine own people free."

Fort Recovery's home-talent cast may have lacked polish, but it responded dutifully to the stern direction given by Harold Breimyer's mother Ella. The production was for Ella her finest hour during her twenty years of membership in Trinity church. Irrespective of halting cadence and a few missed lines, the effect was dramatic. The audience

278

left the church silent and thoughtful, even pensive, sobered.

Why should the modestly-lettered folk in an obscure community feel themselves prepared to sit in moral judgment on civilizations of the ancient past and on their own of their day? Were the German Lutherans singularly capable of doing so, owing to their cultural (including religious) tradition? Or do all common people have an instinctive appreciation that security is in the final test collective, and that moral principles govern it?

Harold Breimyer turned that question over in his mind as he took his small part in the pageant (he was the Negro). He has done so a thousand times since.

The notion drawn from *The Striking of America's Hour,* that a nation is weighed in the balances of liberty, justice, and brotherhood, may have persisted as a chord through Breimyer's career-long studying, teaching, and writing. If that be true, it is not surprising that Harold the agricultural-college entrant chose rural (later called agricultural) economics as his major field. Nor that public policy became his first interest. It was consistent, too, that he drifted into the sub-field known as institutional economics.

Even though he endorsed and practiced Puritan-style individual endeavor, Harold Breimyer always has insisted that the chance for reward is shaped by the cultural environment. Opportunity and security are collectively fashioned. The theme runs through much of this memoir, as the memoir writer credits the over-fulfillment of his expectations to the supportive aid of his community and the enlightened policies of his nation.

As recently as the spring of 1986, speaking at a church-sponsored colloquium on the farmers' debt crisis, Breimyer acknowledged that it is "human nature to claim individual credit" for individual success. But he called attention to the "social component in private opportunity." "Resources and opportunity," he declared, "come out of collective action — of what is done in common effort".[1]

MAN AND NATURE

Another thought pattern in Harold Breimyer's stock-in-intellectual-trade is the relation of Man to Nature. How does enterprising, greedy,

---

[1] Harold Breimyer's speech is in mimeographed form under the title "Origins of the Rural Crisis or How Did We Get Where We Are" (University of Missouri-Columbia, Agricultural Working Paper No. 1986–16) p. 5.

calculating, alternately generous and selfish Man relate to Nature? Does he husband natural resources, or exploit and destroy them? How does he distribute among his fellows the obligations relative to those resources, and the product they yield?

That, in essence, is what agricultural economics is about. Human beings apply their labor to plant seeds in the Earth's soil that is an eternal stock resource if cared for but can easily be destroyed if not. They do so to produce food, fiber, building materials, and even the stuff for vices, to be used by all people.

Increasingly, though, they have taken from Earth some of its depletable stock of minerals in order to enhance the outturn. This is the heart of the exuberantly praised modern technology in agriculture.

In our economy and that of most nations of the Western world, the product of field and forest is allocated partly in proportion to what each agent of production contributes (the Little Red Hen formula), and partly as a payoff to the privileged or as succor to the handicapped.

Harold Breimyer's most distinguished piece of writing was his 1962 article, "The Three Economies of Agriculture." In it he outlined the many meanings of converting husbandry from a simple man-on-land to a complex system drawing heavily on non-farm resources. The first economy, "the production of primary products from the soil," is described in terms of two models. The first is the "primitive" model, in which "land and men are the only existing factors of production." The second is the "industrial" model that is "essentially capital-using" and "fully developed" (pp. 679–682).

The industrial model is the more productive, but it requires human management. "The larger role of variable inputs, partly unharnessing primary agriculture from the binding limitations of native resources, makes it more subject to the individual and collective controls of man" (p.694).

Sixteen years later, at a time when the OPEC run-up in price of oil jolted the world out of its complacency about limitless mineral resources, Breimyer wrote a follow-up article. He did not say the nation's agriculture would go back to its primitive model. But he anticipated, implicitly, the surge of interest in soil conservation and alternative agriculture that would appear soon. He predicted that "the practice and politics of agriculture" thereafter would include taking more care to protect the land base as well as adjusting to scarcer and more costly industrial inputs (p. 46).

The two kinds of action have one common component. Both involve more control by man over his food-producing practices and resources.

So indeed it will be. Man will manage Nature more and more. Whether he does so prudently, effectively, and equitably, is the question above all questions. The answer to it will determine the course of our country and, worldwide, of civilization itself.

To revert to the language of *The Striking of America's Hour,* will the managing be done in a spirit of liberty, justice, and brotherhood? Breimyer is pessimistic. Unless spectacular technological breakthroughs are in the offing, the essential niggardliness of Nature will come to the fore. So will the lamentable incivility of human beings under stress.

Our nation's Golden Age ended in the late 1960s, lost forever in Vietnam. By the 1980s the European-American civilization that had so dominated the world for three centuries found itself eclipsed by the upstart countries of the Rim of Asia, led by Japan. Harold Breimyer doubts that Asia's star will shine long. But as the twentieth century neared its end, the Eastern Star was rising and the Western falling. Had the European-American culture been weighed in the balances and found wanting? Breimyer suspects that may be the case.

FIVE GLORIOUS CENTURIES FOR WESTERN CULTURE

The grand achievements of restless Europeans and their proteges in America during a five-century span that often is dated from the fall of Constantinople (1453) have been delineated by a hundred scholars, or a thousand. And well they should be. It is hardly conceivable that any period of similar length in human history has been so inventive, expansionary, and full of potential for human betterment.

The era began with explosive advancements that have been identified variously, as of the Scientific Revolution, the Religious Reformation (or Enlightenment), the voyages of discovery. Harold Breimyer's favorite high school teacher, the petite Lucile DeSelm, always spoke of the Renaissance, and gave as high status to its flowering of humanistic arts and literature as to advances in the sciences.

Harold Breimyer has put most emphasis on the opening up of whole new continents to occupation and exploitation. Europeans found release for their latent energies — energies in all their colors ranging from the civilized to the piratical. They hastened to occupy North and South America and then Africa, Australia, and New Zealand. They subjugated, enslaved, or killed the native peoples. The newcomers exploited the new lands' resources. They and their descendants also wrought grand achievements in science and technology, the arts, the democratic instrument of government, and maybe, just maybe, religion.

After the new lands had been entirely taken up, a new variety of explorers went into action. They turned in two directions—to the mines, and to the laboratory. Pumps and power-shovels and even the gold miner's pick pulled earth's mineral treasures to the surface. Thereupon they were converted, via the furnace and the chemical retort, into a profusion of material goods, to fill or overfill the horn of material plenty.

By the end of the twentieth century, middle-class Americans were living in more luxury and splendor than earlier royalty had enjoyed. They wallowed in creature comforts. Harold Breimyer has brooded over the rampant consumption—destruction—of mineral resources that goes into the incredible luxury of moving about day and night, at work and at play, in climate-controlled chambers. Or the similar resource-cost of automobile transport, as 150 million U.S. drivers take to the wheel of an almost equal number of passenger cars to satisfy every whim of mobility, whether to see a movie or to cross the country.

For five centuries the new continents were a global frontier. They had all the marks that Frederick Jackson Turner, writing at the end of the nineteenth century, attributed to a frontier culture. Accessibility to new lands and then to non-land resources, all abundantly available for the taking, released the venturesome Europeans and their blood and ideological heirs from the soul-gripping restraints that had characterized crowded feudal Europe.

In the setting there sprouted and flowered a scarcely-shackled individualism and an American brand of democracy. By the time of Turner's writing, the land frontier had closed. Even though the technological wizardry of the twentieth century was yet to come, thoughtful people sensed that social discipline would have to replace rapaciousness.

The Great Depression was the seismic event that forced Americans to take steps to harness individual greed in conformity with social purpose. As has been stated more than once in this memoir, Harold Breimyer was convinced that the New Deal, despite its many flaws, was an enlightened social movement. He believed then, as he has since, that our nation acted during the 1930s and for a quarter-century after World War II to pursue the ideals of liberty, justice, and brotherhood on which, said the authors of *The Striking of America's Hour,* our nation would ultimately be judged. It did so with appreciable success.

LESS USE OF MONETARY INCENTIVE TO SOCIAL ACTION

Almost every historian who has written about the New Deal has insisted that it did not change our basic economic or political system. Most of all, it did not take our beleaguered nation back toward ancient authoritarian governance. Often, the language used is that the New Deal only made our system more humane.

All this is true, but fails to explain what indeed was original and distinctive about the New Deal's policies. One feature of those policies has been so vital a part of policy for agriculture that it merits special mention. It was their relying primarily on monetary incentives to socially responsible individual behavior and business performance. The Franklin Roosevelt government drew on the uniquely American technique of putting monetary restraint on antisocial conduct and, as a companion measure, of offering monetary inducement and reward for individual actions taken in the public interest.

Most textbook definitions of our money economy explain it in terms of using money as a medium for exchanging goods and services, current and contractual. Rarely does an author add that for more than a half century, our country has also made money an instrument of social sanctions. Yet such has been the case.

Monetary Inducement in the First Farm Program. In 1936 Harold Breimyer, as a neophyte agricultural economist newly employed by the Agricultural Adjustment Administration, heard his administrator (and former professor) Howard Tolley describe the essential nature of the new land-retirement program. The program did not mandate, Tolley said, that farmers leave part of their cropland unplanted. It merely invited them to enter into contracts under which they would reduce their acreage planted to wheat, corn, cotton, or other program crop. If they chose to do so, they would receive the "benefit payments" dangled before them.

A few years later, the cotton and tobacco interests were able to introduce a mandatory clause into several commodity programs. The mandatory option remained available only a relatively few years. During the more than fifty-five years of acreage-reduction programs, the prevailing convention has been to offer farmers a Treasury-check reward for voluntary individual action.

Similarly, soil conservation has been induced by offers to cost-share in a farmer's carrying out conserving practices. The Conservation Reserve Program of the 1985 farm law was voluntary rental. Examples of the money-benefit principle in agriculture are many.

Monetized Penalties. Use of money to channel private conduct to public purpose is by no means confined to paying for a desired voluntary action. Money penalties have long served to restrain antisocial action. Admittedly, we use corporal punishment in criminal law, but levying of penalties (including fines) is built into not only civil law but the entire U.S. judicial system as well.

Graduated Income Tax to Fund Monetary Inducements. The most heroic, and most American, of all means of raising government revenue is the graduated income and estate tax. Its message is, in effect, that in our tradition of granting a maximum of individual liberty, tight restraints are not to be imposed on individual conduct, including that of business firms. But in the interest of a social order free of extremes of wealth and poverty, the tax system is designed to be partially redistributive.

Harold Breimyer, in his Extension writings, called the graduated income tax the most civilized form of taxation. It follows that revenues generated by that tax have funded the monetary-inducement arm of government. Thus is a circular system of monetization of social sanctions completed.

Twilight in the 1980s. It has been said often that the counter-revolution of the Reagan years brought nearly to a close the humanization of the U.S. economy that began with the New Deal, continued with the Great Society, and was partially retained through the Nixon and Carter administrations. Not least of the changes was a major retrenchment in the monetary-inducement system just described. During Ronald Reagan's term of office, and partly at his instigation, federal tax laws were rewritten several times. The progressive feature of the personal income tax was watered down so much that Wayne Newton, the entertainer, with his $10 million annual income was taxed at the same rate as the author of this memoir—a retired professor living on an income no more than four-tenths of one percent of Mr.Newton's.

Breimyer declared the 1980s to be the Last Hurrah, the last kick of rampant, unrestrained individualism.

Monetized inducement—paying people to be (do) good—has been

caught in a budgetary pincers. Abandonment of a highly progressive income tax as a revenue source has thrown the federal budget into massive deficit. The action foretold the end of generously funded inducements to private conduct in the social interest. If the Treasury cannot raise money, it cannot pay it out to keep air and water clean and soil in place — or, for that matter, to protect farmers from the shocks of unstable markets, as commodity programs have done since 1933.

What will be the recourse, late in the twentieth century and early in the twenty-first? The options are only two. One is to force socially desirable individual action by mandate, by use of the police power. Some environmental pressures may be so strong, so premonitory of health-risking danger, that mandatory rules will be imposed. The other option is just to abandon social purpose. To the extent the latter is the choice, the villagers of Fort Recovery will have cause to present their pageant once more. "America, thou are weighed in the balances and found wanting."

MAN AND NATURE: THE CONFLICT AHEAD

Harold Breimyer's more distressing forebodings are longer-run than the Reagan years' relinquishing of the humanizing measures and monetary techniques of the New Deal. They stem from what he sees as the end of the marvelously productive five-century era that was inaugurated with Gutenberg, Columbus (or Vasco de Gama), Galileo, and Francis Bacon. He senses and anticipates, as did Oswald Spengler, the decline of the West.

Five centuries of tapping seemingly boundless new resources allowed a maximum of exploitive individual freedom. It minimized social discipline as it had been imposed previously by religious or secular authority. In the United States and some other countries, where socially responsible behavior was sought, it was possible, because of the affluence of those years, to attract it by monetary means.

Moreover, in wealthy nations where Christianity dominates, admonitions to charity softened the worst excesses of social indifference. By the late 1980s every major U.S. city had its food bank and shelter for the homeless. From time to time food was shipped to the starving of Bangladesh, Ethiopia, or other food-short country, victims of too much or too little rainfall or its leaders' improbity.

Man and Nature are conspiring to bring it all to an explosive end. Man is doing so directly, by his breeding habits. He is over-populating the planet. Only in the People's Republic of China and a few other countries are steps being taken consciously to slow the rate of population growth.

In innumerable nations, people are so crowded upon their limited resources that misery is the only foreseeable lot for everyone except the few members of a privileged wealth-holding or ruling class. Not all the aid of international institutions or U.S. Christians, or the fervent preaching about human rights and the merits of democracy as a governmental form, can forestall revolution, bloodshed, and jungle-style chaos.

Resource Pollution, Scarcity. As natural resources are drawn on more intensively and protected less, Nature will make her response. She will do so in two ways.Fouling of air and water will first do visible harm and then will force corrective action by all countries perceptive and vigorous enough to take it. Environmental restrictions are inescapable in the future United States of America.

Specifications and scale of environmental pollution are compiled and published regularly by, among others, the Worldwatch Institute. Its *State of the World* for successive years offers an updated version of the grim story.

It may be a cosmic irony that one kind of pollution, that originating in overconsumption of fossil fuels, will to some extent be self-correcting. Within a relatively few years the burning of petroleum as an energy source will diminish. The wells of England, Mexico, the Soviet Union, and the Near East will trace the same pattern as those of the United States already have done. They will yield less oil. On the other hand, the coal that will partially replace it is more environmentally polluting than oil.

The twentieth century is destined to be known as the petroleum century. As petroleum reserves are gradually exhausted, the shock to all modern industrial nations will be intense. It will force adjustments in how and where people work and live that are too many and complex to be enumerated here. The question at issue is whether the social and political fabric can accommodate the dramatic change without encountering anarchic chaos; which is to say, without a collapse of democratic systems of government and their replacement with some form of tyranny.

Eventually, mankind can survive on planet Earth only insofar as a sustainable means of sustenance is substituted for relying on depletable minerals.

Revolutionizing his technologies will be no more difficult than controlling his own procreation. To date, the breeding of human beings has been little different from that of rabbits. Religiously-based insistence on monogamy, and taboos on promiscuous sexuality, have given way to license. Religious teachings that counseled avoidance of conception did not extend to endorsing abortion of a fetus. The Western world at the end of the 1980s was not prepared to grapple effectively with means of restraining population other than disease, starvation, and homicide.

Eugenics and Euthanasia. Means will eventually be put in place: they will be eugenics for social governing of procreation and euthanasia for life's termination. In the near future the first steps toward social control of procreation will be mandatory sterilization of the criminal and socially irresponsible members of society. In some more distant century, in Harold Breimyer's futuristic conjecture, the creating of human life will be given a ceremonial status equivalent to what the Christian church calls a sacrament. Why is not the creation of a living human being any less sacred—sacramental—than baptism or marriage? It will eventually be so regarded.

And why should human beings, having invented medications to sustain a functional metabolism though the mind be deadened by dementia, deny release? Why should the highest species of life, gifted with cognition, be required to die as animals of the forest do—in even more agony than is allowed household pets? Are these not rational questions?

Euthanasia is in mankind's future.

Brave New World? In past centuries it was accepted that human beings could not improve their well-being and relieve suffering because they lacked the know-how, the technology and instruments, for doing so. Indeed, scarcely more than a century has passed since effective anesthesia became widely available to reduce or dispel the pain of illness, injury, or surgery.

For the future, the limiting factor is not technical, but the age-old one of our collective will. Are we prepared to manage our affairs for civilized survival?

More than fifty years ago Aldous Huxley wrote a novel, *Brave New World,* hypothesizing how a benevolent dictatorial authority would manipulate the germplasm of homo sapiens and foreordain human existence to be free of both stress and satisfaction value. It's unlikely that anyone who read the work at the time has forgotten it. Harold Breimyer surely has not.

Will it be possible to develop the social instruments—religious and secular creeds and a system of government—that draw individual action into socially responsible performance? Can the terms set in *The Striking of America's Hour* be met? Will our nation, and all human society, be weighed and found to meet the criteria of liberty, justice, and brotherhood? This is left as a question. Harold Breimyer's futuristic dreams always end with that question. He cannot hazard the answer.

He knows that Man must manage Nature, which will not be as bountiful in future centuries as in the past five. But first Man must learn to manage himself.

BIOGRAPHICAL DATA

VITA DATA:

Born, 1914, and reared on a farm in western Ohio.

Married to Rachel Styles of Georgia.

One son, Fred, economist, State Street Bank, Boston; three grandchildren.

EDUCATION:

B.S., agricultural economics, Ohio State University, 1934.

M.S., agricultural economics, Ohio State University, 1935.

Graduate work, agricultural economics, University of California, Berkeley, 1935–36.

Ph.D., economics, American University, 1960.

EMPLOYMENT:

Agricultural Adjustment Administration, 1936–39.

Bureau of Agricultural Economics and Agricultural Marketing Service, 1939–59. (in charge, livestock outlook work, 1948–59).

Staff economist, Council of Economic Advisers, Executive Office of the President, 1959–61.

Staff economist, Agricultural Marketing Service, 1961–65, Consumer and Marketing Service, 1965–66.

Visiting research professor, departments of economics and agricultural economics, University of Illinois, 1963–64 (on leave from Agricultural Marketing Service).

Professor, Department of Agricultural Economics, University of Missouri, 1966–84. Also Extension Economist, 1968–84.

FOREIGN ASSIGNMENTS:

Member of exchange delegation in agricultural economics to USSR, July 1958.

Research study for Argentine government, May-July 1961, July 1962; for government of Guatemala, July-August 1965. Project review, CIC-AID, Lima, Peru, July 1967; AID-Colombia, November 1969. Research consultant, Agricultural Research Institute, Zaragoza, Spain, 1974.

PROFESSIONAL ORGANIZATIONS:

American Agricultural Economics Association (Vice-President, 1964, President, 1969).

International Association of Agricultural Economists (Member, U.S. Council, 1967–73).

American Economic Association.

Association for Evolutionary Economics.

Southern Agricultural Economics Association.

Western Agricultural Economics Association.

Agricultural History Society (Member Executive Committee, 1983–85).

HONORS AND AWARDS:

Superior Service Award, U.S. Department of Agriculture, 1954; similar award, group, 1959.

Certificate of Merit, Agricultural Marketing Service, 1963.

Best article award, *Journal of Farm Economics,* 1954, 1957, 1962.

Benjamin Minge Duggar Lecturer, Auburn University, 1970.

Centennial Award for Distinguished Service, College of Agriculture and Home Economics, Ohio State University, 1970.

Extension Publication award (shared), American Agricultural Economics Association, 1971, 1978.

Senior Faculty Award of Merit, Gamma Sigma Delta, University of Missouri, 1972.

Outstanding Educator designation (U.S.), 1973, 1974, 1975.

Elected Fellow, American Agricultural Economics Association, 1973.

Faculty-Alumni Award, University of Missouri, 1975.

Superior Teaching Award (undergraduate), Gamma Sigma Delta, University of Missouri, 1981.

Thomas Jefferson Award, University of Missouri, 1983.

Distinguished Faculty Award, University of Missouri–Columbia Alumni Association, 1983.

MILITARY SERVICE:

Active duty, U.S. Navy, 1942–45. Lt. Cdr., USNR (retired).

CIVIC ACTIVITIES:

Member, Board of Education, Montgomery County, Maryland, 1959–62; president, 1961.

Chairman, Council of Ministries, Missouri United Methodist Church, Columbia, Missouri, 1972–73.

President, Columbia (Missouri) Council of Churches, 1974–76.

Representative-at-large, Missouri Council of Churches, 1978–84.

Lions International.

BIBLIOGRAPHY

Acheson, Dean. *Fragments of my Fleece.* New York: W. W. Norton, 1971.

_____. *Present at the Creation.* New York: Norton, 1969.

Allen, Frederick Lewis. *Only Yesterday.* New York: Blue Ribbon Books, 1931.

Angelou, Maya. *I Know Why the Caged Bird Sings.* New York: Random House, c. 1969.

Aquinas, St. Thomas. *"Treatise on Law."* In *Aristotle, Politics, Books 3–5; St. Thomas Aquinas, Treatise on Law.* Chicago: Great Books Foundation, 1955.

Aristotle. *"Ethics Nicomachea."* In *Ethics, Book 1; Politics, Book 1. Chicago: Great Books Foundation, 1948.*

_____. *Politics, Books 3–5. Chicago: Great Books Foundation, 1955.*

Arnold, C. R. *"What About Overproduction?"* Department of Rural Economics, Ohio State Univ., 1932. Mimeo.

Baker, Gladys. *The County Agent.* Chicago: Univ. of Chicago Press, 1939.

Boroff, David. "American Colleges – What Their Catalogues Never Tell You." *Harper's* 220:1319(April 1960): 33–40.

Boulding, Kenneth E. *Economic Analysis,* revised ed. New York: Harper, 1948.

Breimyer, Harold F. "Sources of Our Increasing Food Supply." *Journal of Farm Economics* 36(1954): 228–42.

_____. "On Price Determination and Aggregate Price Theory." *Journal of Farm Economics* 39(1957): 676–94.

_____. *Demand and Prices for Meat: Factors Influencing Their Historical Development.* U.S. Department of Agriculture, Technical Bulletin No. 1253, 1961.

_____. "The Three Economies of Agriculture." *Journal of Farm Economics* 44(1962): 679–99.

_____. *Individual Freedom and the Economic Organization of Agriculture.* Urbana: Univ. of Illinois Press, 1965.

_____. "Economics and Politics of Extending the 1965 Farm Law." *Economic and Marketing Information for Missouri Agriculture,* Sept. 1968.

_____. "Institutional and Organizational Changes Necessary to Facilitate Improvements in Programs in Research and Related Teaching and Extension Activities in Agricultural Economics." Univ. of Missouri–Columbia Agricultural Economics Paper No. 1971–43. 1971. Mimeo.

_____. "The Problem and its Setting." *Bargaining in Agriculture: Potentials and Pitfalls in Collective Action,* edited by Harold F. Breimyer and Wallace Barr, Univ. of Missouri Extension Division C-911, June 1971, pp. 3–7.

_____. "Farming's Non-Instinct for Self-Preservation. Univ. of Missouri–Columbia Agricultural Economics Paper No. 1972–17. Mimeo.

_____. "The New Farm Program." *Economic and Marketing Information for Missouri Agriculture,* Nov. 1973.

———. "Where Money in Farming Comes From." *Economic and Marketing Information for Missouri Agriculture,* Sept. 1975.

———. *Farm Policy: 13 Essays.* Ames: Iowa State Univ. Press, 1977.

———. "Agriculture's Three Economies in a Changing Resource Environment." *American Journal of Agricultural Economics 60(1978): 37–47.*

———. *"The 1977 Farm Bill." Economic and Marketing Information for Missouri Agriculture,* Jan. 1978.

———. "Our Common Future—Atlantis, Armageddon, or Something in Between?" Univ. of Missouri–Columbia Agricultural Economics Paper No. 1980–19. Mimeo.

———. "The Fallacy of Macroeconomics." *Newsletter,* American Agricultural Economics Association, Jan. 1981.

———. "Viewpoint." *Newsletter,* American Agricultural Economics Association, Sept. 1982.

———. "Statement . . . Before the Subcommittee on Government Information, Justice, and Agriculture of the Committee on Government Operations, U.S. House of Representatives, July 11, 1983." Washington, DC: U.S. Government Printing Office, 1983.

———. "The Payment-in-Kind Program." *Economic and Marketing Information for Missouri Agriculture,* Feb. 1983.

———. "The University as a Community of Service-Giving Scholars: Retrospect and Prospect." Univ. of Missouri–Columbia Agricultural Economics Paper No. 1983–8. Mimeo.

———. "The Education of Harold Breimyer." Univ. of Missouri–Columbia, Department of Agricultural Economics, 1984. Mimeo.

———. "Agriculture and the Political Economy." *Challenge 28:6* (1985): 15–21.

———. "Causes, Consequences, Correctives, and Christian Responses to the Farm Crisis." Univ. of Missouri–Columbia Agricultural Economics Working Paper No. 1986–34. Mimeo.

———. "Origins of the Rural Crisis or 'How Did We Get Where We are?' " Univ. of Missouri–Columbia Agricultural Economics Working Paper No. 1986–16. Mimeo.

———. "Targeting as a Principle in Farm Policy." Testimony given before Committee on Agriculture, Nutrition, and Forestry, U.S. Senate, Washington, DC, March 18, 1987. Univ. of Missouri–Columbia Agricultural Economics Working Paper No. 1987–5. Mimeo.

———. "The Place of Domestic Agricultural Policy in an Internationalized Agriculture." In *Agricultural Policies: The New Reality.* Univ. of Missouri–Columbia Agricultural Experiment Station Report 370, 1987, pp. 22–38.

———. "Unsung Heroes: Farm Family Counselors." *On the Economy,* July 25, 1987. Columbia, Mo. Mimeo.

———. "Reflections on Communication in Agricultural Economics." *Journal of Agricultural Economics Research* 40:1(1988) pp. 47–48.

———. "The Irresistible Appeal of Tax Concessions." *On the Economy,* April 16, 1988. Columbia, Mo. Mimeo.

———. James Tucker, Hoy F. Carman, Richard S. Fenwick, and W. Fred Woods. *How Federal Income Tax Rules Affect Ownership and Control of Farming.* North Central Regional Extension Publication 40, Univ. of Illinois at Urbana-Champaign, Cooperative Extension Service, Special Publication 38, Sept. 1975.

_____. and Abner Womack. "The 1981 Farm Bill." *Economic and Marketing Information for Missouri Agriculture,* March 1982.

Brewster, John M. *A Philosopher Among Economics,* edited by J. Patrick Madden and David E. Brewster. Philadelphia: J. T. Murphy, *1970.*

Brown, Lester R. (and various co-authors). Worldwatch Institute. *State of the World.* New York: Norton, 1984 and successive years.

Caldwell, Erskine. *Tobacco Road.* New York: Grosset & Dunlap, c. 1932.

Cochrane, Willard W. "My Views on Agricultural Policy—How and Why They Have Changed." In *Agricultural Policies: The New Reality.* Univ. of Missouri–Columbia Agricultural Experiment Station Special Report 370, 1987, pp. 29–34.

Conkin, Paul K. *Tomorrow a New World: The New Deal Community Program.* New York: Da Capo Press, 1976.

Copenhaver, Laura Scherer, Katherine Scherer Cronk, and Mathilde A. Vossler. *The Striking of America's Hour.* Philadelphia: Women's Missionary Society, Lutheran Church in America, 1925.

Eggert, Jim. "Consensus Forecasting—A Ten-Year Report Card." *Challenge* 30:3(1987): 59–62.

Ezekiel, Mordecai J. B. *Methods of Correlation Analysis.* New York: Wiley, 1930.

Foster, William Trufant, and Waddill Catchings. *Money.* New York: Houghton Mifflin, 1924.

_____. *The Road to Plenty.* New York: Houghton Mifflin, 1928.

Gray, Lewis C. "Rent Under the Assumption of Exhaustibility." *Quarterly Journal of Economics* 28(1914): 466–89.

Gunsallus, Brooke L., Harold F. Breimyer, Aaron J. Blumberg, and Edgar C. McVoy. *Manufacturing Brick and Tile to Serve Your Community.* U.S. Department of Commerce, Industrial (Small Business) Series No. 49, 1946.

Hadwiger, Don F. "Farmers in Politics." *Agricultural History* 50:1(1976): pp. 56–70.

Hardin, Charles M. "The Bureau of Agricultural Economics Under Fire: A Study in Valuation Conflicts." *Journal of Farm Economics* 28(1946): 635–68.

Hayes, H. Gordon. *Our Economic System,* Vols. 1, 2. New York: Holt, 1928.

Hoffer, Eric. *The True Believer: Thoughts on the Nature of Mass Movements.* New York: Harper & Row, c.1951.

Hotelling, Harold. "The Economics of Exhaustible Resources." *Journal of Political Economy* 39(1931): 137–75.

Huxley, Aldous. *Brave New World.* New York: Harper, 1932.

Iacocca, Lee. *Talking Straight.* New York: Bantam Books, 1988.

Johnstone, Paul H. "Old Ideals Versus New Ideas in Farm Life." *Farmers in a Changing World,* Yearbook of Agriculture, 1940. Washington, D.C.: USDA, 1940.

Kant, Immanuel. *Fundamental Principles of the Metaphysics of Morals.* Chicago: Great Books Foundation, 1959.

_____. *Prolegomena to Any Future Metaphysics.* Chicago: Great Books Foundation, 1956.

Kennedy, Paul. *The Rise and Fall of the Great Powers.* New York: Random House, 1987.

Keynes, John Maynard. *The General Theory of Employment Interest and*

Money. New York: Harcourt, Brace, 1936.

Kirkendall, Richard S. *Social Scientists and Farm Politics in the Age of Roosevelt.* Columbia: Univ. of Missouri Press, 1966.

Kohls, Richard L. "Bargaining Power in Livestock Marketing." Purdue Univ. Department of Agricultural Economics, c. 1968. Mimeo.

Kraenzel, Carl F. *The Great Plains in Transition.* Norman: Univ. of Oklahoma Press, 1955.

Ladd, George W. *Agricultural Bargaining Power.* Ames: Iowa State Univ. Press, 1964.

Lerner, Max. "Our Constitutional Government: Of, By and For the People." Mimeographed notes of Gerald Engelman, taken in Graduate School, U.S. Department of Agriculture, April 28, 1965.

Lewis, Sinclair. *It Can't Happen Here.* Garden City, N.Y.: Sun Dial, 1935.

Locklin, David Philip. *Economics of Transportation,* 7th Ed. Homewood, Ill.: Irwin, 1972.

Manchester, William. "FDR Thunders." *A Sense of History: The Best Writing from the Pages of American Heritage,* Introduction by Byron Dobell. Boston: Houghton–Mifflin, 1985.

Michener, James. *Centennial.* New York: Random House, 1974.

Morhart, Hilda Dischinger. *The Zoar Story.* Strasburg, Ohio. Gordon Printing, 1981.

National Academy of Sciences–National Research Council. *Resources and Man.* San Francisco: W. H. Freeman, 1969.

Nord, Warren A. "Liberals Should Want Religion Taught in Public Schools." *Washington Post National Weekly Edition,* July 21, 1986, pp. 23–24.

North Central Public Policy Education Committee. *Who Will Control U.S. Agriculture?* North Central Regional Extension Publication 32, Univ. of Illinois at Urbana-Champaign, Cooperative Extension Service, Special Publication 27, Aug. 1972.

Ohio Historical Society. *Zoar: An Ohio Experiment in Communalism.* Columbus: Ohio Historical Society, 1970.

Olson, Mancur. *The Rise and Decline of Nations.* New Haven: Yale Univ. Press, 1982.

Parsons, George Frederic. *The Atlantic Monthly,* September 1886. Quoted in "100 Years Ago," *The Atlantic* 260:9(1986):p.12.

Perrett, Geoffrey. *America in the Twenties, a History.* New York: Simon and Schuster, 1982.

Potts, Mark, and Peter Behr. *The Leading Edge: CEOs Who Turned Their Companies Around and How They Did It.* New York: McGraw-Hill, 1986.

Rasmussen, Wayne D., ed. *Agriculture in the United States: A Documentary History,* Vol. 3. New York: Random House, 1975.

Reich, Robert. *Tales of a New America.* Quotation in *Common Cause Magazine,* Jan.–Feb. 1987, p.16.

Reno, Milo. "Why the Farmers' Holiday?" Department of Rural Economics, Ohio State Univ., 1932. Mimeo.

Rohr, Martha E. *Historical Sketch of Fort Recovery.* Fort Recovery Historical Society, Fort Recovery, Ohio, 1974.

St. Augustine. *Confessions,* Books 1–8. Chicago: Great Books Foundation, 1948.

Saloutos, Theodore. *The American Farmer and the New Deal.* Ames: Iowa State Univ. Press, 1982.

Santayana, George. *The Last Puritan.* New York: Charles Scribner's Sons, 1936.

Santmyer, Helen Hooven. *. . . and Ladies of the Club.* New York: Putnam, 1982.

Schlesinger, Arthur Meier. *Political and Social History of the United States, 1829–1925.* New York: Macmillan, 1925.

Schlesinger, Arthur M., Jr. *The Cycles of American History.* Boston: Houghton-Mifflin, 1986.

Schultz, Theodore W. *Agriculture in an Unstable Economy.* New York: McGraw-Hill, 1945.

Steinbeck, John. *Grapes of Wrath.* New York: Heritage, c.1940.

Terkel, Lewis. *Hard Times: An Oral History of the Great Depression.* New York: Pantheon, 1970.

Thompson, Silvanus Phillips. *Calculus Made Easy.* London: Macmillan, 1946.

Torgerson, Randall E. *Producer Power at the Bargaining Table.* Columbia: Univ. of Missouri Press, 1970.

Turner, Frederick Jackson. *The Frontier in American History.* New York: Holt, 1920.

U.S. Department of Agriculture. *Farmers in a Changing World,* Yearbook of Agriculture, 1940. Washington, D.C.: USDA, 1940.

_____. *Century of Service: the First 100 Years of the United States Department of Agriculture.* Washington, D.C.: USDA 1963.

_____. *A Time to Choose: Summary Report on the Structure of Agriculture.* Washington, D.C.: USDA, January 1981.

U.S. House of Representatives, Special Subcommittee on Cotton of the Committee on Agriculture. *Industrialization and the South.* Project VII of Study of Agricultural and Economic Problems of the Cotton Belt. Hearings, July 7–8, 1947. Washington D.C.: U.S. Government Printing Office.

University of Illinois at Urbana-Champaign. Who Will Control U.S. Agriculture? Series of North Central Regional Extension Publications under the title, 1972–74.

Wallace, Henry A. "The Department as I Have Known It." (pp. 19–21). *Growth Through Agricultural Progress: Lecture Series in Honor of the United States Department of Agriculture Centennial Year,* edited by Wayne D. Rasmusson, Washington, D.C.: 1962.

Wallich, Henry C. *The Cost of Freedom.* New York: Harper, 1960.

Ward, Barbara, and Rene Dubos. *Only One Earth.* New York: Norton, 1972.

Washington, Booker T. *Up From Slavery.* Garden City, N.Y.: Doubleday, c.1901.

Watkins, Frederick. *The Political Tradition of the West.* Cambridge: Harvard Univ. Press, 1948.

Wheeler, Leslie A. "The New Agricultural Protectionism and its Effect on Trade Policy." *Journal of Farm Economics* 42(1960): 797–810.

White, Theodore H. *In Search of History: A Personal Adventure.* New York: Harper & Row, 1978.

Wilson, Edmund. "The Hudson River Progressive." *The New Republic,* April 5, 1933.

Woods, W. Fred, Harold D. Guither, Leonard R. Kyle, C. Allen Bock, Ralph E. Hepp, Gerald A. Harrison, Harold F. Breimyer, and Michael D. Boehlje.

Death and Taxes: Policy Issues Affecting Farm Property Transfers. North Central Regional Extension Publication 40, Univ. of Illinois at Urbana-Champaign, Cooperative Extension Service, Special Publication 39, Sept. 1975.

Wouk, Herman. *The Caine Mutiny.* Garden City, N.Y.: Doubleday, 1951.

INDEX